SUCCEEDING TOGETHER?

Schools, Child Welfare, and Uncertain Public
Responsibility for Abused or Neglected Children

Succeeding Together?

Schools, Child Welfare, and Uncertain Public Responsibility for Abused or Neglected Children

KELLY GALLAGHER-MACKAY

UNIVERSITY OF TORONTO PRESS
Toronto Buffalo London

© University of Toronto Press 2017
Toronto Buffalo London
www.utppublishing.com
Printed in Canada

ISBN 978-1-4426-5064-0

♾ Printed on acid-free, 100% post-consumer recycled paper with vegetable-based inks.

Library and Archives Canada Cataloguing in Publication

Gallagher-Mackay, Kelly, author
Succeeding together? : schools, child welfare, and uncertain public responsibility for abused or neglected children / Kelly Gallagher-Mackay.

Includes bibliographical references and index.
ISBN 978-1-4426-5064-0 (cloth)

1. Abused children – Education. 2. Abused children – Care.
3. Child welfare. 4. School social work. 5. Teacher-student relationships.
6. Education – Parent participation. I. Title.

LC4801.G34 2017   371.7   C2016-907669-5

This book has been published with the help of a grant from the Federation for the Humanities and Social Sciences, through the Awards to Scholarly Publications Program, using funds provided by the Social Sciences and Humanities Research Council of Canada.

University of Toronto Press acknowledges the financial assistance to its publishing program of the Canada Council for the Arts and the Ontario Arts Council, an agency of the Government of Ontario.

 Canada Council for the Arts / Conseil des Arts du Canada

 ONTARIO ARTS COUNCIL
CONSEIL DES ARTS DE L'ONTARIO
an Ontario government agency
un organisme du gouvernement de l'Ontario

Funded by the Government of Canada / Financé par le gouvernement du Canada   Canada

Contents

Acknowledgments vii

1 Collective Responsibility for Maltreated Children and Its Dilemmas 1

2 Separate Spheres and Closed Systems: Reporting and Communication between Schools and Child Protection 25

3 Schools "Disciplining" Families' Cultural Difference through Child Protection 64

4 Not "in the Game of Maximizing Potential": Corporate Parenthood, Policy Silence, and Limited Services for Children Who Stay at Home 71

5 Regulating Aspirations: Teachers' Responsibility and "The Whole Child" 98

6 Between Labour and Love: Individualizing Teachers' Responsibility for the Work of Care 121

Conclusion – Revisiting the Dilemmas of Collective Responsibility: Implications for Research, Practice, and Policy 140

Appendix 1: Notes on Methodology and Methods 159

Appendix 2: For Whose Protection? Gatekeeping, Ethics, Research Review, and Access in Studies of the Front Line 167

*Appendix 3: Regulation of Teachers' Work: Sources and
            Responsibilities* 180

Notes 181

References 189

Index 207

Acknowledgments

I am extraordinarily grateful to the sixty people who took the risks and time to share their experience and knowledge with me as participants in this research. Without them, there would be no book.

I'm particularly grateful to Jane Gaskell, who provided incisive and challenging feedback on the research, for the wise and ongoing mentorship of Joseph Flessa, and to Professor Shelley Gavigan for contributing her expertise in law and society, as well as to colleagues at the Ontario Institute for Studies of Education and Faculty of Social Work at the University of Toronto. Professor Barbara Fallon and the Child Welfare Journal Watch group provided excellent support and background in my cross-disciplinary endeavours.

I also must express my persistent gratitude to supporters from earlier life who helped me make the move across disciplines, having always emphasized the social and political aspects of both law and education. In particular, Harry Arthurs, Andrew Petter, Anne Crawford, Beverly Browne, Scott Clark, and Nora Sanders have each had a lasting influence on my career and supported me in my emphasis on the social and political aspects of both law and education. I always reflect with pleasure and satisfaction on what I learned from them. The students at Akitsiraq Law School helped define my focus on educational opportunity. Further thanks to my colleagues at People for Education, particularly Annie Kidder, for giving me the impetus and time to finish this work, and for helping find new ways to move between research and policy change on some of the issues in this book.

Douglas Hildebrand, editor at the University of Toronto Press, has been patient and helpful for the transition of this work into a book. The manuscript benefitted considerably from the thoughtful feedback and recommendations of the anonymous referees, and careful copyediting work of Lara Friedlander and Avery Peters. Kelsey Blackwell provided cover inspiration. I thank them, and the production team at the press.

This research received funding support from Social Sciences and Humanities Research Council of Canada and the Ontario Graduate Scholarship. It is unlikely it would exist without that crucial assistance.

Finally, my heartfelt thanks go to friends and family who have been incredibly supportive through this long process. Particular thanks to Jeannie Samuel and Janna Promislow, who were fellow-travellers on this road. Joanna Birenbaum, Rosemary Gallagher, David Szablowski, Judith Pyke, Joe Pernice, Joan Green, Ian Mackay, Geoff Gallagher-Mackay, and Eleanore Cronk all talked me through different questions and parts of the process. I count on love and support from Samuel Law every step of the way.

My children, Xin Ke and Nuan Qi, inspired the work, as did my mother, Sally Gallagher. This book is dedicated to her memory.

SUCCEEDING TOGETHER?

Schools, Child Welfare, and Uncertain Public
Responsibility for Abused or Neglected Children

Chapter One

Collective Responsibility for Maltreated Children and Its Dilemmas

How do schools and child welfare authorities work, together and apart, to respond to the educational needs of abused or neglected children who remain at home with their parents? This practical question inevitably raises the vexed – and under-theorized – question of collective responsibility. How is collective responsibility put into practice in the lives of particular children? How is it managed between institutions? How do policymakers, social workers, teachers, and families understand this responsibility? Based on the experiences of mothers and front-line workers in schools and child welfare agencies, this book looks at the exercise of collective responsibility for educational success of maltreated children in practice, while analysing the complex policy framework and underlying assumptions that shape that exercise.

Children experiencing abuse and neglect – including the vast majority of children in the child welfare system whose situation does not require that they be removed from the home – are by definition an extremely vulnerable group. Moreover, the literature on education and child welfare points to gaps in achievement, higher levels of involvement with special education and discipline processes, and lower levels of participation and engagement at school (see Blome, 1997; Brownell, M.D., Roos, N.P., MacWilliam, L., Leclair, L., Ekuma, O., Fransoo, R., 2010; Kortenkamp & Ehrle, 2002; Scherr, 2007; Wulczyn et al., 2009; and more detailed discussion later this chapter), suggesting the need for strong positive and education-specific supports for these children. Their vulnerability and these gaps engage schools' and child welfare agencies' responsibilities for well-being and equity.

Yet the policy response to these children's needs raises significant theoretical and political issues because of the children's situation on the borderline of public and private responsibility. The reality of abuse and neglect creates a rupture in the comfortable narrative that all parents naturally and capably do what is necessary to support their children's well-being, a narrative (among others) implicitly used to justify the division between private and public responsibility for the care of children. There is an underlying assumption that public supports exist to supplement the essential, unpaid, and politically invisible labour of care and socialization that is presumed to occur in the home (e.g., Daly & Lewis, 2000). The work of care and socialization becomes a public or government responsibility only where there is a strong justification for collective provision (e.g., schooling), or where a threshold of failure in the private sphere has been met (e.g., child protection). In the more extreme cases of child protection, the state finds substitute care through fostering and/or adoption. But as a matter of sound, evidence-based public policy, the vast majority of abused and neglected children remain with their families, and in these cases parents' labour of care continues alongside state intervention.

To improve outcomes and experiences for this group of children, strong public systems are needed to provide meaningful support to children, and to the parents – overwhelmingly mothers – who maintain the responsibility to care for them. The extent to which educational supports are deployed in a way that effectively contributes to the success of these children, whether by schools alone or working with child welfare, provides a case study of how public responsibility for extremely vulnerable children is – or is not – operationalized. Yet mobilization of state support for vulnerable children and their families is exactly the type of complex, messy endeavour that poses a key challenge to effective state action in our time. The challenge arises both because the underlying problems are significant, and because goals, processes, and responsibilities of the various actors are ill defined. In this light, the book frames a series of "dilemmas of collective responsibility" from both an institutional and theoretical perspective.

The heart of the book is a series of analyses that explore how these dilemmas play out between schools, Children's Aid Societies (CAS), and families:

Separate spheres of knowledge and mutual distrust (Chapter 2)
– In the area where there is the most explicit coordination – mandatory reporting of child abuse and neglect – it is clear from front-line accounts as well as legislation and detailed protocols

that information sharing is both expected and valuable across separate spheres of knowledge. Teachers are expected to know and report on what is readily observable at school, while the CAS is responsible for active investigation and knowledge of the home and to make contact with key professionals (collaterals) in a child's life. Yet in practice, data suggests very limited collaboration or even sharing of knowledge; teachers and family service workers express serious reservations about communicating between these two institutions. Moreover, the emphasis on the shared public responsibility to scrutinize families may limit the extent to which professionals in either child protection or schools see as their role to advocate and ensure that other institutions are meeting the children's needs.

Some educators conceive of child protection as a resource to police cultural difference (Chapter 3)
− Defining particular behaviours as problematic and warranting intervention also establishes a boundary between matters of public and private concern. A process of surveillance can reinforce that boundary. Where the problematic behaviours are associated (whether or not accurately) with particular groups, systemic and discriminatory effects can result from these processes of surveillance. There is a worrying congruence between the frequency with which educators identified CAS as a resource to help them address issues of cultural difference and the large-scale data showing an overrepresentation of racialized groups in reports of child abuse or neglect by professionals.

A lacuna in the responsibility of child protection for the well-being of children who remain with their parents (Chapter 4)
− When child protection takes on custody of a child in need of protection, it has been described as "corporate parenthood," where the state must ensure that the full range of parenting supports are provided to a child. But how does "corporate parenthood" operate where children are receiving services from CAS but remain at home? The provision of educational supports provides a case study. Officials offer widely varying accounts of the scope of public responsibility for these children. In practice and policy, though, it is clear that most CASs see themselves as having relatively limited responsibility for organizing proactive educational supports for

this group of children. Instead, their focus is on ensuring mothers' appropriate exercise of responsibility, while public support is *not* subject to oversight. This reflects a very weak accountability framework that does little to ensure that the needs of this group of children are met.

Challenges regulating teachers' caring work (Chapters 5 and 6)
– Teachers' professional responsibility for children's well-being appears to be both expected and valued but not planned for or institutionally supported in the current school setting, a shortcoming that is particularly important where children are exceptionally vulnerable. The framework of professional responsibility includes a minimal enforceable definition of teacher responsibility that coexists with a set of maximal expectations. In particular, the work of caring is considered a hallmark of exceptional teaching, yet there is an aspect of the work that goes "beyond the job." This paradox effectively personalizes this important work and leaves it unsupported, even where the very nature of teachers' work provides them with little choice but to handle the need "right in your face," in the words of Cory, a school social worker. Most educators acknowledge the widely varying capacity for and commitment to the work of supporting young people with significant issues.

Taken together, these dilemmas reveal significant holes in the exercise of collective responsibility for these extremely vulnerable children. More effective support for these children requires both improved coordination and mutual scrutiny, and, perhaps equally significantly, higher expectations around public responsibility for children's well-being within each domain. While there are significant challenges in asking institutions (public or otherwise) to promote it, there is an urgent need to ensure that action to improve children's well-being is not written-off as a worthy but unattainable goal in the real world of schools and child protection.

Abuse, Neglect, and Child Welfare Case Outcomes in Canada

The third Canadian Incidence Study of Reported Abuse and Neglect (CIS) conducted in 2008 (Public Health Agency of Canada, 2010) provides an overview of the incidence of reported abuse and neglect in

Canada, and of child and family characteristics of those involved with the system.[1]

- The overall incidence was 39.16 cases of investigated maltreatment per 1000 children, a rate that has been fairly stable since 2003. Of all investigations, 36 per cent of cases were substantiated, and 30 per cent were considered to be unfounded; the remainder of the cases were categorized as suspicious or representing degrees of future risk.
- Schools are the single most common referral source for maltreatment investigations – 24 per cent of all referrals come from schools. Schools refer more cases than the police (22 per cent) and constitute at least twice the number of referrals from any other source (Public Health Agency of Canada, 2010, p. 26).
- 92 per cent of investigations do not result in an out-of-home placement, whether in the form of foster care (4 per cent), formal or informal kinship care (4 per cent), or a residential or treatment program (< 1 per cent).
- In 27 per cent of investigations – an estimated 62,715 cases across Canada (including those where an out-of-home placement occurred) – the case was kept open for services after the initial investigation. This book focuses on children in this group whose cases do not include an out-of-home placement. I refer to them, variously, as the children who remain with their parent(s) or families, or children receiving services in the community.
- Since the CIS was first conducted (1998, 2003, 2008), the proportion of cases that remain open for services has decreased by 8 per cent since 1998, but the absolute number of cases has increased by more than a third.

From a school perspective, a national incidence rate of approximately 4 per cent suggests that teachers encounter suspected or actual abuse or neglect with relatively low frequency. Moreover, three out of four reports to CAS will result in a decision to close the case after investigation, a statistic that is not typically discussed when emphasizing the duty to report suspected maltreatment. Even in a case where CAS decides to provide ongoing services, a child is much more likely to stay with his or her parent(s) than to go into care or any kind of out-of-home placement – an involvement that may not be visible to the school. Thus, as a group, teachers rarely encounter CAS and often when they do will not be aware of any outcome from the encounter.

As a final note on the outcomes of child protection investigations, only 5 per cent of cases result in any kind of application to the court (Public Health Agency of Canada, 2010, p. 29). Many of the substantive accountability measures in the Child and Family Services Act – for example, the requirement that CAS demonstrate that services to support a child have been considered, and that any placement is the least disruptive alternative for a child – are based on review by a court. These accountability measures operate at the level of indirect influence (if at all) in the majority of cases that never get to court.

Educational Vulnerability of Children Experiencing Abuse or Neglect

Education is a key determinant of health and well-being in Canada and internationally (Public Health Officer of Canada, 2009). School is a key environment for children's development, healthy or otherwise (Biglan, 2014; Lerner, Rothman, Boulos, & Castellino, 2002). At its finest, school can open a child's mind to understanding and provide rich new experiences and opportunities. Succeeding in school is both an achievement in its own right and a prerequisite for many jobs or further educational opportunities that are in turn strongly correlated with higher incomes and greater self-determination. Some argue that success at school is even more significant for children in the child welfare system, since they will often have fewer other assets to draw on as they transition into adulthood (e.g., Geenen & Powers, 2006). In a recent, registry-based study of child welfare outcomes in Sweden, researchers Marie Berlin, Bo Vinnerljung, and Anders Hjern (2011) concluded:

> Youth who age out of long-term foster care have very high excess risks of future psychosocial problems compared to other peers. Up to 55% of these overrisks were statistically attributable to their dismal school performance. The general message from this study is: If society wants to improve life opportunities for care leaver, it is necessary to give them effective help with their schooling and education while they are in care.
>
> Poor educational performance should be regarded as a main determinant for care leavers' future life chances. It can be influenced and improved while children are in societal care ... We do not subscribe to the hypothesis that the results reported here are inevitable, just because adverse early childhood experiences are common among care leavers from long term foster care. (p. 2496)

A large body of Canadian (see generally, Ferguson & Wolkow, 2012; Kufeldt, 2006; Trocmé & Caunce, 1995) and international evidence (Eckenrode, Laird, & Doris, 1993; Heath, Colton, & Aldgate, 1994; O'Higgins, Sebba, & Luke, 2015; Pecora et al., 2006; Pecora, 2012; Smithgall, Gladden, Howard, Goerge, & Courtney, 2004; Wulczyn, Smithgall, & Chen, 2009) points to markedly inferior educational outcomes for children in the foster care system. For example, the Gateway to Success survey of Children's Aid Societies showed that only 42 per cent of 19- and 20-year-old Crown wards or former Crown wards graduate from high school, compared to 75 per cent in the general population (a low estimate). Further, 21 per cent of youth don't attend school despite a legal requirement to attend to 18 years of age, and only 21 per cent of Crown wards or former Crown wards were enrolled in post-secondary, compared to 40 per cent of the general population. The overwhelming majority of those in post-secondary were in apprenticeship and college programs (Ontario Association of Children's Aid Societies, 2008).

A smaller body of evidence suggests that maltreated children, *regardless* of foster care placement, also have significantly worse academic outcomes (Brownell et al., 2015; Brownell, et al., 2010; Leiter, 2007; Leiter & Johnsen, 1994). A recent population-based study in Manitoba showed that, among children born between 1989 and 2003, 66.8 per cent of students who had ever received care from Child and Family Services graduated from high school, compared to the 89.3 per cent of students whose families had not received any services from child welfare authorities (Brownell et al., 2015). In an earlier study, the authors had shown that the graduation rate was dramatically worse if the child's family received income assistance or if the child's mother was a teen when she gave birth to her first child. For the 3.9 per cent of children with all three of these risk factors, fully 84 per cent would not finish high school (Brownell, et al., 2010).

International evidence, mostly focused on those in foster care, has shown that children who had experienced abuse or neglect and were receiving services from the child welfare system faced numerous challenges to educational success relative to the general population, including far higher levels of identification for special education needs, higher levels of suspension and expulsion, greater absenteeism, lower levels of self-reported engagement and extracurricular participation, and lower achievement on large-scale assessments (Burley & Halpern, 2001; Goerge, Voorhis, Grant, Casey, & Robinson, 1992; Jackson & Simon, 2006;

Kortenkamp & Ehrle, 2002; Scherr, 2007; Jackson, Ajayi, & Quigley, 2005; Tilbury, Creed, Buys, Osmond, & Crawford, 2014).

A historical review shows how explanations for these poor academic outcomes and experiences have changed over time (Jackson and Simon, 2006). The first wave of explanations suggested the gap simply reflected the relatively disadvantaged background of most children in the child welfare system. More complex statistical analyses demonstrated that foster care status was an independent factor, above and beyond poverty, affecting outcomes. Since then, explanations have ranged from the organic – "most children who come into the care system are so damaged by their previous experience that it is unrealistic to expect them to achieve educationally at anything like average levels" (Jackson & Simon, 2006, p. 49) – to the social:

> Educational problems of children in care were caused more by the failure of social services and education to work together and by social workers' ignorance and neglect of educational matters than by any characteristics of the children themselves ... Even when joint training was arranged for teachers and social workers (an uncommon event in any case), the agenda was that of social services, usually focusing on child abuse and protection. Promoting children's educational attainment was not considered relevant, since expectations of what they could achieve were so minimal. (ibid., p. 49)

Swedish research showed that children in out-of-home care had lower school performance and post-secondary involvement than other children with similar IQs, and described the situation of children in state care as one that frequently amounts to educational and cognitive neglect. The researchers pointed to low expectations of educators, social workers, and caregivers as a key factor contributing to the poor outcomes (Tideman, Vinnerljung, Hintze, & Isaksson, 2011, citing published Swedish-language, large-scale cohort studies).

Debate about causes may influence the types of remedial efforts undertaken. A detailed critique of the literature on schooling and maltreatment (Stone, 2007; see also, Berridge, 2012) argues that in the child welfare literature, generally, schools and the education system are conceptualized like a black box. Relatively little attention is paid to the types of factors typically considered by educators and education policy makers to affect student performance, including attendance, motivation, and opportunity to learn at a school and classroom level. At an expert conference in 2010, there was a consensus that there is effectively no research on the factors that contribute to resilience and high performance in school for children in the child welfare system (Berliner, 2010; but see e.g. Dryfoos & Nissani, 2006). A recent "scoping review" of the literature on educational interventions for children in care found almost no research about educational interventions. Even stretching the bounds to a systematic review, they were able to find only eleven studies that contained "surprisingly few evaluated attempts to do something about foster children's poor school achievement" (Forsman & Vinnerljung, 2012; see also Liabo, Gray, & Mulcahy, 2013).

Finally, there is very limited published research or policy, in Canada or internationally, that looks at the *distinct* educational experiences children who remain with their parents – who are the majority of those involved with the child welfare system because of maltreatment. While these children do not experience the discontinuities or trauma of removal from the home, and in many cases they have fewer immediate safety concerns, they remain vulnerable. As the Ontario government noted in its (ongoing) Child Welfare Transformation project: "Lower risk cases, however, would not be seen as necessarily requiring less service. While these may not be cases where there are immediate safety concerns, the long term effects of chronic maltreatment can be more severe than in more acute cases that may have received a full protection investigation" (Ontario Ministry of Children and Youth Services, 2005, p. 9).

As a group, they face at least some of the same obstacles that create challenges for children in the foster care system. However, the range of supports that are in place institutionally on the part of both child welfare and schools appear to be much more limited, the scope of public responsibility is far more amorphous, and issues of coordination are even more complex.

Collective Responsibility, Accountability, and the "Problem of Many Hands"

In practice, any shared responsibility – particularly what I am terming "collective responsibility," which often includes state provision – is neither apolitical nor without institutional context. A "problem of many hands" (Bovens, 1998; Thompson, 1980), the *shared* responsibility for the well-being of children who have experienced abuse or neglect and who live at home, for example, requires coordination between quite different arms of the state – most prominently, but not exclusively, schools and child welfare agencies – *and* the active participation of parents and caregivers.

In Ontario, the legal framework for education and child protection is, at the broadest level, fairly explicit about the scope of public responsibility for children's well-being. The Education Act requires school boards to *"promote student achievement and well-being,"*[2] and its preamble proclaims that *"all partners in the education sector … have a role to play* in enhancing student achievement and well-being." Similarly, the "paramount purpose" of the Child and Family Services Act is "to promote the best interests, protection, and *well-being* of children" (italics added).[3]

Preambles or purpose statements are intended to set direction for agencies and to assist in the interpretation of responsibilities under legislation (Sullivan, 2007). Both the education and child welfare systems have identified child well-being as central to their mandates. Notably, child well-being is a secondary goal in each system, coming after student achievement in the Education Act and after protection in the Child and Family Services Act. This overlapping responsibility for well-being, however ill-defined, suggests the need for coordinated effort.

Yet these broad purposes quickly founder in some of the key dilemmas of contemporary policymaking, notably the complex, "decentred" nature of regulatory activity characterized by "complexity, fragmentation, interdependencies, ungovernability, and the rejection of a clear distinction between public and private" (Black, 2008). Those who seek to understand and build systems to improve educational experiences and outcomes for maltreated children must face "the problem of many hands" (Bovens, 1998; Thompson, 1980), because the participation of so many interdependent actors is required. The involvement of one actor does not obviate the need for the work of another; no one can effectively fulfil their responsibilities – or be subject to discrete accountability, or claim full credit – without the engagement of others.

Theoretical Challenges: Towards a Theory of Collective Responsibility for Well-Being

Prior to the theoretical challenge raised by "the problem of many hands" – in this case looking at the schooling of children in the child welfare system but not in care – is the need to strengthen the understanding of "collective responsibility for dependency," which the philosopher and legal theorist Martha Fineman (2005) argued is a central feminist project. Collective responsibility, in this sense, means that the continuing role and importance of the family is not a defence or an estoppel against the need for public resources and support. For her, strengthening the basis for asserting this collective responsibility is "perhaps the most important task for those concerned with the welfare of poor mothers and their children" (pp. 180–1). In her view, the theory must be developed as a claim of right or entitlement to support on the part of caregivers. Those who need or want help with this valuable work should be able to get it – from potentially diverse public sources. Moreover, a person seeking support should not have to concede the right to collective control over individual, intimate decision-making. Unfortunately, as this study will illustrate, Fineman's notion of a collective responsibility for dependency, in many ways, operates contrary both to the logic of child welfare and to the intensified role for parents in contemporary schooling.

In the context of schooling, there has been long-standing acknowledgment of the importance of home life as a key – if not *the* key – determinant of educational outcomes (starting, historically, with Coleman, 1966; see also Frempong & Willms, 2002; Organisation for Economic Co-operation and Development, 2014; in the child welfare context, see Berridge, 2012). The later studies also point to strong evidence that socio-economic status or even early experiences are not, in fact, destiny. However, research that seeks to explain the correlation between poverty and limited educational achievement has often focused on dissonance between family and school. Sara Lawrence Lightfoot, in a classic ethnography, *Worlds Apart*, characterized this literature indelibly as sexist and individualizing: "Within the literature on family–school dissonance, therefore, we find the sexist tradition of blaming mothers for the perceived inadequacies of their children, for the perpetuation of their own poverty and for the creation of social deviants and social chaos" (Lightfoot, 1978, p. 13).

This literature appears to see *schooling* as the key to well-being and successful futures for children, almost in opposition to the maternal contribution. Lightfoot argues, in fact, that "mothers are evaluated in terms of how well they have prepared their children for school … The notion is that there is a need for strong teachers when mothers are perceived as being less than adequate" (p. 61). The ways in which mothers provide for their children, often in extremely adverse conditions, is less visible in the eyes of the education system than the fact that their children are not "ready to learn." The emphasis is more on the shortcomings than the achievements of the mothers.

Since the 1980s, the literature on the connection between home and school has taken on a more prescriptive tone (Alexander, 2010, p. 73), with greater attention to appropriate parent involvement practice on the part of both schools and parents (e.g., Epstein, 1998; Pushor, 2007). Some researchers have found that, particularly on the part of schools, the rhetoric of parent–school connection-building outstrips the reality (Corter & Pelletier, 2005). Others have argued that the increased emphasis on parent involvement at school may in fact be particularly problematic for more disadvantaged parents (a classic study: Lareau & Shumar, 1996; for a review, see Mapp, 2011; and see Hong, 2011 for a distinct approach). Alison Griffith and Dorothy E. Smith (2005) described "the mothering discourse," which provides developed categories of knowledge and "a moral logic of responsibility, that subordinates those who participate to a universalized public education system, aligning parenting practices with educational requirements, without reference to practical limitations affecting mother's actual work" (p. 40). It is undeniable that the rhetoric of parent involvement in schools is primarily oriented towards the question of how parents can support their children's schooling, rather than seeing schools as part of the support system for vulnerable families. This "common sense" treatment of parents as either a resource to be put to use for the school or a potentially blameworthy source of children's problems is at odds with a notion of collective responsibility for dependency, which must take into account the conditions and needs of caregivers.

The case is even more extreme in the context of child protection. Socio-legal scholars have long argued that the child protection mandate, however universal, has in practice operated to police familial ideologies (Chunn, 1988; Gavigan, 1996; more recently, Pelton, 2008), and in particular, to limit and stigmatize public support for struggling families (Scarth & Sullivan, 2008). Karen Swift (1995), in her classic *Manufacturing Bad Mothers*, wrote about "help" and "authority" in child protection. Contrary to Fineman's model of "collective responsibility for dependency," Swift argues that far from making help or support available while preserving a role for individual decision-making,

> The "good parent" model, through which help and authority are apparently merged, continually produces the mothers as unworthy of help. Their own lived experience disappears through procedures designed to

examine their present suitability for the job of parenting. The same procedures produce children as actually being helped through the exertion of state authority over their parents. We may notice that most of the help that in fact is provided [to] children is theoretical. They are rescued from dangerous situations to be sure, but their futures are far from ensured through these repeated rescue operations. (pp. 170–1)

Swift suggests that the child welfare system's focus is on rescuing children – and on enforcing parental responsibility – more than providing the support the children need for their continuing well-being.[4] Public responsibility for children's well-being is exercised by pressuring parents to provide "good enough" parenting, through a combination of "support" and compulsion due to the ever-present threat of removal. She argues, finally, that this approach is insufficient to provide for children's well-being, because ultimately it does not provide the supports that are necessary for parents, particularly mothers.

As such, Swift's work can be seen as part of a general feminist critique of privatization in public institutions and discourse, as "a broad policy impulse to change the balance between private and public responsibility in public policy" (Cossman & Fudge, 2002, p. 18). Feminist scholarship of the welfare state has examined the categorical ways in which responsibility for social reproduction have historically been heavily gendered as the private responsibility of mothers, or as "women's work" within the family, and have been legitimately defined as being beyond public concern (see e.g., Daly & Rake, 2004; Jenson, 2004). Strikingly, in its modern, more gender-neutral state, women's responsibility for dependency and/or reproduction continues, largely unabated. As women are recast "equally" as worker-citizens, their ongoing work raising children and caring for other dependents "has either been rendered invisible (at best) and relegated to no one (at worst)" (Gavigan & Chunn, 2007, p. 737).

Child welfare is another area where continuity is more marked than change. Public support for the hands-on work of parenting has *always* been sharply limited, and social issues that deeply affect parenting options – such as the epidemic of poverty among single mothers – have always been individualized. Individualization is a process by which issues are understood "both with respect to causes and solutions, in highly individualized terms ... Social and structural analyses are displaced in favour of individual solutions to individual problems" (Cossman, 2002, p. 21).

Parental responsibility is among the most deeply naturalized or taken-for-granted of private responsibilities; under normal circumstances, the social construction is invisible. In the context of child protection, this naturalized order is made more visible as different aspects of parenting explicitly become part of the state's responsibility. But at the same time as the state becomes involved, the ongoing exercise of responsibilities by mothers in the family becomes subject to scrutiny ("assessment") and even enforcement. By establishing a threshold of adequate parenting, this public involvement in fact reinforces the boundaries of private responsibility.

A theory of collective responsibility for dependency would assume that some public help is necessary for most parents at different times, promoting a more fluid boundary between public and private. It would support measures to ensure that the help provided was effective to meet the needs of children and their caregivers. In my view, such a response would be consistent with the paramount purpose of the Child and Family Services Act, "to promote the best interests, protection and well-being of children."[5] However, when we turn our gaze to the actual machinery of children's services, it is hard to know where to start in attempting to operationalize this type of public responsibility.

Practical Challenges: Scale, Complexity, and Operational Silos in Ontario

Education and childcare are both provincial responsibilities in Canada, and delivery of services is significantly decentralized, even fragmented. Local governance structures, including school boards and Children's Aid Societies, were developed to ensure responsiveness to the needs of different communities; even though the province is the sole funder and establishes the framework for operations, provincial policy can often seem quite removed from operational realities at the level of the individual child, worker, school, or community.

In Ontario, the Ministry of Education has legal responsibility for education, and is exclusively responsible for funding public education in the province (CAD $22.53 billion in 2014–15) and setting province-wide policies. In 2014, there were 1.35 million elementary school students, and more than 73,000 certified elementary school teachers. Authority is delegated to 72 district school boards, which are organized into four "systems" (English Public, English Catholic, French Public, and French Catholic). Accordingly, in a given geographical area, there are four different educational authorities, all with almost identical legal authority but somewhat distinct policies. There are significant differences between individual schools, both in terms of the composition of the student body and policies and practices; there are often even greater levels of differences in abilities, achievement, and social background between individual students and classes (e.g., the classic study by Raudenbusch & Willms, 1991). In 2014, there were 3980 elementary schools across Ontario.

On the child protection side, funding (CAD $1.6 billion in 2014–15) and authority for child welfare (and related areas such as children's mental health and youth justice) is exercised by the Ministry of Children and Youth Services (MCYS), which sets province-wide policy under the Child and Family Services Act. The act authorizes non-profit Children's Aid Societies to deliver services; in 2012 there were 46 in Ontario, with 8800 staff (Commission to Promote Sustainable Child Welfare (Ontario), 2012a, p. 8).[6] A Provincial Child and Youth Advocate[7] is directly appointed by the legislature to investigate and report on conditions and services for children in the child welfare system throughout the province. Some areas are served by a single Children's Aid Society, but in others there are multiple CASs with distinct religious or cultural mandates. For example, in the City of Toronto, there are four different Children's Aid Societies. Children from any school board can be served by any agency, resulting in a high level of bureaucratic complexity and significant challenges in terms of developing working relationships between schools and particular CASs.[8] In 2010, the Commission to Promote Sustainable Child Welfare reported that CASs showed important differences in capacity, services delivered, and interpretation of mandate. The commission also criticized low levels of collaboration between CASs and with external partners, excessive variation in the kinds and availability of services, and insufficient accountability between the CASs and MCYS. Even at the ministry level, the commission found considerable fragmentation of ministry functions (2010, pp. 2–3). This operational fragmentation is an important contributing factor in the relatively low levels of data available about the system or, more dramatically, about individual cases (MacKinnon, 2006); there is even less data about outcomes for children receiving services in the community (Commission to Promote Sustainable Child Welfare, 2012b, p. 47).

Particularly given the shocking legacy of residential schools and problematic child welfare intervention with Indigenous families (see Truth and Reconciliation Commission, 2015), it is disturbing to note that the situation of First Nations, Metis, and Inuit (FNMI) children is marked even further by fragmentation and gaps. Jurisdictional disputes are a unique disadvantage faced on a regular basis by First Nations children, as is significant relative underfunding for First Nations child welfare services (Blackstock, 2011). These differences in treatment have been recognized as discriminatory by the Canadian Human Rights Tribunal, in a decision that will not be appealed by the Government of Canada (*First Nations Child and Family Caring Society of Canada v. Attorney General of Canada*, 2016). Many agencies serving FNMI children have fewer community services to draw upon in supporting children, and, as is widely recognized, First Nations, Metis, and Inuit families face far higher than average challenges in terms of poverty, ill health, under housing, and education – all of which contribute to poor child welfare outcomes.

In the past decade, a number of provincial initiatives have been introduced to improve coordination between child welfare and education in Ontario. The "renewed vision" for education in Ontario specifically references children and youth in care of the province, and commits schools to supporting their "unique transitions" (in and out of foster care, and between placements) and monitoring results (Ministry of Education, 2014a). With the exception of a new Joint Protocol for Student Achievement, these initiatives are limited to those children in care.

In 2015, the province, with the support of the Ontario Association of Children's Aid Societies, released an ambitious template for a Joint Protocol for Student Achievement, which the government is encouraging CASs and school boards across the province to sign (Ministry of Children and Youth Services and Ministry of Education, 2015). The protocol establishes a regime for information sharing, administrative processes around school registration, and dispute resolution where there are concerns about registration, services being received, or discipline. The key tools are a REACH (Realizing Educational Achievement for Children/Youth) team to put in place proactive and preventative measures for children in care or children receiving services from a CAS, and an Educational Success Plan (ESP) for every student. The REACH team includes someone from the child's school, someone from their CAS, a parent or caregiver, as appropriate, and the child. The team may also include a student advocate; other staff (e.g., special education teachers); community stakeholders; or First Nations, Metis, or Inuit community representation. The team is expected to meet at least twice a year to plan for appropriate supports and experiences to promote the student's short- and long-term educational success. Some of these supports may be within the school, others may be provided by the CAS (e.g., tutoring, social skills programs). The Educational Success Plan, drafted by the REACH team, is meant to track plans, and to incorporate other educational planning tools such as an Individual Education Plan. The ESP addresses special education needs and planning for the student's future, with a focus on transitions to further education or work.

What is particularly interesting about the joint protocol template, in the context of this study, is that it specifically includes children receiving services in the community; for those children, parents must consent to the sharing of information and participation in REACH and ESP activities. In all cases, children 12 years or older must also consent. This significant change occurred after my research took place, so it is beyond the scope of this book to assess them – but the research clearly identified a need for mechanisms of this type. It will be very interesting to see how many CASs and schools implement REACH teams, and, in the case of students living in the community, whether they routinely seek and obtain consent from parents to harness these tools for the benefit of these students.

Another key area of co-operation is in the area of outcomes measurement and publication. In Ontario, the Child Welfare Outcomes Expert Reference Group developed a list of desired outcomes for children in the child welfare system, including those receiving services in the community. These outcomes include (basic) measures of educational progress (Ontario Child Welfare Outcomes Expert Reference Group, 2010). The Ministry of Children and Youth Services, working with the Ontario Association of Children's Aid Societies, in turn developed a list of agreed-upon service performance indicators in the areas of safety, permanency, and well-being. Students' educational progress is measured using age-to-grade data. But data on indicators relating to well-being, including education, are limited to children in care. There has been considerable internal controversy over which indicators will be reported publicly.

To build stronger bridges to post-secondary education, the province has established "Crown Ward Education Championship Teams" (Ontario Association of Children's Aid Societies, 2007), again, specifically for children in care in several regions (as of 2016, there are approximately 20 teams across Ontario). The teams promote collaborative mentoring for students, peer support, and guidance supports to help students look ahead. The province has also guaranteed free tuition to children in care in universities and some colleges to promote post-secondary education.

Individual CASs have done a range of work to improve educational outcomes for children in their care. For example, one CAS actually began to operate a KUMON tutoring franchise, and was able to show improved outcomes for students receiving tutoring support; that same CAS worked actively to develop an "education culture" to boost expectations for their students, to minimize school changes, and to train foster parents to be better prepared to manage educational issues (e.g., O'Brien, 2012). In addition, the province has been supporting pilot projects to improve supports for children in care (e.g., Flynn et al., 2012; Harper & Schmidt, 2012).

While these efforts represent progress, it is important to contrast the situation in Ontario with that found in other jurisdictions. A large-scale, cross-national European study found that most countries have made very limited moves to improve educational outcomes for children in the care system, with one exception: England (Jackson & Cameron, 2012). Through its "Every Child Matters" reforms, England established a legislated duty to co-operate between schools and children's services, an integrated set of child outcome measures, a set of integrated inspections of schools and children's services, a Common Assessment Framework for diverse professionals working with vulnerable children, and an exception to privacy rules when it is important for children's well-being (e.g., Chief Inspector of Schools, 2005; Government of England, 2004; Government of England, 2005). The government has also put in place a range of practical innovations around managing the shared responsibility, such as pilot projects to bring educational experts to identify children's educational needs at the local authority level through "Virtual School Headteachers," which were found to be highly effective (Berridge, Henry, Jackson, & Turney, 2009). The newly established Rees Centre for Research in Fostering and Education at Oxford University is developing a significant body of studies on research, practice, and policy information relating to child welfare and schooling, including research on these initiatives.[9]

The United States has increasingly emphasized child well-being as a priority for child welfare services (see Administration for Children, Youth and Families [U.S.], 2012). The Department of Health and Human Services has identified schools as one of the three key proximal influences on healthy child development, alongside family and peers, and begun to develop recommendations for schools' role in contributing to healthy child development in general, and particularly for children experiencing maltreatment (see Biglan, 2014). The federal government conducts cyclical Child and Family Services Reviews (CFSR) of all states, which include monitoring well-being outcomes. The reviews track a specific outcome that "Children receive appropriate services to meet their educational needs." Education is the *only* one of the 21 outcomes in areas that include safety, permanence, and well-being, on which a significant number of states (10) are in "substantial conformity" with federal standards. Nonetheless, in the most recent publicly available CFSR Aggregate Report, an analysis showed that in 30 states, the educational needs of children were not assessed; in 24 states there were challenges maintaining or coordinating educational services for foster children due in part to a lack of communication between schools and agency, as well as delays; and in 23 states, the children's educational needs were not addressed (Health and Human Services, 2011).

The examples of England and the United States highlight the relatively underdeveloped levels of co-operation between schools and child welfare in Ontario. As we have seen, the institutional context for the interaction between child welfare and education in Ontario is marked by considerable scale, by fragmentation, and by persistent operational silos. Local initiatives to improve coordination are also underway, but they are not yet broadly disseminated. In spite of significant efforts to improve coordination at the provincial level in the last several years, it is too soon to judge the impact of important initiatives such as the Joint Protocol for Student Achievement, and it is worrying that performance indicators continue to report only partially on children in the community.

Investigating Collective Responsibility: Multi-Sited with an Emphasis on Linkages

This research developed out of my interest in a very general question: given that mothers, child protection authorities, and schools all have a powerful interest in the well-being and success of children who are receiving services from a Children's Aid Society and living at home, how do these groups interact? And how are those interactions shaped by their policy context?

A central challenge was to grasp how institutional routines and assumptions shape the actions of front-line workers in a policy area requiring co-operation between bureaucracies and active maintenance of relationships with both children and their parents. These routines and assumptions operate in the shadow of serious concerns about neglect or abuse. This research question recognizes that a complete analysis of "decentred" regulatory activity includes not only formal, written law, and policy, but extends to the informal processes which bind rule-making and compliance together through social interaction (e.g., Tamanaha, 1995). This approach is consistent with longstanding traditions in implementation research in education and social policy (Elmore & McLaughlin, 1988; McLaughlin, 1987; Pressman & Wildavsky, 2005) and theories of street-level bureaucracy which emphasize the extent to which public policy is not what is proclaimed on high but "the decisions of street-level bureaucrats, the routines they establish and the devices they invent to cope with uncertainties and work pressures" (Lipsky, 1980, p. xii; for an update, see Maynard-Moody & Portillo, 2010).

To address the challenge, I drew on the sociological approach of institutional ethnography, which is "not meant as a way of discovering the everyday world as such, but of looking out beyond the everyday to discover how it came to happen as it does" (Smith, 2006b, p.3). Rather than focusing simply on the perspective of one group, the study looked at the issues of shared responsibility from multiple perspectives. I used accounts from mothers, teachers, and child welfare workers alongside interviews with policy officials and review of legislation and policy documents, to connect micro-level, narrative data with macro issues of context and institutions.

The initial design of the study called for linked interviews about particular children to tell a story about how the different parts of the system work together (or do not). After recruiting and interviewing parents whose child or children's CAS cases were recently closed across a large metropolitan area, I sought their consent to interview the family service worker and a teacher who had worked with their child or children while the case was open. This strategy meant that the teachers and workers I interviewed came from five different school boards, three different agencies, and twenty-one different schools. In this urban context, institutional heterogeneity is one of the features affecting how child welfare and schools work together, and it is one of the factors that makes regulation of the field organizationally challenging. Strikingly, there were strong similarities between the observations of front-line workers across boards and agencies.

Naturally, there were numerous layers of permission-seeking involved before I could conduct linked interviews with mothers and the professionals involved in their children's lives. Although one large Children's Aid Society was extremely facilitative, a number of school boards and agencies did not approve the research, despite ethics approval from University of Toronto. Ultimately, the research was able to proceed based on a revised ethics protocol, relying on section 2 of the *Tri-Council policy statement on ethical research involving humans* (Interagency secretariat on research ethics, 2005),[10] which specifies that institutions such as corporations or government are not required to consent to research about them and should not have the right to veto research.

The lack of institutional support from different boards and agencies shaped my sample, because it limited certain types of recruitment and because some professional participants were unwilling to proceed in the absence of approval from their employer. At one level, the lack of support is indicative of a guardedness and defensiveness that itself forms a barrier to inter-agency co-operation. The terms of the refusals also reflected institutional attitudes particularly towards the mothers in the sample. Those who chose to participate – in some cases consciously ignoring institutional preferences otherwise – provided very frank accounts of their experiences, which did not noticeably differ between individuals from organizations with looser or tighter efforts to control participation of their staff. On the other hand, the lack of institutional support may have made it easier for some workers who had difficult experiences to decline to be interviewed. A detailed discussion of the ethical questions raised in this research, institutional gatekeeping and its effects on my research, and implications for my subject, is included in Appendix 2.

Ultimately, I supplemented the linked interviews with a series of unlinked interviews with teachers and social workers who were not involved with the mothers I interviewed. Early interviews also emphasized the importance of school personnel other than teachers – particularly principals and school social workers – in supporting children where there were concerns about abuse and neglect and managing relationships with Children's Aid Societies. In the interests of better understanding my subject, I added interviews with those groups.[11]

In total, I interviewed eight mothers (six linked), ten teachers (five linked, five unlinked), eight family service workers (two linked, six unlinked), six school principals (unlinked), and six student support workers (unlinked) as my front-line group. There were only two fully triangulated cases. In addition to front-line personnel, I also interviewed leaders from different points in the structures of CAS and school systems, conducting a total of fifty-seven interviews which ranged from forty minutes to more than two hours in length. I've used pseudonyms throughout.

The role of mother, teacher, and principal is self-explanatory. Family service workers are one group of social workers in children's aid societies whose primary responsibility is to work in an ongoing way with families (unlike an intake worker). Student support workers can include school social workers, guidance counselors, or child and youth workers; they do not have daily classroom interaction with students but may play a key role in supporting students at school. In the past several years, a number of CASs have created a new position, "education advocate." This position has the responsibility of supporting students in care in their dealings with schools and building stronger relationships between schools and CASs. Education advocates have significant background working in the school system (e.g., former principals or trustees), but are now working on behalf of the CAS.

The use of multiple data sources – informants positioned differently in the system – and textual analysis allowed useful analytic triangulation. It not only helped enhance trustworthiness of the data, but it helped illuminate the points of overlap and disconnect between the systems and shed light on participants' understandings of their own and their shared responsibilities in light of the expectations of others.

Terminology: Parents versus Mothers

According to Fineman (2005), the concept of collective responsibility for dependency is particularly important for poor women. Fineman's position is one of "substantive equality," defined by the Supreme Court of Canada as taking into account social, political, economic, and historical factors concerning a group (e.g., Andrews v. Law Society of British Columbia, 1989; see also, *Withler* v. *Canada* [*Attorney General*], 2011). Substantive equality, the main thrust of Canadian equality jurisprudence since the introduction of the Charter of Rights in 1982, "repudiates a formalistic 'treats like alike' approach." Formal equality is associated with the individualistic use of gender-neutral language such as "parents," in a way that ignores the traditional allocation of work within the family as a social institution. Like all institutions, the family changes over time, which may affect the distribution of work within it and certainly affects the ways in which policy constructs and regulates that division (Eichler, 1997a). Substantive equality requires explicit recognition that caring work – and its associated costs – continues to be, overwhelmingly, the responsibility of women, both within the institution of the family and in interaction with public institutions such as schools and child welfare. Social expectations of mothers are significantly different than they are for fathers, and this book focuses on the social category of motherhood.

Significantly, all the social/occupational categories in my study – parents involved with CAS,[12] elementary school teachers, and social workers[13] – are dominated by women. This reflects the reality that those who do the majority of the work caring for, educating, and keeping these children safe, in the private or the public sphere, are overwhelmingly women. The work they do is undeniably part of the powerful historical and ongoing category of "women's work" (Daly & Rake, 2004), which fundamentally shapes its visibility, perceptions of its value, and the public support it receives.

Like Sylvia Biklen in her study of women teachers (1995), while I understand my work as an exploration of the ways that the responsibility of mothers is framed, my vocabulary follows that of the research participants as they reference mothers and parents, in order to respect their perspectives on mothers and parenting. Like her, whether participants talk about parents or about mothers, I find the gendered positions of my participants lurk as the subtext of each encounter (p. 127–8).

I also recognize that the language is highly politicized. For some, efforts to talk about "parents" rather than mothers, represents an effort to redefine responsibility within the family in a way that creates stronger expectations for fathers. Promoting a larger role for fathers in caring work within the household, as well as in sharing the associated costs, is an important equality strategy. For others, avoiding the specific terminology of women or mothers in favour of language such as gender or parenthood, may be an effort to "dissociate an author [or speaker] from the (supposedly strident) feminist politics of inequality or power" in a quest for academic legitimacy or social acceptability (Scott, 1986). In this study, I have opted for the sociological use of gender-specific language, and endeavoured to keep my politics explicit.

Collective Responsibility for Dependency, and Its Dilemmas

The concept of building collective responsibility for dependency necessarily challenges the existing relationship between public and private. This study focuses on a group of adults – mothers, social workers, and teachers – who work and interact at the margin between public and private. Parents, mostly mothers, and the front-line state actors who represent the public sphere in these families' lives give the collective responsibility for the well-being of this group of children its meaning in practice. Through interviews, the participants articulate what they understand to be the public responsibility for the well-being of these children.

The book takes up five specific areas of responsibility in the chapters below:

- The interaction between schools and child welfare with respect to their shared responsibilities around the duty to report abuse and neglect, which reveals support in principle but not always in practice.
- The definition of aspects of cultural difference as problematic by some educators, using the tools of child protection – which may contribute, in turn, to issues of overrepresentation of certain groups in the child welfare system.
- Child welfare's responsibility, if any, to provide educational services for children who remain with their parents, which highlights the limited policy and accountability framework around it.
- The difficulty pinpointing – let alone prescribing – the scope of teachers' irregular work. Minimal and maximal definitions of teachers' responsibilities coexist in law and the understandings of teachers and parents. While high aspirations are widely held inside and outside the profession, a definition of what can fairly be expected of teachers is ultimately individualized.
- Teachers' responsibility to provide care and maintain relationships with students which are ultimately privatized, leading to a "hit and miss" system of determining whether students will encounter a teacher who make a difference.

Each area illustrates different aspects of the broad issue of collective responsibility for dependency. The chapters illustrate shifting boundaries between private and public, and between support, autonomy, and compulsion. Taken together, the analysis highlights the need for a more robust conception of public responsibility, for enhanced opportunities for two-way communication, and for better tools for coordination at the local and system levels. Meaningful change will be anchored in a deepened commitment to the achievable goal of broad, deep, and practical public support for the well-being of very vulnerable children.

Chapter Two

Separate Spheres and Closed Systems: Reporting and Communication between Schools and Child Protection

Home and School: Different Worlds?

In this chapter, I focus specifically on the aspect of the relationship between schools and child welfare agencies where there are the clearest formal requirements for coordination – the responsibility of educators to observe, report, and take action on situations that raise significant concerns about abuse or neglect. A prerequisite for effective child welfare and protection work is the capacity to identify children who are being abused or neglected or who are at risk of maltreatment. It is obvious that child welfare, acting alone, does not have the resources to pick up on all the situations of harm or risk to children. Accordingly, Ontario's Child and Family Services Act creates a duty to report suspected maltreatment that delegates responsibility for observation and judgment about harm and risk to children to the broader public, and particularly to professionals such as educators. Child welfare workers in Ontario, in turn, have a less-publicized obligation to be in contact with "collaterals," those who work closely with children outside child welfare, such as teachers or doctors. The duty to observe and, in limited ways, to share information is an essential part of a collective responsibility to take action to protect children.

A report of neglect or abuse has the power to define both a child and a family in ways that are beyond the control of the individual reporter. It has the potential to activate needed support, or to unleash powerful machinery that can (sometimes necessarily) result in huge consequences for children and parents, and which is very likely to result in stigma.

The notion of "separate spheres" is a historical (Victorian) notion of distinct, naturalized realms of responsibility for women and men, where women were ascendant in the private world of the home, and men out in the public world of politics and market. Critique of, and engagement with, the metaphor of separate spheres, "social space divided into dichotomous and gendered realms of public and private" (Downs, 2010, p. 14), has been a focus of feminist theory for decades (e.g., Pateman, 1997; Rosenberg, 1983; Scott, 1986, 2008). Critics have pointed to the essential inter-dependency of the "separate" domains, the hierarchical ordering of public and private, and the ways in which a focus on a particular dichotomy systematically displaces analysis of other crucial, constitutive aspects of social structure such as class, race, and epoch. However, used critically, the notion of separate spheres provides scholars and activists with a powerful model for "analyzing in context the way any binary opposite operates, reversing and displacing its historical construction rather than accepting it as real or self-evident or in the nature of things" (Scott, 1986, p. 1074). In this chapter, I make critical use of the concept of separate spheres, but not by examining "separate" domains or responsibilities of women and men. Instead, I show how the responsibility of family service workers and teachers to protect children is divided, respectively, into spheres of home and school. From the perspective of educators and parents, at least, home and school map onto private and public realms. This constructed dichotomy establishes an accepted limit on the responsibility of each professional group, and simultaneously defines the appropriate focus of scrutiny.

While both child protection and schools have mandates to watch and report on possible risks to children, the legislative and policy scheme assumes "separate spheres" of responsibility. The different agencies watch and collect information about different aspects of the children's lives. Specifically, the school has a limited mandate to scrutinize children's home lives, and child protection, in turn, tends to assume that the school is meeting children's educational needs. Separate spheres of responsibility for surveillance provide considerable operational benefit, particularly for schools. However, a review of front-line practitioners' practice reveals that while the scheme is clear and widely acknowledged, there are considerable gaps in its operation. Finally, an unintended effect of separate spheres of responsibility for vigilance is that front-line workers from each institution each fail to scrutinize the performance of the other. This failure potentially deprives the children involved of important advocates. Scrutiny is focused on mothers, a relatively easy target, and is based on possible deficits in the private sphere, not emphasizing the considerable potential for deficits in the policies or responses of multiple systems that one school trustee in a leadership role described in an interview as "masses of bureaucratic red tape that are hard to navigate."

The Legal and Normative Model of Complementary Scrutiny

An Area of Detailed Law and Protocol

Section 72 of the Child and Family Services Act (CFSA) imposes an ongoing, statutory duty on all persons to report any reasonable suspicion of abuse or neglect. For teachers, among other professionals who work with children, the CFSA makes it an offence to fail to personally report such a suspicion. Each board across the province has put into place extensive procedures to ensure that educators, particularly principals, have detailed guidelines about how to respond to a suspicion of abuse or neglect. These guidelines are based on extensive protocols and policies in place between boards of education, Children's Aid Societies, and police services.[1] The purpose of these policies and protocols is not only to reiterate the duty to report but also to define and distinguish the responsibilities of educators (mostly principals, who are required either to comply or ensure that others do) from those of CAS. Educators have the duty to report, but their role stops there. At the point child protection has been informed of a suspicion, it is the exclusive responsibility of child protection to investigate and take the necessary action to protect a child. There is an urgent, practical purpose for this division of labour – investigation of child abuse and neglect is extremely complex and very easily compromised (e.g., Myers, 2005, chapter 1). But in effect, the law puts in place a system where teachers' responsibility towards the safety of children is to constantly be on lookout for what is readily observable, to report, and, if there are ongoing concerns, to follow up through the principal or the child protection agency.

CAS workers' duties are prescribed under the CFSA, its regulations, and agency-specific policies that do not have the force of law but are binding on workers as employees. The CFSA is largely silent about the obligation of child protection to work with other agencies, including schools.[2] The regulations prescribe Standards of Practice (Ministry of Children and Youth Services, 2007), which anticipate the involvement of collaterals – usually understood as community services such as schools, family doctors, hospitals, or other services. Collaterals are identified as important to monitoring (mandatory) safety plans for children (Standard 5), assessing family and child strengths and needs, and service planning for cases receiving ongoing service (Standard 9). Collaterals are also a mandatory part of the process of closing a case, either at the stage of investigation or ongoing service (Standard 11). Each Children's Aid Society in Ontario has a policy manual – a detailed, mandatory guidebook for workers' practice in the field. A policy or service manual does not have the force of law, and there can be differences between policies at different CASs. However, at all the CASs where I conducted interviews, there was a specific policy in place requiring workers to contact collaterals within two weeks of opening a case.[3] The duty to contact collaterals is constrained by the requirement – consistent with privacy legislation[4] – that a parent consent to the contact. It does not necessarily imply two-way information flow, as the objective for contact is, in many cases, information-gathering.

"They are your eyes on the child": Child Protection Relies on Teacher Surveillance

Interview data shows that the mandated division of the labour of surveillance appeared to be well-understood, and generally widely accepted, by child protection workers, teachers, and parents. All the child protection workers I interviewed underlined teachers' capacity as ongoing observers as an important part of the safety net for children. For example, one family service worker, Mallory, explained: "The school in every case should be aware that you are working. I would say pretty much. They are the major collateral. They are seeing the child every day. They are the eyes. The parent could be saying everything is great. But the school could be saying, she's coming to school with no lunch, or inadequate lunch ... they are your eyes on the child."

This explanation also emphasizes schools' role in surveillance, acting as an agent for child protection, and that the school's view is, in many ways, preferred to that of mothers. Another social worker working with the CAS, Kira – someone to whom I was referred by another CAS worker because of her reputation as a strong advocate for children within the school system – described CAS's expectations of teachers during ongoing casework:

I would love to hear from the school. It's kind of a low-risk case – that's why it is not critical that I speak to the school. But for that 360 degree–view of the family – they are going to have insight on his situation, his social skills, is his homework being done, hygiene, how he is faring socially, emotionally, academically. When you are asking mom, or asking the child, especially as a child protection worker – it makes sense that their vested interest is putting the most positive face on the situation. Talking to the school gives you much more of the picture.

Another school social worker, Zelda, who had worked for several years at CAS, was quite analytical about the kinds of information teachers have that can be very helpful:

Teachers, because they see the kids every day, all day, they should be able to pick up the patterns more, especially around issues of neglect. As a social worker, if I see a kid every week or two weeks, there is lots of information I don't get. I think teachers have a lot more interactions with parents than I do, so they would have more of a bigger picture of the family than I might as someone who parachutes in. And, oftentimes, teachers have a history with families through teaching siblings.

In turn, the teachers I interviewed were unanimous that their typical role in a child protection investigation had been to provide background information, at the investigation stage or possibly at case closing. One special education teacher, Laura, commented:

They are interested in meeting with me, because there is a perception that I know more about these kids than anyone else does because I work with kids for several years – so they'll talk to me if they are trying to get a quick history, especially if they feel the parent is not candid ... they want to know background, behaviour, how the child is doing socially. I always feel like it is more like I am helping them get on their way than anything reciprocal.

This perception was echoed by other educators. For example, Evelyn, a very experienced teacher working in a challenging neighbourhood, commented, "Usually they just come in and do the interview and you never see them again."

"We don't know what they know": The Boundary on Teacher Surveillance

Although schools have an important mandate to report on suspected abuse and/or neglect, and they often play a role in initial investigations because they know a great deal about their students, most of the school personnel I talked to recognized that CAS had important knowledge that lay beyond the parameters of what they normally know as educators. They expressed the view that CAS should know what is going on at home, and that they themselves have a limited knowledge – or responsibility for this knowledge. One principal, who identified herself as an activist problem-solver and who prided herself on her ability to connect with parents who were struggling, commented, "Sometimes we have a discussion [with CAS], we might be saying this kid is not going to survive in high school. We have a lot of information about what is going on – but we don't know what they know." Marika, a teacher who was very frustrated with the lack of resources she had as a classroom teacher facing large numbers of children with significant educational and social needs, commented that "We always just report – and then, here it is. I put this case in your hands – then obviously, *you* have the resources to continue solving this problem." She acknowledged that social workers working with CAS were no doubt also overwhelmed, but in the face of the demands that she faced in the classroom, she needed to believe that CAS was able to fulfil its responsibilities.

Laura, the special education teacher, explained that CAS was "in the home, very involved, they really know what is going on." Another teacher, Antonio, defined CAS's responsibility as "to have contact with the family, make sure they go to home visit, make the parents aware that they are aware of what is happening in the home and at school." In some cases, educators rely on CAS's role in dealing with the family to reinforce a view of the school as a "place apart" in children's lives. For example, when asked to define success in school, Gabriella, a guidance counsellor, responded by talking about the school as an institution separate from the messiness of the home life: "If we're looking at it through the scope of an abused or neglected child: We've succeeded if we're protecting the child. We've succeeded if we've provided safety, if the school has provided, hopefully, safety, nurturing adults, things to do ... a separate life from their home life." By contrast, she defined the responsibility of CAS to "follow through with the family, longer term."

A third-year teacher, Kanti, frustrated that CAS had never responded when she had reported a child missing school without his mother's knowledge, remarked, "The lady I talked to tried to downplay the whole thing. I know they deal with really serious stuff, and something could be more urgent on the day I was talking to her – but I feel that neglect *is* very serious, and has serious impact. I felt like the situation I was reporting was serious enough that I expected some kind of monitoring or observation of what was taking place at home."

Based on the interviews, it appears that teachers and other school personnel, including those who describe their practice as involving extensive contact with families, expect child protection to have significant knowledge of, and impact on, children's home life that is categorically different from the kinds of knowledge and impact they feel that they can, should, or wish to have, as educators. Teachers *and* child protection workers expect school personnel to be vigilant observers of what happens in school, to have a sensitivity to risk to children, and to communicate their observations, but they do not expect that the teachers should be probing or otherwise intervening in children's home life; that responsibility belongs to child welfare.

A Useful Boundary

The extent to which both parents and educators see these separate spheres of responsibility as appropriate and beneficial is striking. Both groups, for the most part, emphasize the importance of boundaries in maintaining positive relationships between the school and parents. Teachers and even principals may in fact be grateful for the opportunity to pass on responsibility to a figure beyond the walls of the classroom or even the school itself. In addition, a number of the administrators and social workers I interviewed emphasized the importance of being able to delegate home concerns so as to allow teachers to maintain academic focus.

Maintaining Positive Relationships
Between Home and School

MOTHERS

The mothers I interviewed largely accepted that the school would have some knowledge of the background facts of their situation, up to and including their involvement with CAS, where there was a clear nexus between direct concern with the child and the background knowledge. At the same time, at least some of the mothers were also concerned that the school not push too far into their affairs.

I asked all eight mothers whether the school was aware that CAS was involved with their children. Six of them reported that the school was aware (although in one of those cases, the teacher said he had *not* been aware of CAS involvement, and in another, where the family was being served by a child protection agency that did not call itself a Children's Aid Society, the teacher knew the child was troubled and seeing a counsellor but was "not sure" whether she had been aware that child protection was involved). In only one case did the mother report that the school did *not* know about her family's child welfare involvement. One did not know whether the school was aware of the involvement of child protection. The school learned of each family's involvement with CAS in different ways. In three cases, the school had learned about CAS's involvement during a period when the child was temporarily removed from the mother's home. Two mothers reported calling the teachers to tell them themselves. For example, Caroline reported, "I told them about Ali's foot [which was extremely badly burned] because the kids had to go ... they went and lived with my sisters for a week or so. So I had to tell the school 'okay, my children ain't here, this, this and that.' I told the school." In two cases (including that one), the parents also knew that someone from school had called to report suspected abuse or neglect. In another case where there was a concern about exposure to ongoing domestic violence, a mother had told the principal, in order to try to ensure that the father (from whom she was temporarily separated) did not take the child from the school without her knowledge. She hoped CAS could convince the principal to put a safety procedure in place, in the absence of a court order. One mother reported that social workers from CAS routinely visited the school to see how the kids were doing.[5]

The mothers I interviewed, on the whole, saw it as necessary and useful that the school knew something about what they were going through. One mother, Ruby – a relatively recent immigrant, learning English, with very little formal education – even saw CAS as a resource for the teacher if there were problems with her children (one of whom was in a behaviour class).

Do you think there's anything CAS can do to help your kids with school?
Yeah.
   What do you think?
When they go to school, they ask teacher ... They come in free to do everything to do with learning, because they know they don't have problems. If they have problems, even when they go there, I know the teachers know if they do something, they can call Children's Aid. So they help them.

The teacher helps them to see the things they are doing, so they know more too. If their children don't do good, or the teacher don't teach them good, Children's Aid know. Yeah.

This mother appeared to see CAS as actively providing support in managing the behaviour of her children both at home and at school.

More often, it seemed that the mothers saw the school's knowledge of their situation as allowing for some special understanding or extra support for their children. For example, Rachel, who had informed the school about her abusive relationship and the fact her child was getting help from outside agencies, said:

Because Jamie's missed a bit of school – not months, but some days he'll get up and say "oh, my stomach hurts," and it doesn't ... but his teacher told me to keep him home – because with everything he's going through, he might need some extra mothering, like to feel safe. She said if he's really pushing the envelope, just keep him with you – just don't let him take advantage of it long term.

Deborah, a mother with a Cree background, now living in Toronto, described how the school had been extremely supportive of her and her family in a number of ways (helping her youngest child register for kindergarten at the last minute when the school was full, waiving activities fees, providing holiday hampers). She clearly saw the school's knowledge of her general situation as important to this support. Deborah observed, "I don't want to say it's favouritism, it's just they have seen me for a long time, they have seen me struggling ... they were looking out for us."

The mothers I interviewed appeared relatively unconcerned about the school's knowledge of their involvement with child welfare. There is a strong body of research that shows high levels of stigma associated with child welfare involvement (e.g., Kemp, Marcenko, Hoagwood, & Vesneski, 2009; Scholte et al., 1999; Sykes, 2011). Also, I observed considerable stigmatizing behaviour on the part of some of the educators I encountered in the process of recruiting participants for this research (see Appendix 2). There are a number of possible explanations for the mothers' expressed comfort with their school knowing about their child welfare involvement. Scholte et al. (1999) found that receipt of preventative services was much less stigmatized than actual child removal. The mothers who were willing to speak to me – and even more, to let me talk to their children's teachers – could well have had fewer concerns about stigma than the general population of parents involved with child welfare. Perceptions of stigma may also be an issue that shapes the perceptions of service providers as well as clients.

Although the mothers accepted some level of knowledge on the part of the school about their struggles and even the involvement of CAS, several of them were wary of the school having too much knowledge or involvement with their home situation, or actively seeking it out. Deborah, though she appreciated the school looking out for her and her family through "the hell we were going through," also said she didn't want the school asking questions:

Do you think your relationship with school changed when child welfare got involved?
No, because the school had nothing to do with it. Once I got them back and everything, it was just normal. They handled it quite well, actually, without inquiring or anything … they didn't go there, they didn't question anything about it, it was just the relationship we had had before.
  Did that surprise you?
No, it didn't surprise me. It's just – I [pause] was grateful that they didn't bug me. I knew they wouldn't.

Caroline, a mother who had been reported by the school on a suspicion of abuse, expressed confidence in the school's judgment. While she had been very angry with her own psychiatrist who had reported her on another occasion, she was comfortable with the school's scrutiny – partly because the staff involved knew when to stop asking questions:

I got very angry with my doctor … I got over that after a while, but at first, I wouldn't even see the doctor any more. I told her, "Up yours. I hate you. You've been my doctor forever, I let you into my personal world."
  You never had those kinds of feelings with the school, though, even though they reported you?
No. Not the school because [pause] that's their job. I know my doctor. I feel that my doctor was "my" doctor. She's trying to help *me* and I just felt that I was betrayed a bit there. With the school I wasn't as angry. With my doctor, I was a bit more angry. I was like "how dare you. I'm telling you everything and you're … " But the school, I'm cool with.
  They're there for the kids? That's their job?
Yeah. They're there for the kids, yeah. And like I said, a few of them know a bit more of our personal life … Because I know quite a few of the teachers,

I feel comfortable to talk to them. If it helps my kids, sure. Now if they poke into maybe me going out, what I do with all my free time or something, I'd say "hey, that's really ... " But they don't. They're pretty good.

Another woman, Anisha, a pregnant young mother of three, expressed frustration with a new school her son started to attend when she moved into a shelter:

I haven't been there too long so I can't really judge them yet, but to me they're more busy trying to be in my business, maybe because of my living situation ... One day, I sent one of the women from the shelter to pick up my son, because he's there half-day, and the teacher was asking her questions, "Oh, do you live in the shelter too?" I pick up my son every day – can't you ask me questions to my face? ... I feel like an outcast because they know my address. I feel like they're being biased because of my address ... Don't feel as welcome as I did at my other school.

This was clearly a major concern, because Anisha raised the same point again later:

Do you think you and the school see their responsibilities same way?
At the old school, yes. At the new school, they are too busy trying to know why this and why that. Sometimes I feel they question my children ... the old school, they cared about what was going on outside of school but they more cared about what was happening with M. when he was in school.
How can you feel that difference?
Just a vibe – you know sometimes, when your spirit just doesn't take to somebody. At his new school, I don't feel that they care as much for my son. At his old school, they cared about him, they went out their way to make sure he had what he needed.

For Anisha, the ability to have the school *uninvolved* in her own situation – her "business" – was an important part of what it took for her to be comfortable with the school environment. She perceived questions about her own situation as nosy, inappropriate, and potentially judgmental – certainly not reflecting care for her son. By contrast, she appreciated the types of concern that the old school had shown, where they would "answer my questions" and "go out of their way to contact me if there was an issue, a problem to be dealt with, with his academics, I felt they really put their time in it."

She particularly appreciated the positive feedback that she received from her child's teacher, and, in that context, she was receptive to some chiding by the teacher:

> She told me he was her best student, and if she could have him every year, she'd love to have him. She said he was a really good student, he listened, she never had to speak to him twice, he always got his work done on time. The only thing was his attendance, sometimes, but that's me ... because he doesn't go to school on his own ... other than that she had really good feedback about him.

When CAS was involved, Anisha presumed that the report had come from the old school, since her child was apprehended from there, but she never talked about it with them. She noted, again with appreciation, that before, during, and after the period of CAS involvement including a temporary apprehension, "I felt like they treated me the same, maybe they didn't know to the extreme what happened, but I didn't feel like they were treating me different."

To a large extent, the parents in my study accepted that the school would have some knowledge about the presence of CAS in their lives, but they did not wish the school to actively inquire into their cases or into what was going on at home. The capacity of the school to remain a constant in the lives of the families where I conducted interviews was, in part, a result of a practice of not pursuing these issues with the parents, and limiting communication (and efforts to help) to more typically academic or material supports.

For other parents, school knowledge of CAS involvement, and the circumstances that might have led to it, could be more problematic than for the mothers in my sample. A number of the family service workers and other social workers I interviewed said an obstacle to family service work with schools is that parents are anxious to ensure that schools *don't know* about their involvement with CAS. As a social worker in a community agency said, "often the parent is going to be reluctant to have Children's Aid contacting the school, they don't want the school to know Children's Aid is involved, you know, the stigma piece." Similarly, an experienced worker in a school-based parenting centre commented that the more marginalized the parent is – and especially if there may be criminal activity in the home – the more likely he or she is to be resistant to school inquiries into her home life. In these circumstances, which may represent a significant minority of families involved with

CAS, it may be even more important for schools to maintain a position of limited inquiry into children's home lives.

EDUCATORS

Educators, too, share the view that it is advantageous for schools to have only a limited responsibility for knowing about children's home life, where they can refer to and rely upon CAS playing a role of monitoring and investigating issues of concern. Mirroring the comments of the mothers in my study, teachers see non-intrusiveness as an important part of maintaining positive relationships with parents of children in their classes.

Several of the teachers I talked to indicated that they had been careful about how they communicated with parents, even where they perceived potential risk to children at home, in order to maintain a positive tone in working with the parent of a child in the class. They saw that tone as being important for maintaining open communication and ensuring they could be of greatest help to the child. This issue seemed to come up most in the context of discussions about relationships *after* teachers reported a suspicion of abuse or neglect.[6]

One of the teachers I interviewed, Sabine, was unwilling to confirm that she had reported a child to CAS, although she conceded it was possible she had done so. She had certainly been aware that CAS had temporarily apprehended the child. Sabine was the kindergarten teacher whom Anisha had found to be engaged and helpful – who she saw as non-intrusive, and actively communicating about his needs. While we talked, Sabine appeared to be really struggling with her conflicting responsibilities. She said: "I knew that *something* was going on at home, but I didn't know what. I don't think everything was OK there. It might have been prostitution, or drugs, or something. But how was I supposed to find out about that and still keep focus on how the child was doing in my class in kindergarten?"

Her emphasis was on maintaining communication and, to the extent possible, an allied front with the mother in dealing with the child about his educational needs. Anisha's comments seem to reflect the benefits of this approach in terms of her appreciation for Sabine's concern, effort, and the academic focus of communication.

The observations of an experienced school social worker, Alexandra, suggest that Sabine's dilemma – and discomfort with her solution – was not atypical. She observed, "When it comes to home life … teachers seem to be a little bit more hands-off. I will say, 'have you asked them who they go home to?' My sense is that they are afraid to go into this." Another school social worker, Zelda, mirrored that comment when she observed: "In my experience, schools don't usually follow up – they just don't want to get involved. CAS is seen as something negative or adversarial and teachers want to keep separate from that. They don't want to become involved in the dirty stuff. They need to have a relationship with the kid for the year. They are protecting themselves by not getting too involved in a potentially messy investigation, a messy home life."

In her view, teachers' desire to avoid conflict – strongly associated, here, with CAS and the underlying circumstances that might lead to their involvement – is a logical outflow of the daily, sustained contact between teacher and child, and to a lesser extent, teacher and parent.

Fernanda, a principal, also talked about the need to maintain a positive relationship in order to be able to work with parents to solve problems that fall within the domain of the school:

I talk to parents more informally – allow for light-hearted exchange. When they start calling me [Fernanda] I know I am getting somewhere. It allows me to dig in – to know why parents are taxed, to bargain together on what's doable, to get feedback. We need to be a team to strategize ... I am trying to get to the same goals as parents – most parents want their kids to have high school, have opportunities.

There was only one example, among the ten teachers I interviewed, of a teacher who articulated his responsibilities as encompassing knowledge of the home, and even, where necessary, confrontation with parents. As a teacher in a behaviour class, Antonio's starting point was to include among his responsibilities ensuring that his students "feel safe at home":

I put myself in [students'] shoes, when there is CAS involvement. I think they must be scared going home knowing their mom is in trouble. I try to reassure students.
How do you help them feel safe at home?
With me it is so different – we have eight students. The big thing is the parents, so I make sure that I have constant and direct communication with parents at all times. They call me freely – we're communicating every day. I create such a trusting relationship with them they open up to me. When something goes on at home, I call and say, "this is going on and what are you doing about it?"

Are there challenges communicating in cases where there is CAS involvement?
I work hard to develop trust, and then there are times when I have to break that trust with them and call CAS. Parents are going to say, "What! Mr. L called CAS!" Then I have to rebuild that trust – it is hard, but it does happen ... it is day by day and letting them know that you are there for them. I try to be supportive.

As noted above, this teacher's position was exceptional among the ten teachers (indeed, all eighteen educators) I talked to. While his bottom line was similar to most of the teachers – you do what you have to do to get parents' support – the extent to which he saw engaging with parents on home turf as a way of getting there was very different, even relative to four other special education teachers. In this case, it is also notable that though his stance was one of intense parent engagement and knowledge of the home situation, he was completely surprised to learn that CAS was involved with the child whom we were discussing. This was striking because the mother described significant CAS involvement with the family, including a temporary apprehension and, at one period of time, nightly help with bedtime for the child the teacher taught, in addition to social worker visits to the school. Unlike Antonio, most of the other teachers were more likely to avoid conflict, and explicitly limited the home knowledge that they sought, or were willing to share with me.

Maintaining a Focus on Academics

The principals and social workers I interviewed identified a specific educational benefit of CAS involvement for children and teachers: it meant that teachers were able to focus on meeting children's academic needs, rather than "playing social worker" in the words of principals Fernanda and Simon. Most of the teachers I interviewed defined educational success for the children they teach in substantially social–emotional terms. To provide two quick examples from among the many, Laura, a special education teacher just beginning a career in administration, explained that, for her, "success is social–emotional, and then academic. If a child feels self-worth, has friends, can be happy, feels they have power of some kind, and actually enjoy school – that is a success." Dana, who worked in an inner-city school, suggested that "success would be that a child would be able to learn for themselves in their day-to-day life – not necessarily your three R's, but including health, social management, and emotional health as well – being a learner of themselves and of the world around them, and even at this young age, to have the confidence that they can do and be who they have been created to be."

It was interesting to note that others in the school seemed to have a stronger – and more conventional – definition of teachers' main responsibility as essentially academic. For the principals and social workers I interviewed, CAS's primary responsibility for the home situation helps teachers to put aside the distracting "black hole" of supporting students with significant social needs in favour of instruction. As Simon, a reflective and pragmatic principal, said:

There is a fine line for teachers; they always want to play social worker. Really, you want to neutralize the social worker mentality and get them to focus on academic success. So we need to put the referrals in place to allow the teachers to focus on academic progress. They should be asking, what does this child need to learn – do they need program modifications? Quiet space? They need to know the difference between the two roles. Social workers get involved when the home problems mean the child can't learn. Sometimes teachers want to parent children – we need to make sure that agencies are here, are visible, so we can get on with our teaching. I think it is crucial that the agencies be visible, not only to kids, but also to staff.

Simon actively seeks out a larger presence on the part of Children's Aid Societies as a way of creating a better-defined division of labour between the work of CAS and schools. Knowing that teachers frequently say that kids can't learn when their basic needs aren't being met, he wants someone else on hand to visibly take responsibility for meeting those needs. CAS is the residual agency that is the most obvious candidate. This perspective was echoed by two of the four other principals I interviewed.

Similarly, the school social workers I interviewed talked about the challenges for teachers who are facing children with pressing social needs. Having stated that the bar for CAS to intervene with a family is very high, sometimes creating problems for teachers, John, a school social worker, explained his own role as follows:

What is a teacher's responsibility towards abused or neglected children?
Last spring I ran a workshop on dual relationships, supporting staff being teachers, not social worker, police officer, therapist, parent ... As a social worker, I make a conscious effort to protect teachers from dual relationships.

Generally, teachers are not trained in mental health. They don't want the responsibility. Occasionally a teacher will be more involved, meddling, interested in the juicy information – but by and large dealing with kids' abuse and neglect flatly depresses them. They just want to teach.
So what is the teacher's role?
To teach. To be advocates in an academic environment.
What do you mean by advocacy?
Work with the kid academically, bring the kid into context, flag learning exceptionalities. Flag SES (social–economic status, i.e., family income and education) stuff, though that sometimes moves into the social worker role. Mostly advocate within the system – to administrators. Try to get material supports. Teachers can urge for tolerance – I know my kid best, let's not react too quickly with the whole protocol.

This social worker is expressing a particularly critical view of his fellow professionals. As an ideal type, however, a teacher who is confident that social workers (in-school or CAS) are able to meet the social needs of the child, which they place at the centre of the child's learning, will be in a position to focus more intensely on instruction. The critique of teachers being overly involved in addressing students' social problems may be rooted in a concern that this approach deflects from the responsibility to focus on student achievement, or an excuse for student under-performance. But if that is the concern, surely having social workers on hand is a blunt instrument to overcome some teachers' excuses for lowering expectations for students who have difficulty learning. As is, however, the realities of limited information flow (see discussion of one-way communication below) tend to work against teachers' confidence that CAS is meeting students' needs, much less allowing for compartmentalization of their work with students into a purely academic box.

Teachers and social workers both talk about the importance of teachers' capacity to safeguard children through vigilant observation. Each group recognizes a boundary in terms of teachers' responsibility to observe and know; they are expected to know what is going on in the classroom, but they are not expected to actively seek out knowledge about the home situation, leaving that responsibility with child protection. It appears this boundary is extremely useful for educators. First, it helps parents and teachers maintain positive home–school relationships, even through hard times. Second, administrators and social workers see it as a way that teachers are able to maintain their focus on academics. Third, at least some teachers see the ability to call on CAS to monitor parents as a strategy that, in itself, operates to help define and prevent behaviour that they find unacceptable (see chapter 3). CAS is particularly useful to educators because they do not see it as the appropriate role (or competency) of the school to challenge parenting behaviour at home, even where they have serious concerns.

Limits on the Model

The conception of the school working alongside child protection to contribute information to full-time child welfare workers may be entrenched in legislation, but it runs into numerous obstacles in practice. Some obstacles reflect deep ideologies, and some are more explicitly practical.

Contested Views of the Role of the School

One practical limitation of the model of complementary surveillance between school and child protection are teachers' ideas about the appropriate role of the school in connection with other parts of the state. We have already seen some evidence that at least some educators see the school as a refuge or place of safety for children. In some cases, the way the school protects children may be through reporting perceived risk. But in other cases, having the school watch students on behalf of other agencies may actually contribute to greater distrust, both for children and families. Such distrust can weaken attachment to school, limit help-seeking by students, and ultimately have a negative impact on learning.

Social workers, in particular, are aware of the negative conceptions of child protection, and that too close an association between the school and child protection can lead to problems. As one school social worker, Alexandra, noted, "even as a *school* social worker, kids think if I get involved, they will be taken from their families. They need to know it doesn't work that way." Melanie, a mother with a positive relationship with her school social worker, talked about several of her friends, other mothers who, although they could use some assistance, would not go to the school social worker because they feared being reported to CAS. John, the social worker who talked about teachers not wanting to be involved in addressing students' abuse and neglect, articulated his vision of the school as a place apart:

You don't want schools becoming too collaborative with CAS because then you lose the uniqueness of school. If school is working too much with agencies like CAS, it becomes a panopticon for the kids – they are always being watched. Kids are very protective of school as a place apart. Kids are sometimes uncomfortable dealing with social work in school. They see all of social work as part of CAS. For example, there was a teenager, a Crown ward, walking down the stairs after me today, muttering so I could hear him – "informer, informer."

The notion is that children and families are well served by the school as a place apart – where too close a connection with the coercive power of CAS is likely to affect the kinds of essential learning relationships.

Others within the school community have quite a different view. For them, both safety and children's access to services that can make a difference to well-being are enhanced through greater co-operation – as well as through the public appearance of co-operation – between the schools and other children's agencies including CAS. For example, Simon, the principal who wanted to overcome teachers' "social worker mentality," commented:

It is uncomfortable, but parents need to know – it is important that they know we are not separate entities. It's like with the police. Our local division, police are in the school in plain clothes all the time, playing ball with the kids. CAS needs to do that. It has helped to overcome the distrust. And really, the only way to get to parents is through the kids. If CAS can hook the kids, the parents will come. CAS should be visible in the schools.

In this view, ongoing communication and a visible presence for child protection is the key factor that leads to de-stigmatizing child protection work and improving children's and families' access to services.

These differing perspectives on the role of the school in relation to other child-serving agencies reflect, in part, research participants' differing views of the agencies in question. Those who see the other agencies as largely benign tend to be more receptive to co-operation. Those who see them as dominantly coercive are more likely to be sceptical.

Teachers' Limited Knowledge

The model of complementary surveillance works on the assumption that teachers, because they see children daily, have relatively high levels of knowledge about how the children are doing. Though they may not know the details of the home situation, they will be in a position to assess risk to, and identify supports for, children. The teachers I interviewed, however, were quite sceptical about their own knowledge, and they appeared to find expectations unrealistic. Sabine, the kindergarten teacher whose discretion was appreciated by Anisha, asked rhetorically, "You can't ask people about problems at home if they are not bringing it up. So how are you supposed to find out if something is going wrong?"

As an illustration of the gaps in teacher knowledge about children's situations, one of the more striking findings of my research was that a number of the educators I interviewed did not know that the child I was interviewing them about had been involved with child protection. Of the eight mothers I interviewed, I was able to speak to educators in six of the cases (five teachers and one school social worker). Of those six, two had *no idea* that the family in question was working with CAS; one was aware the child was working with a counsellor, but not that the child had a case with CAS. Of the others, either the school had made the report, or the school had been notified in the case of a temporary removal. In the two cases where I was unable to speak to someone at the school, the mothers reported that the school knew of their child welfare involvement; this was likely the case because there had been temporary removals in those cases.

Several of the school social workers I interviewed also spoke of limits on teachers' – and their own – ability to learn about children's home situation. When asked how often CAS is working with a family without the school's knowledge, one school social worker, Cory, responded, "It's more often than I could even guess." When asked how she generally learned about cases where CAS was involved, Alexandra said, "I wish I knew more about them – it is almost by default that you learn about a case where CAS is involved. Usually, it is because of a crisis – or you have a teacher who is perceptive and they will reach out to you. You very seldom learn from the families." Zelda said she always asked families what supports they had, and would ask specifically about CAS involvement, but that they did not always disclose.

Another school social worker, John, pointed to policies that actually limit their capacity to get more information when a teacher is concerned: "Control over information is always tightening up – for example, there is directive from the board's lawyers that the social worker can't even see a student without a signed referral from parent or guardian. This is really problematic if there is a concern about maltreatment. Often, social workers will see the child anyway to help the teachers make a decision [about reporting]."

Taken together, these observations suggest that teachers, social workers, and other administrators concur that, although they see children every day, they are often unaware of problems in the home and/or the kinds of services that may have been mobilized to address a child's needs.

Teachers' Concerns About Reporting

Although the legislative and normative model is that teachers who suspect abuse or neglect will share that information with CAS, there is pretty strong evidence that many teachers *do not* consistently pass information along. There was almost complete agreement among my informants that many teachers are reluctant to make a report when they suspect abuse and neglect. This finding is consistent with numerous studies showing that teachers often do not report suspected abuse and neglect (e.g., Abrahams, Casey, & Daro, 1992; Alvarez et al., 2004; Kenny, 2004; National Committee for the Prevention of Child Abuse, 1997).

Most of my informants talked about this issue in the third person. For example, Laura, a special education teacher and acting administrator, noted that "probably five or ten times a year for our school, when someone discloses to a teacher, the teacher may come to me, saying 'I think something is wrong, but I don't want to continue' – that happens often, especially my mentee." Fernanda, the hands-on principal with an obvious drive to help struggling families, and an active interest in child welfare issues, remarked: "There are some teachers where something reportable has happened and they haven't done anything, they've played social worker and hoped it would go away ... I become aware after the fact when a student has told me something in my office."

One teacher, Kanti, disclosed her own hesitation about reporting in a situation where CAS had been involved in the past. She explained that she had been working closely with a father who was struggling, but she hesitated to report him despite concerns about how his son was doing, because she knew he was making every effort to improve.

Teachers gave a variety of reasons for this reluctance. Two prominent reasons were concern about the impact of reporting on ongoing relationships with children and parents, and concern that a report would make things worse for the child – either because they might lead to problems at home, or that CAS involvement would lead to a child being removed. These reasons were sometimes intertwined. Gabriella, a guidance counsellor, remarked, "I wish CAS could protect us so we aren't breaking the trust with these kids. A lot of teachers are reluctant to call – they are scared."

The importance of maintaining relationships with children and parents was clearly central to many teachers' sense of themselves as professionals. As one said, "I try as a classroom teacher to create an environment of trust – I really try to create a classroom that is about helping a holistic child – through parent connections, by building [a] team within a classroom and within a school." A report jeopardizes the working relationship they have developed with parents, which is, as discussed above, often premised to some degree on positive communication and avoidance of over-involvement in the home situation. In some cases, the closer the working relationship, the greater the internal struggle about whether to report. John, a school social worker, explained: "For teachers, reporting is almost always traumatic, especially [for] more inexperienced teachers. They don't see themselves as a social worker. They see it as a terrifying betrayal – sometimes harder if there is a close relationship. Teachers are afraid they will 'lose the family.' They will argue within the school that they can't be the one to make the call."

In reply to a question about whether there was any staff training or discussions of child protection issues in the school, one of the principals, Simon, noted:

We have a few staff meetings during the year to talk about student issues. For example, if there is a disclosure, [we are] trying to make sure the teacher is not focused on the negative relationship with the parent but on how this will assist the child. Generally, when a call is made, the teacher is doing it from her good heart. Sometimes there has to be tension for something to get to a better place. Teachers are sometimes unwilling to do that.

Another principal, Margaret, who was notably direct as well as kind, commented along the same lines, "Maybe teachers are not always willing to make the calls. Sometimes teachers forget their job is to protect the kid; they worry about breaking the connection they have."

It is widely understood that reporting results in a rupture in relationships. Brenda, a former principal now working with a CAS as an education advocate, remarked:

There is no question in my mind that the relationship is always tenuous after that. Once a report is made, it is up to the principal to rally around the parents and get them back on track. You have to get them in, try to explain why the action has been taken. You have to hope the groundwork has been laid – [that] there has been lots of information sharing before the report ... but at a certain point, you are into your conflict resolution models.

Educators talked about having observed, if not experienced firsthand, situations where a report led to a direct confrontation. Brenda also described a situation where an angry father had actually pushed a principal over as she was helping children get on a school bus. John, the social worker, commented, "Teachers are sometimes dealing with parents where there are big problems – there can be yelling, spitting. It's not why you went to teacher's college. But the biggest issue is the betrayal of trust."

Apart from potentially damaging their relationships with a child or family, teachers' hesitation about reporting is also related to concerns that a report to CAS may create additional problems for children. At least some of the teachers I interviewed identified a fear that a report and investigation would lead to children experiencing additional maltreatment at home. One teacher, Anabel, described a situation in her first year of teaching when she had reported suspected abuse. To her horror, the child had come back to school having been badly beaten, and this was after child protection had investigated and decided to leave the child at home. She said, "it changed my view of child services, as I realized the violent ramifications the student faced due to my reporting. I felt that I had worsened her situation, not made it better." These unintended consequences meant she was much less likely to report next time. Among my interviewees, a larger number expressed concern that calling CAS could trigger a process leading to children's removal from the home. Laura, the special education teacher moving into leadership roles, commented: "There are some teachers that don't want to call because they are worried the child will be taken from the home ... CAS should advocate for themselves as a service provider in the community – *not as someone you tattle-tale to*. It would be different if teachers really felt like they were making a call in hopes that a parent would feel supported. I wish it wasn't seen as so negative."

Zelda, an experienced school social worker who had also worked for children's aid, commented, to the same effect, that CAS doesn't have a very good reputation in the schools in which she works, which may lead to limited co-operation. When asked what accounts for CAS's reputation, she reflected, "Well, there is a misconception that Children's Aid are babysnatchers."

Both of these situations appear to be a result of limited knowledge about the operations of CAS and, in particular, a misconception that the usual outcome of CAS involvement is removal from the home. This misconception can lead to two contradictory responses on the part of teachers, neither of which is particularly helpful to CAS. Some teachers will experience disappointment or a sense of betrayal when an expected outcome – such as removal – does not occur; others will be reluctant to call in any but the most extreme cases because the assumed outcome of a call is removal.

At least some of my school informants also confessed to limited knowledge about CAS processes, including how to communicate with CAS if there are ongoing concerns. Gabriella, the guidance counsellor, suggested:

Maybe CAS could come into the schools and explain what they do as a result of the call – explain what they do. We don't know.
Does anyone from school call and ask what's happened?
No, not usually. Earlier this year, we had a case where we had made a call, the child came in and told the teacher, "my father took me for a walk last night, bought me a hotdog, told me what to say." So the teacher called them and gave them a heads up that this kid has been coached. But I don't think anyone from our school has ever called to say, "hey what did you do?" And the kids don't tell us either ... Sometimes, we get parent referrals – CAS will tell the parent to go into the school and ask for social work. This father came in, asked for a social worker because CAS told him to. But it stopped there, he didn't ever follow up, didn't ever return the paper. We sent it home a couple of times. I don't know what we should do in this case.

An unpublished survey of administrators in one board (approximately one third responded) confirms real gaps in knowledge about the workings of CAS (Hill, 2009). A majority of respondents – between two-thirds and three-quarters of respondents in that survey – were not familiar with aspects of CAS service such as kinship care or community links, nor were they familiar with the concept of differential response, which calls for child welfare responses to vary depending on the situation and needs of a child and family. When asked what they wanted to learn about in relation to CAS, the overwhelming majority replied that they were interested in learning about available community resources and supports – almost twice as many as expressed interest in learning about the characteristics or patterns of different kinds of maltreatment (Hill, 2009). If school personnel don't know what CAS does or how and when to communicate with its staff, the odds of working together effectively goes down sharply.

This lack of general knowledge about how CAS operates is compounded by what was very widely cited as the major problem in dealings with CAS, which was non-communication with the school in specific cases. A community agency social worker (and former family services worker), Donata, described this as a dilemma for child protection: "It goes both ways – I think in the community in general, teachers included. They are mad when the kids are not taken, and they are mad when the kids are taken. There is always that dilemma when you report. You are required by law. You are supposed to inform them. But that's where it stops. It's not that Children's Aid will inform you back."

In the next section I discuss the impact of non-communication in particular cases, both as a deterrent to reporting and as a problem for ongoing working relationships.

Communication Is One-Way: Educators' Concern that CAS Doesn't Communicate

With only two exceptions, the educators I interviewed commented that child protection does not communicate with them. This criticism of CAS was very consistent across the interviews. Alexandra, a school social worker with CAS experience, described it as "a rigid kind of closed system." "Whatever they are doing, it's happening behind closed doors," commented a teacher, Dana. Another experienced teacher, Evelyn, said, "In general, I wouldn't have said they were very helpful. I have always found them closed, very closed." Fernanda, a principal who had actively reached out to CAS in the different districts where she worked, remarked, "Workers don't generally share with us. CAS doesn't routinely share information. It is a concern because you have to know what you don't know to ask the right question."

Margaret, another principal, reported that she always asks CAS if they can give feedback, but "they don't always do that ... they'll generally just give us a little insight." A guidance counsellor, Gabriella, when asked what she expects from CAS, said: "I would like follow up, but we never get it. They have actually told me they don't have to tell me. They usually use the words, 'I'll leave this with my supervisor, or at a team meeting' ... and then we don't hear anything."

Three school social workers compared communication with CAS unfavourably with their experiences working with other community agencies such as children's mental health.

These comments are supported by other evidence, such as the administrator survey data discussed above (Hill, 2009). While broadly expressing satisfaction with their dealings with CAS, roughly three-quarters of administrators reported roadblocks in their dealings, and in response to an open-ended question about the major roadblocks, specified a lack of sharing information, lack of follow up, and slow response times.

CAS may simply be fulfilling its obligations under the Freedom of Information and Protection of Privacy Act by maintaining the privacy of the families it is dealing with. But to state the obvious, non-communication has a significant impact on coordination and relationship building.

A few research participants explained that experiences of not hearing back from CAS had led them (or their colleagues) to decide not to report in the future. Laura, the special education teacher, commented, "The lack of follow up means that teachers tend to report less and less, or call anonymously." John, the school social worker, commented, "[teachers'] jaws hit the floor when they see what CAS doesn't respond to – most reports get thrown back. Most veteran teachers rarely disclose. As a social worker, there is more buzz from junior teachers." He appeared to see the issue as one of learning CAS's threshold, and it is also possible that the more experienced teachers simply feel less pressure on their professional judgment about their own work. Much of the discussion about CAS communication centred on follow up for reports, because – as was very clear in all my interviews with educators and CAS personnel – the vast majority of children's aid–school contact happens in the context of intake, initial investigation, or case closing.[7]

But perhaps just as significantly, not hearing back from CAS also creates difficulties in ongoing work with children. Without some knowledge about what is happening at home, at least one teacher, Laura, felt like she needed to be careful about reaching out to a child where she suspected abuse: "I wish communication was more ongoing – the one thing I hear everybody saying is that I had this really intense moment for me and for the child ... and then there's nothing. I don't even know what happened next ... and because you don't know what's happening, you also don't want to talk to the child."

Although, as discussed, educators may feel hesitant about getting too involved in a child's home situation or with CAS, at least some of them saw that a more open relationship with CAS would help them provide support to the children. A school social worker, Alexandra, who had five years of experience with CAS, commented: "I wish CAS would be more open. They could contact me in September. I don't need to know the details of why they are working with the family – just, 'this is how we are supporting the family and we need you to support the family this way.'"

Another social worker saw the situation in reverse. She worried that schools, knowing that CAS was generally involved with a family but not in direct communication, might assume that CAS was taking steps to meet a child's needs (such as enrolment in an extracurricular program to help with social development), and therefore be less likely to pursue exceptional supports for vulnerable children. A CAS worker, Kira, echoed this concern, citing an interaction she had recently had with a principal who said she would take a family out of their school's "holiday program" when she learned that CAS also had a way of providing support for families at the holidays. "I downplayed our role so that we could both support the family, especially since we were closing the case. That support wouldn't be redundant for this family."

Very few of my educator informants, whether teachers, principals, or social workers, had participated in a meeting where CAS had worked with the school and family to try to agree on a strategy or coordinate support for a child. Several people had heard of such meetings occurring and thought they might be useful, but they were unaware of anything like that happening at their own school. Only one teacher, Laura, had first-hand experience with a CAS-initiated strategy meeting. As a special education teacher with more than a decade of experience, she dealt quite regularly with CAS. She estimated CAS was involved with one to three of the children she taught each year, and she often dealt directly with CAS because she was recognized as a good information source. She explained: "There was one time when there wound up being a huge meeting – CAS, us, another agency – needing to deal with the emotional needs, make sure there is consistency, a lot of programming decisions. But only the once."

However, while citing that experience of joint-agency work involving CAS, she again expressed frustration at the lack of communication from CAS. "The huge meeting I mentioned – we had this big meeting, and then I haven't heard from her since. It doesn't feel like a backup because there is no ongoing communication." Similarly, Zelda, a school social worker, commented: "There is not a lot of co-operation between us and CAS workers – it's always one-way conversations, where they get information from the school and then go manage their case. I haven't been in a lot of situations where we are all rounding up the support around the child, with CAS leading that process."

Only one teacher – Antonio, a special education teacher in a class for students with behavioural exceptionalities – talked about having CAS regularly involved in working with children in an ongoing way. He said it was always his practice to invite CAS to the annual Identification, Placement, and Review Committee (IPRC) meeting, at which a child's needs and services are discussed:

Have you been involved in an IPRC where CAS was present?
Yes, many times. If there is [CAS] involved in the home and there is an IPRC, it's so important, are you kidding me – so important – they need to be privy to that. So if there is CAS involvement with any of my students, they are always invited. We're making decisions about these kids at these meetings and CAS is an important part of making those decisions.
How are they important?
They let us know about any progress or difficulties, and it's all kind of out on the table so we can make the best decisions in the best interests of the child.

Something that distinguishes his situation was his practice, as a teacher, of inviting CAS to be involved. For all the frustration that most of the educators I met mentioned in dealing with CAS, and with the limited communication, it appears to be quite unusual for educators to follow up with CAS. Many of my teacher interviewees didn't know that they even could follow up. Some may not want to. Those principals who did follow up on a routine basis – Simon, for example, and Margaret – reported that they could usually get the basic information about what was happening with a case. A few social workers also indicated that they would be asked to follow up by a principal, and were able to obtain information. Otherwise, school personnel rarely described themselves as reaching out to CAS for support *or* follow up, and CAS workers report that it is fairly unusual for teachers to follow up with them.

"We don't want students be seen as problems"

Despite support in principle, educators have issues with the model of complementary scrutiny. Educators have questions or concerns about the role of the school, teachers' limited knowledge, seeing reporting to CAS as risky for the child, and a lack of ongoing communication. The model also falls short from a CAS perspective. While the family service workers I talked to were articulate about the potential benefits of working with the school, they often chose not to do so, or to have quite limited contact, in practice. As a manager of community programs at one CAS noted, "There may be ongoing consultation between the worker and the school ... The reality is that teachers and principals have so much information, but often that communication just doesn't happen."

They cited a number of reasons for having limited communication. A common reason was logistical challenges in contacting educators, especially teachers. Both groups are extremely busy. Because teachers are in the classroom all day, several of the social workers mentioned they found it difficult to reach them in the time frames they needed. For this reason, several workers said they would usually work with an administrator at the school rather than the teacher. All the parents and all the social workers I talked to agreed that CAS monitored how things were going at school by asking the parents to look at children's report cards. Workers explained that asking parents was much simpler than being in touch with the school. Nobody mentioned that a report card check-in with the parents presented an opportunity to get information about the parent's perception of the child's progress at school, but that may also be a factor in this approach.

Quite apart from logistical challenges, several social workers articulated a number of concerns about the desirability of being involved with the school. Many family service workers I interviewed identified their role as supporting the parent to be more able to deal with the school system, rather than taking over the responsibility of dealing with the school directly.

Some of the reasons CAS gave for not working with schools, however, were based on concerns about how schools would handle information.

Many of the front-line workers I talked to were concerned that if they worked directly with the school on an issue of social support, the result of the intervention would be to have that child seen as a problem. Mallory, an experienced social worker who had extremely positive relationships with the mothers I interviewed, said simply:

You don't want the school focused on the child as a problem or having difficulties, because if you do, then they are always seeing a difficulty. With children, I don't define a problem unless they are defining a problem – unless it's really horrific. If you start targeting them, I am always concerned that the kid is seen as a problem ... So, unless there seems to be a huge issue with the school, I try and back off a little bit. I don't want the kids labelled: "they have a Children's Aid worker." It depends on the age of the kids, but ... sometimes you will find that the school, not so much the inner-city schools, that the school will attribute *anything* to them being "with the Children's Aid."

Mallory almost whispered "with the Children's Aid," making visible air quotes. She was articulating a concern that CAS involvement will lead to stigma that will have a negative effect on children's opportunities or perceived potential. Another social worker, Delilah, explained that if a child was not having a problem at school, she would not contact the school. Indeed, she would go so far as to pretend to be a relative if she had to meet a student at the school to keep school personnel from identifying the child as involved with CAS. She explained, "Once a kid goes into care, he's labelled. I think we have to be very careful with that; I think schools really overreact to that: 'This kid's a CAS kid, he's trouble.' So as a worker, if a kid doesn't have a problem, I try not to go to the school at all." When asked about limited information sharing between CAS and schools, Mark, an education advocate, pointed to a fairly extreme example of stigma, saying that although health and safety issues are required to be shared, "[CAS social workers] are often afraid if they tell school about something where there is a safety issue, the school won't accept the student."

The perception that informing the school about CAS involvement might lead to targeting or stigma was not universally held, however. Another social worker, Dani, when asked about the possible effect of stigma arising from an association with CAS, said:

I would say the opposite. My experience has been you'll get the teacher who goes out of their way – they can tell, there's often a flag with those sort of kids, whether there has been a disclosure or not ... I can think of a number of situations where a teacher was able to develop a very good rapport with the child. I remember one child receiving support because the teacher had the kids do journals every day. The teacher used that as a communication tool. She would write supportive stuff back, or if there was something hard, she would spend ten minutes with the child.

While there are many stories of how schools and teachers have been exceptionally helpful, the concerns raised by some of these workers – that schools will use information about CAS involvement to define a child as a problem or otherwise single them out for lower expectations or even unfavourable treatment – is a strong indictment of the school system. They are describing a situation in which many workers assume a child will *not only* not get the supports he or she needs but also will likely face unchecked discrimination within the schools on the basis of knowledge of CAS involvement (and possibly other aspects of his or her identity as well).

Keeping Information within CAS: Questions of Confidentiality and Consent

The final major reasons for limiting the flow of information to schools, from a CAS perspective, were issues of confidentiality and consent. According to educators, the major reason that CAS cites for declining to share information is confidentiality. A school social worker, Zelda, when asked why she observed limited co-operation with CAS, immediately answered, "Confidentiality has to be a part of it. And they are territorial – this is my case, my family, I know what they need, and the school doesn't." Another school social worker, Alexandra, commented that the school only finds out about CAS involvement where there is a crisis, asking rhetorically, "Could there be more of a system in place? For sure, absolutely. I wish CAS would be more open ... you run into the whole confidentiality piece of it. They can't even communicate that Jane Brown is going to be in grade four, so we don't know." An experienced teacher, Dana, commented, "We talk about not knowing, and the confidentiality piece – when a child comes into my classroom – if the school has reported something, I would see it in my OSR [Ontario Student Record] file. [The OSR is a mandatory record kept for each student that contains information on, for example, a student's grades, special education needs, or (some) discipline issues.]

If the school has not reported something, I wouldn't have any access to that information."

Where children are working with CAS, and remain in the community, CAS does not stand in the place of the parent,[8] so the parent (and child) retain the same rights to privacy as any other individual in society. Privacy of the child and family is protected both under the Freedom of Information and Protection of Privacy Act (FIPPA),[9] where personal information is exempted from the assumption that records should be public, and under the Education Act.[10] FIPPA extends to both child protection and schools. Personal information is defined as "information relating to the education or the medical, psychiatric, psychological, criminal, or employment history of the individual ..." (FIPPA, s.2). As noted above, apart from the privacy rights of the families, and the real risk of stigma and discrimination, confidentiality is crucially important at the investigative stage of a child abuse case. At that point, particularly if it is a serious case where charges may be contemplated, it is important for witnesses to give investigators independent information that has not been contaminated with word of mouth or suggestions (see Myers, 2005). The policy of CAS is consistent with the legislation, in that it prohibits the sharing of personal information (a violation of confidentiality) without the consent of the parents.

Accordingly, a family service supervisor, Mary, explained that she expected information would be shared with schools if and only if the parent consented. In her experience, parents often did not consent. She explained, "A surprising number of parents will say, 'I don't want you talking to the school – they made the report, I don't want you going back.' Once that happens, you can't do anything." In that case, the agency's position is that no information can be shared, and Mary relies on educators' understanding of their continuing duty to report to find out if there were problems at school. Another family service worker talked about a case where the mother had declined to consent, and she could not get information from the school even though she "would really love to get that 360 view the school has to offer." She – and one other worker – said it was her invariable practice to ask parents to consent to share information with the school. Several of the other workers, however, indicated that they did not routinely seek consent. This appears to be an area of considerable professional discretion with significant implications for the potential for coordination and communication. In other words, sharing information with schools depends not only on parents' consent but also on workers' decisions about whether to seek consent in the first place. This is an archetypical example of the gap between law as enacted, and law in practice.

The complexity of the issue of privacy and confidentiality is reflected in the 2015 review of the Child and Family Services Act, which recognized calls for "a legislative framework for information management within and across services for children, youth and their families," noting inquest findings and other investigations which demonstrated the risks of current, fragmented, and inconsistent information sharing (Ministry of Children and Youth Services, 2015, p. 19). Nevertheless, the review also highlighted the importance of privacy protection; it stressed the desire to limit the burden on children, youth, and families to repeatedly share their stories as they moved between institutions; and it contained concern about sharing information on any basis other than consent and necessity. The review did not appear to generate any concrete recommendations about how to balance these competing concerns, but it appeared to place a continuing emphasis on consent and privacy as opposed to some of the models adopted in England where there is a duty to share information that may be important for children's safety or well-being.

Apart from the provisions of FIPPA, to which teachers and social workers made only occasional reference, Mark, a CAS education advocate and former principal, suggested that a major barrier to communication was that CAS workers lack confidence in the educators' commitment to maintaining confidentiality. He commented that the different training they receive may underlie different practices around confidentiality between the two disciplines:

Teachers have about zero training in confidentiality and consent. Social workers have very intense training. I asked two teachers about their training around this issue. They thought and thought, but they couldn't think of anything until I mentioned the OSR [Ontario Student Record]. Then they said, "Oh yes, we learned about keeping the OSR confidential." I asked a social worker about the training, and her response was "every fucking class, every fucking day." The training is totally different, however, because workers are so aware of confidentiality. They don't share things that need to be shared or should be shared. That's partly because they are suspicious of teachers – they know they talk about students. They walk into a staff room and hear teachers talking about students. That's shocking, because a staff room can be quite public.

Mark observed that, apart from differences of training, there are institutional factors that make teachers less likely to observe strict confidentiality: "It's natural that teachers would talk – and teachers don't have any debriefing process in their workplace. There is no process where they can talk with another adult properly. But social workers don't see it like that."

A front-line family service worker similarly commented on her perception of educators' relatively lax practice around confidentiality. She commented that schools will often share information with CAS without the same sort of formalized consent as would be required from other professionals. She noted, "The schools are very cooperative with us, for the most part. They will talk to us without a consent. I am guilty of talking to a school with just a documented verbal consent – whereas doctors always require us to fax a consent. As workers, we know professionals that will require consent and those that won't."

Certainly, from educators, there were widely varying accounts of practices around confidentiality in schools. Most teachers acknowledged that information about CAS involvement could be highly sensitive and needed to be treated with caution, or on a need-to-know basis. One teacher, Dana, commented that in her school the rules were "pretty tight," citing as an example a specialist teacher who made a report and told only the principal; no one notified the classroom teacher who had to confront a very upset parent (a scenario shared with me by several teachers). A school social worker, Cory, indicated that she would get a written consent from parents to share information with the teacher and principal, and would respect a parent's decision not to do so unless she perceived a real risk to the child. But for others, definitions of "need to know" appeared to be more flexible. Accounts from other teachers tended to suggest a much wider flow of information. As Evelyn, a teacher in a low-income downtown school, said:

We never talk about what to do in a case, never. I wouldn't say it's taboo but it's one of those big issues that people don't talk about. You may see a CAS worker but you'd never discuss it in a meeting. You probably could find out who they were there to see – an LTO [Long-Term Occasional – a teacher on limited term contract] probably wouldn't tell you. But if it was a permanent teacher, I would be told. The information is not *so* closed.

Is there a purpose for sharing that information?

It could be useful if you are teaching a sister or brother of the child. Generally, it's just sort of that nosy curiosity – which doesn't really have any use at all. [CAS reports] always go into the file so if I got that child I will find out.

Zelda, the school social worker, commented: "There really should be no talking among staff about families. Sometimes, depending on the school or how many teachers are teaching different kids in the same family, there is some information sharing, but that should only be 'as needed.' Sometimes I might facilitate sharing of information. Although they should be respecting confidentiality, do they always? No. In certain schools, they do talk about families."

Margaret, a principal, also expressed the view that some information sharing was part of the normal way of doing business, and that it was in fact helpful to a child. She remarked that "The policy says we're not supposed to disclose information about abuse or neglect to anyone, but it makes sense to have people aware in a way that won't get out of control. We want to make sure they're getting the extra attention. It's just typical teachers sticking together."

In summary, then, there are numerous reasons why a CAS will decline to share information with schools. Workers may be worried that a child will be stigmatized on the basis of their involvement with CAS, or that schools will do less for a child believing that CAS is looking out for them. The privacy protections of the Freedom of Information and Protection of Privacy Act bind CAS workers, though some workers made relatively little reference to the act, and the question of whether to seek consent to share information is clearly the subject of considerable administrative discretion. In this context, workers' decisions about how and whether to share information are shaped not only by formal prohibitions but also by their perceptions of the schools as a safe environment for children – a place where information will not be used to stigmatize or discriminate against a child, and where there are adequate protections for the child's privacy.

The Paradox of Non-Communication

Thus, despite a fairly high level of formal coordination of the responsibility of surveillance between child protection and schools, the formal coordination and relatively well-understood interdependence falls down in practice. Teachers may not always have the knowledge that is imputed to them – in particular, knowledge of CAS involvement – and they often do not report what they know, either because they think it is futile, or because they are concerned about what will happen to the child or relationships with a family. Children's Aid Societies are far from consistent in their dealings with schools. While acknowledging the important information schools can provide, it is often the case that family service workers intentionally choose to keep schools ignorant of a child's involvement with the agency, and they may rely on claims of confidentiality to keep communication with schools "one-way." As one school social worker, John, commented, "There is distrust in closed systems. One system doesn't really trust the other system."

At the level of individual workers, of course, there is a wide variety of practice. I talked to one social worker, Kira, who said, "We're involved with the schools a lot – if there are behavioural concerns, or neglect, school plays a pivotal role. It's hard to have a comprehensive case plan and exclude the school." More typical, however, was the response of another worker, Delilah. When asked whether her involvement with the school usually came about because she contacted the school, or because the school contacted her, Delilah explained, "Because of our workload, to be honest, it's probably when they contact me. The only time I contact them is if I need more information – if Mom says kids are not going to school. With our caseload, we don't have time."

Even in some cases where there would appear to be quite serious educational issues – my interviews included Melanie, a mother who was charged with parental harassment and banned from the school premises; Hua, whose child was a victim of a pattern of bullying; and a teacher whose student was moved from a behavioural to a learning disabled special education designation – a child protection worker did not contact the school or get involved to support the child or parent. In some cases, at least, an invitation from the school was what it took to get the social worker through the door. Melanie reported: "[Our social worker] has witnessed my kids' behaviour and what was happening – every day – but these new schools never called. Now, when the middle school called, he wants to go to a meeting. I asked him, 'Where were you when I told you about the other things?' He only went to the school when the school asked him to get involved."

If CAS workers wait for invitations from the school to get involved in educational planning or problem-solving, then, from the perspective of a child potentially facing significant educational challenges with potentially compromised home support, it is problematic that the school frequently doesn't know that CAS is involved. From a protection perspective, schools are definitely less likely to communicate if they are not aware a case is open.[11] Although there is an *ongoing* duty to report suspected abuse and neglect, and workers are required to remind anyone who reports maltreatment of that duty, most teachers cite lack of follow up as a major reason that teachers don't always report their suspicions.

If the school doesn't know they are involved, CAS institutionally needs to be confident in their own capacity to assess educational well-being, and/or confident in schools' capacity to fully meet children's education needs. But most of the education advocates I talked to expressed doubts about many workers' understanding of school processes. One commented, for example, that many workers had considerable difficulty understanding a report card, particularly if a child had an Individual Education Plan (IEP) for their special education needs. All the workers I interviewed could readily tell stories of quite problematic actions on the part of schools in dealing with children they served. More generally, one of the major reasons that CAS chooses not to involve schools relates to doubts about the school's misuse of information – concerns about maintaining confidentiality or using information to label and stigmatize children. Taken together, these factors seem to suggest that workers' assessment of progress and problems may be limited, and their confidence in schools' ability to meet children's needs is also limited. With schools unaware of CAS involvement, and therefore unable to use their power to convene this particular type of support for children, the picture is one of significant gaps in children's educational safety net.

The Myopia of the Model: A Missed Opportunity for Advocacy for Children

We can see that there are significant gaps in the system through which schools and child protection coordinate their responsibility to protect children by seeking out and sharing relevant information. These gaps may arise through numerous factors, including overwork and practically boundless mandates,[12] lack of knowledge, and, sometimes, mutual distrust. But perhaps the system itself has an important myopia in terms of its focus on the family as the primary object of surveillance. Particularly if the goals of child protection and education go beyond keeping children safe and towards helping children achieve well-being, there is a relatively strong consensus that an approach that emphasizes strengths as well as challenges will ultimately be most fruitful.

The theory around resilience, in particular, directs attention to how people thrive through hardship. One of the key findings of resilience research is that people thrive through maintaining strong relationships (e.g., Howard, Dryden, & Johnson 1999; Rutter, 1987). There is no doubt that workers in child protection and schools have the potential to be an important source of the positive relationships and positive experiences that contribute to better life outcomes for more children. But at the same time, both schools and child protection are large bureaucracies within larger bureaucracies that can be quite hard to navigate, facing more demands than they are able to meet. A strengths-based position on supporting the well-being of this highly vulnerable group of children requires that each institution try to hold each other to a very high standard. In other words, the subject of surveillance and advocacy should not only be families but also be the government institutions that have been created, in part, to be positive forces in young children's lives.

The case for mutual oversight is strengthened because both are compulsory institutions for children and their families. A key premise of administrative justice is that there should be greater checks on the power of institutions that have greater power over individuals (e.g., *Baker* v. *Canada* [*Minister of Citizenship and Immigration*]).[13] Children in the child welfare system who live at home have relatively few mechanisms for challenging the services they receive,[14] and there is relatively limited systemic oversight either at the level of institutional reporting or by the Office of the Provincial Advocate for Children and Youth. In schools, remarkably, mechanisms for oversight are perhaps even weaker. The Provincial Advocate commented freely that while he had doubts about responsibilities to those receiving child protection services in the community, "It seems like there is an even a greater lack of accountability in the education system. There is nobody to ask."

If formal checks and balances for both schools and CASs are limited for children living at home, more transparency in inter-sectoral work between professionals may provide informal visibility that can open doors for children and families. One of the family service workers I talked to, Kalpana, saw a key role for child welfare in advocating for children at school. She explained her role in school meetings: "There are still some CAS muscles we can use ... even for a child in the community. We can help increase the priority for that child. You can't just sit back. Parents go into these meetings with schools ... they tend to accept what is given. They don't see there are other options, other things that can be provided."

At the very minimum, child welfare workers should be evaluating not only whether a child is progressing but also whether the school is making a positive difference in a child's life and whether there is the potential to improve these experiences. Obviously, social workers shouldn't be telling teachers how to teach, but there is definitely room to make sure a child has a champion at the school, ideally someone to whom both the child and the parent can relate to. Social workers should expect to know if there are learning supports that could help improve a student's performance, and whether the necessary assessments and/or services are happening. They could expect to be aware as to whether alternatives are being considered if serious discipline is taking place. If they see evidence of stigma or discrimination, they may want to flag the issue with administrators or even superintendents.

Teachers and administrators should actively follow up after making a report, and should expect to know if services are put in place for a child who they have perceived to be struggling. They should also ensure their educational expertise is taken into account in the development of service plans for families. A teacher is well-positioned to say whether a child would benefit from certain types of assessments or supports, or whether they need something different at school, or, for youth, whether they will require certain courses to achieve their goals. This is not expertise a social worker would usually be able to bring to the planning process. There may be objections to putting goals beyond the direct control of parents in service plans (e.g., ensuring a child is assessed for special education services) as inconsistent with the widely held principle of minimal intrusiveness and the desire of many parents to have child protection out of their life. However, it may provide an opportunity for dialogue and/or pressure that will lead to improved outcomes for children. If educational outcomes for maltreated children are to be improved, this opportunity should not be missed.

Chapter Three

Schools "Disciplining" Families' Cultural Difference through Child Protection

Institutionalized child protection and routine teacher observation of children's home life are – among other purposes – part of the way the normal family is defined and enforced. The further a family falls from the norm, the more likely it is to be exposed to intrusive scrutiny. It is almost a cliché to observe that what is defined as deviant or problematic occurs through a process of social construction – through the development of shared understandings – and that these understandings or social categories may be given real-world effects through other social processes and institutions. Where particular groups – for example, racial or cultural minority groups – are consistently identified with a need for scrutiny or intervention, it has the capacity to shape perceptions of the groups and the work of institutions, contributing to a vicious cycle.

Educators readily invoke the power of Children's Aid Societies to affect family's behaviour through surveillance, and, perhaps surprisingly, a significant number of them specifically and spontaneously talked about CAS as part of their toolkit to help manage cultural differences. These findings are consistent with research showing professional reporters are the main source of reports about visible minority children, perhaps suggesting one potential cause of recognized disproportionality in the child welfare system.

Michel Foucault's writings have been canonical in understanding the development and impact of social categories. One of his key concepts is surveillance, in which power is commonly exercised and produced not so much through direct coercion but through observation, comparison, and assessment. Those subject to surveillance experience a "state of conscious and permanent visibility" that makes the functioning of power almost automatic: "surveillance is permanent in its effects, even if it is discontinuous in its action ... the perfection of power should tend to render its actual exercise unnecessary" (Foucault, 1977, p. 201). Foucault further identified the family as "the privileged locus for the disciplinary question of the normal and the abnormal" (p. 215) through the work of fields such as medicine, psychology, and education. To be disciplined is both to be "individualized" and to be made to play a part in an embedded social order. The way in which certain behaviours are defined as problematic establishes a boundary between matters of private and public concern but also, through attribution, it has the power to define certain groups as warranting particular scrutiny, again, with real world effects.

Racial Overrepresentation in Child Welfare and Professional Reporting

There is by now a sizeable literature that demonstrates patterns of overrepresentation of racial and cultural minorities in the child protection system in both Canada and the United States (Contenta, Monsebraaten, & Rankin, 2014; Courtney et al., 1996; Lavergne, Dufour, Trocmé, & Larrivée, 2008; Roberts, 2008; Trocmé, MacLaurin, et al., 2005). Again, one of the basic insights of the literature is the recognition that rates of reported maltreatment – and other indicators tracked through the child welfare system, such as placement rates – are a product of intersecting social and institutional forces; they do not straightforwardly reflect differences in the underlying phenomenon. Lavergne and colleagues (2008) used census and Canadian Incidence Survey data to show that in Canada, Aboriginal, black, and Latino children are overrepresented in child maltreatment investigations relative to their representation in the general population, and whites, Asians, and Arabs are underrepresented. However, where the analysis is restricted to reports of physical abuse alone, black and Asian families are overrepresented, and Aboriginal families are much less frequently investigated. There are no differences between any of the groups in terms of reports of physical harm (p. 69).

One of the key drivers of these patterns is who reports. Lavergne et al. (2008) noted that "reports about children from visible minority groups came chiefly from professional referral sources, whereas those involving Aboriginals and whites originated primarily with non-professional sources" (p. 68). Teachers are one of the important groups of professional reporters making up just under a quarter of all reports (Public Health Agency of Canada, 2010).

In the first-hand accounts of a significant number of the educators I interviewed, they described CAS as being most useful to them as a form of indirect control and visibility for families where there were signs of potentially worrying behaviour. Particularly striking was the extent to which teachers appeared to see surveillance (in terms of actual eyes-on coverage, and invoking the possibility of critical scrutiny) as a tool not only for protecting children, but, particularly, for reinforcing social norms about parenting. It is clear, too, that a significant number of the educators (at least a third of those I interviewed) wanted to invoke the potential coercion of the CAS alongside the soft power of the school to discipline – and limit – cultural difference.

The teachers I interviewed appeared to be quite aware of the extent to which the potential to be scrutinized was a powerful tool of social control. Teachers wanted to know CAS was paying attention and actively scrutinizing worrying situations. This is illustrated with comments like Kanti's, when she said, "I felt like the situation I was reporting was serious enough that I expected some kind of monitoring or observation of what was taking place." But also, these teachers expect the process of being observed, in and of itself, to have an impact on families. For example, Antonio explained it was beneficial to have CAS involved because "parents knowing there is involvement by CAS – it makes them more aware in how their parenting is affecting them [the children]."

Seeking "support with the re-culturing of families"

A significant number of the educators I spoke to, without prompting, very candidly expressed the view that one of the main functions that they saw for CAS was to shape the socialization of immigrant families attending their schools. In these accounts, children's home cultures were clearly seen in starkly negative terms: associated with physical abuse, lack of capacity, and a general lack of parenting skills. Gabriella, a guidance counsellor, for example, when asked what help she could expect from CAS, responded immediately:

Mostly, I want support with the re-culturing of families. There is a huge cultural divide between where these families are coming from and the Canadian way of life, Canadian law. I think CAS is doing this work with families. The families don't understand that if kids are bruised or hurt, there are schools out there, there are social workers out there, and we're going to try to stop them – CAS needs to work on the education piece about the alternatives to beating, parenting strategies.

This articulation of the role of child welfare services is based on a stereotype that abuse is more acceptable in certain ethnic groups (e.g., Maiter, Alaggia, & Trocmé, 2004), and also on an idealization of Canadian parenting practices, given that North American evidence suggests over 60 per cent of parents use physical discipline (p. 219). The way this guidance counsellor expressed her concern started with the notion of physical discipline but quickly shifted to a broader concern with parenting strategies more generally. This shift may reflect a broad psycho-sociological and popular literature that emphasizes prevention and "positive discipline" (e.g., Dreikurs & Soltz, 1964; Sears & Sears, 1995). However, issues of physical discipline provide an opening both to reinforce stereotypes about other cultures and to scrutinize parenting more broadly. This broader parenting is found wanting, particularly with reference to a "Canadian" norm constructed in opposition to it. When asked later in the interview whether parents' responsibilities change with the involvement of CAS in the family, Gabriella answered: "I hope so. CAS is working on educating and re-culturing. Parents need to know they are being watched, they have to know that this is not going to go away, have to see the seriousness of CAS's involvement – they should be watched, I think."

This is a classic articulation of belief in the power of visibility to shape behaviour and, ultimately, to reshape the norms within society.

Although that educator was particularly explicit, several others had similar comments. One principal, Margaret, when asked whether anything changed after a report to CAS, replied, "It depends, it really depends on the parent, whether the call was a wake-up for them. If it is a cultural thing – if abuse was more condoned – there can be a good change." Another teacher, Dana, when asked whether there was such a thing as a "typical case" that warranted a call to CAS, explained: "Neglect is the big reason CAS gets involved. Also, cultural differences – in terms of knowing that we don't hit children, people coming from their home cultures and not being sure how to discipline their children. For some parents, with CAS being called in, it's around education, teaching parents strategies and skills, and letting parents know what is and is not appropriate."

Again, we see the view that one of main ways some educators see CAS is as a mode of compulsory cultural re-education. The teachers see this as helpful to their work in schools, and, presumably, perceive it as beneficial to the children they teach. They also see this work lying outside of the role and responsibility of school personnel.

Through engaging CAS, as a distinctive public agency with a responsibility for children's safety and well-being, and with coercive powers over parents, educators see themselves as having helped clarify the norms and requirements of parenting for particular groups of parents. This is very consistent with Foucault's notion of effective discipline, which takes place through "centres of observation disseminated throughout society."

Similarly, emphasizing that any issue precipitating a call to child protection is often nested in a larger set of social needs. Fernanda, a principal who emphasized her connection to parents and students, commented: "We have two large public housing developments in our catchment. Those families often have broader issues; we try to support them. For example, some communities have different approaches to disciplining a child. We let CAS help them understand we don't do that here. That's not the schools' job."

Fernanda identified a need to change a cultural norm; however, she distinguished between the role of the school and that of CAS. She saw the role of CAS as reaching out to individuals (here, defined by their community and housing status) and changing parenting practice at home.

Although the perspective I have identified was surprisingly common, it is important to note that at least one of my educator interviewees, Evelyn, a teacher with many years of experience in an urban school setting, saw it as inappropriate to involve CAS:

The two [students] I have been in an investigative interview with, it was sort of a new to the country situation. I think a lot of cases get referred where some parenting courses could be helpful. I know that a lot of new immigrant families have been allowed to rule with the rod at home, so to take their children away here ... it makes more sense to educate them in how to parent. Parents will say I can't control my child because I can't hit my child here – then we do see problems. It's amazing how quickly kids learn the rules.

This educator still linked certain cultures with physical punishment, but she thought it inappropriate to use the coercive power and scrutiny of CAS as an intervention.

Recognizing that Racism and Prejudice Exist

Notably, none of the CAS informants I interviewed saw helping schools police cultural boundaries as part of their role. Several of them initiated conversations about how race and culture have an impact both on services they provide and on referrals they receive, but they were more likely to talk about possible discrimination in the schools. For example, a director of services for one CAS emphasized the importance of ensuring that Children's Aid Societies "recognize that racism and prejudice exist. There is too much denial about that now." An educational advocate, Carla, talked about recognizing the need for advocacy in a school that has a very poor track record in terms of suspensions of immigrant youth. Front-line workers, too, acknowledged that cultural gaps could be a factor in children's educational success. One family service worker, Kira, was identified by her colleagues as particularly effective in working with schools. After talking about the value of input from the school in understanding particular cases, she commented, "But the school can also be very oppressive and judgmental and discriminatory. There are times when the school's input can bolster the family's position. Rather than giving a helpful clinical assessment it actually bolsters a family's report that they are being targeted." In light of her knowledge about systemic patterns of poor outcomes for racialized children, she felt it was her duty to take parents' concerns about racism at their children's school very seriously. The example she provided was not about reporting but about the need for advocacy. CAS had become involved in the case of a middle-school girl, whom she described as "uncooperative" with "behaviour issues." Her mother would not consent to a special education designation (IEP) for behavioural exceptionalities. The mother was quite concerned about the school's treatment of the girl, including "expelling her without expelling her," by telling the girl that she could not come back to school and refusing to agree to a boundary variation (which would allow the girl to change schools) unless her mother would consent to an IEP (which would identify her daughter as having behavioural exceptionalities).

Mallory, a worker who worked closely with a mother, Saliha, to help her leave a violent home, acknowledged that cultural gaps could sometimes be a factor in ongoing CAS involvement. She was more inclined to see cultural difference as being part of a set of background challenges for clients rather than a matter of different groups' practices or cultures needing to be adjusted. For example, she commented about Saliha's son: "in the first year or two of school, he wasn't doing very well, didn't make friends very well because he was different, you know, different culture." Or, explaining ongoing CAS involvement with some older children, she commented, "You will find if the families have held on to their traditions ... the kids sort of break out and create a bit of hell because they want to be 'Canadian.' Different cultures may struggle a little bit more to feel successful in our schools." She used air quotes around the word Canadian, distancing herself a bit from any conventional interpretation of it. Unlike the educators whom I interviewed, none of the CAS personnel or policy officials I talked to articulated their role as one of monitoring cultural compliance, nor did they identify concerns about physical abuse as being attached to certain groups.

A Matter of Public Concern?

A key argument in this book is that the border between private and public responsibility for children is a shifting one with political consequences, and that the involvement of child welfare is not only a signal of vulnerability or "risk," it also specifically represents a judgment that there is a need for public intervention to ensure protection and well-being. Although the sample in this study is small, it is striking that several of my educator informants, entirely without prompting, identified the policing of culturally non-mainstream families as a key role for CAS. They sought to actively involve a public institution in defining and enforcing acceptable behaviour on the part of these families, explicitly expressing concerns about cultural patterns.

If it is indeed a part of the taken-for-granted practical judgments of a meaningfully large group of educators that certain groups are disproportionately likely to practice or condone physical discipline amounting to abuse, it could contribute to the problem of overrepresentation in child welfare. The negative impacts of overrepresentation of certain groups with child welfare has been clearly identified, as has the need for studies that look at organizational factors beyond child welfare directly – including the interrelationship between schools and child welfare – as a driver for patterns of disproportionality. This study, while far from definitive, strengthens the case for the importance of addressing the way that educators contribute to the child welfare pipeline. It also suggests that as a part of professional development around how schools and CAS work together, work to challenge racial and cultural stereotypes around abuse or neglect would be a useful contribution.

Chapter Four

Not "in the Game of Maximizing Potential": Corporate Parenthood, Policy Silence, and Limited Services for Children Who Stay at Home

It is becoming more clear what Crown Wards should expect. But what is the obligation of the state towards the child they are serving in the community? It is not clear to me, nor, I think, to the agencies. I still don't think they have figured it out.

Provincial Advocate for Children and Youth

Through child welfare, the government endeavours to ensure that the needs of maltreated children are met. That includes both the provision of supplementary, transitional services and supports, and – where children stay at home – oversight and even enforcement of comprehensive parental responsibility, mostly exercised by mothers. Through the limits placed on the supports available through child welfare, and the core responsibilities that are enforced, the boundary between public and private responsibility for children becomes visible. Through examining the availability of supports for educational well-being, we see that mothers' responsibility to provide for their children when they stay at home is affirmed and enforced through child welfare practice. But if the focus is shifted away from enforcement of mothers' individualized responsibility towards scrutiny of the exercise of *public* responsibility, an analysis of the regime reveals responsibility that is ambiguous in scope, intermittent and discretionary in practice, and subject to very, very few formal mechanisms to address the adequacy of support for children and families receiving services from child welfare. The power of residual conceptions of parental responsibility – even in the context of limited capacity – is such that the government is able to express commitment to supporting vulnerable children's well-being without being held responsible for putting in place effective resources or supports; ambiguity is a shield for limited action.

It does not seem like a coincidence that accountability mechanisms to ensure support for these children are weak. This tendency is rendered more significant in light of the current wave of child welfare reforms based on principles of differential response. This model places a greater emphasis on avoiding adversarial child welfare involvement, flexibility, and individualization of services provided in the community. But a clearer articulation of public responsibility for supporting these children, combined with meaningful individual and systemic accountability measures, is required in order for child protection authorities to avoid the recognized risk that vulnerable children in the community whose cases are not identified as "high risk" will suffer long-term harm.

Does the Corporate State Parent Children Who Stay at Home?

Under the Child and Family Services Act, when a child becomes a Crown ward or a ward of the society,[1] "the Crown (acting through a Children's Aid Society) has the rights and responsibilities of a parent for the purpose of the child's care, custody and control."[2] Correspondingly, a child in care has "rights to care." But simply to assign parenting responsibility to the Crown doesn't answer the urgent question of how children will be raised or cared for. Roger Bullock, Mark Courtney, and Roy Parker and their colleagues (Bullock, Courtney, Parker, Sinclair & Thoburn, 2006), considered to be among the Anglo-American world's leading child welfare experts, articulated a theory about the exercise of parental responsibility for children in the care of the state in their article, "Does the corporate state parent?" They point to a consensus that:

> Parenting for children in care has several facets – legal, social, psychological and biological. At a national level, the state establishes a legal framework and provides resources for services that orchestrate broad welfare aims, such as regulating those who select, vet and train carers. At the local level, professionals, usually social workers, assume responsibility for various aspects of the child's life, such as placement in a family, safety, education and health. At the personal level, parenting responsibilities are allocated to carers who provide the face-to-face aspects of looking after children and therefore the long-term benefits. (p. 1348)

The authors discuss the challenges of parenting in the context of this divided model.[3] They are silent about another group of children: those who are involved with child protection but not "in care," where there is no out-of-home placement or transfer of custody.

For those children, too, responsibility is divided. But the responsibility of the state is even more ambiguous. Parents continue to provide the face-to-face aspects of looking after children and therefore, as Bullock, Courtney, and Parker point out, provide the major short- and long-term benefits to the child. But professionals become involved with various aspects of a child's life, and the state's legal framework and resources are engaged. There is, however, an important lack of clarity about the ends for which child welfare services are involved with these children. This shapes the accountability framework that exists to assess the appropriateness or adequacy of services provided to children or families in this situation. This situation is further complicated when the services in question are provided by a different arm of the state, such as public schools.

Bullock, Courtney, and Parker suggest two ways of looking at parenting: one, in terms of end states of healthy psychosocial development, and the other, emphasizing the tasks or work of parenting. The original working party on caring for separated children (Parker, 1980) coined the language of "corporate parenting" to describe the state's role with children who were in care. They saw normal parenting as a collection of ingredients, such as affection, nurture, stimulation, control, partisanship, and unqualified aid in times of emergency. Taken together, these elements of care produce "normal" development for individual children. This "normal" parenting was contrasted with the more discontinuous and divided experiences of those in the care system. There are many other sociological approaches to understanding the parenting role, including those that – in addition to valuing commitment and attachment – put a greater emphasis on parents' work and what they do (provide care, teach social behaviour, maintain responsiveness, and "organize their own support" [e.g., Quinton, 2004, p. 27]).

Where a child is in care, child protection agencies have a duty to select a substitute caregiver and to "[seek] to ensure that all the aspects of parenting listed in the previous paragraphs are provided in a coherent way to those who need to enter public out-of-home caretaking" (Bullock, Courtney, Parker, Sinclair & Thoburn, 2006, p. 1349). In a situation where a case is opened for family services, with the child or children staying at home, the comprehensive care and attachment, the tasks, behaviour, and relationships, remain with the original family. In this case, does the state retain a duty to ensure that "affection, nurture, stimulation, control, partisanship, and unqualified aid in times of emergency" are provided in a coherent way? Or is public responsibility somehow understood in a way that is primarily transitional or supplementary? The state's duty here is ambiguous at best.

Mothers' Responsibility in the Context of CAS Involvement

The main emphasis in my interviews was on issues of education rather than the full gamut of responsibility for parenting. But even though questions and answers were often framed around educational issues, it quickly became clear that the mothers whose children lived at home while CAS was involved with their families did not see CAS in any way diminishing or lightening their responsibilities. "Comprehensive" parental responsibility rested on their shoulders, often heavily, as one can see in Saliha's heartfelt call: "Because I am a single mother, if anything happens to them, everybody is going to blame me: 'OK, you didn't take care of your children properly. This is why they are like that.' It is a big fear. 'You did it – it is all your fault.' If there is anything bad, 'you did it.' If there is a good thing, God did it. Or, anybody can do it."

Later, when she was asked whether CAS involvement changed her responsibilities in any way, Saliha replied simply, "No. They are very helpful. But it didn't change anything." This mother, who described extremely busy days managing her schedule as a full-time student and her time with her young children, much of which was dedicated to their schoolwork, had a very positive experience with CAS in helping her leave an abusive relationship, but she did not see CAS as taking on any of her responsibilities in the course of doing so.

Other mothers tended to see their responsibilities in terms of helping their children achieve "end states" of healthy development. Caroline wanted her children to have a good life, to have and achieve high aspirations. She saw her role as supporting those aspirations as well as providing a positive role model, despite her challenges with mental health, lack of education, and poverty:

I don't want to see my children struggle. I want to see them have a good education and to be able to have a good job afterwards. Not like their mother ... So, I'm thinking if I could show them, too, that this is the way that it goes, you just don't sit home every day and take care of children, you go to work and everything. I tell them, "you can be a doctor; you could be a teacher." I want them to have a better life than what I had ... where my dream was sort of squashed. I don't want them to squash their dreams early ... I'd just like to see that they get the good education and probably the good job, and the house and the husband and the dog. All the good stuff, a picket fence ...

I think this quote, and many of her other comments in the course of the interview, show her clear understanding of the complex ways in which parents contribute to their children's development. It also reflects the "bonds of affection" that she feels for her children that so powerfully undergird naturalized assumptions of complete responsibility.

Another mother – a new immigrant learning the language and also learning to read and write – directly connected her own work protecting and maintaining some control over her children to her aspirations for them to grow up and become contributing members of society. Ruby explained:

When they grow up, I want them to become a good people. I don't want them to stand in the streets or outside and do bad stuff. I don't want them to become like that. So, even now, I'm not giving them a chance to go out for themselves because I know if you give them a chance ... they find friends from outside. So, I'm not keeping them too much, I give them chance to play, but not "go outside and play with your friends." No, I'm not doing that, because any time you leave them, they can find friends from the Centre, if you give them a chance, they can make them become bad. I know when I go out with you, I take you to park, I take you to somewhere, if you are happy, you are not going to make friends too much to give you bad ideas. So, I try to do that.

At other points in the interview, she described her efforts to secure academic help and caregiving from her neighbours. Even though she had, for a time, needed and received considerable help from CAS with her very challenging son, this mother was a classic example of someone who "was the organizer of her own support," despite significant obstacles. Comments from the other mothers heavily emphasized this role of actively building relationships and seeking out formal and informal supports for their children. Melanie proudly explained that she had been able to get an updated psycho-educational assessment for her older son: "With the whole psych assessment, I just picked up the phone and did what I had to do. The school wasn't going to come to me – never mentioned it. I just happened to find that out. There are a lot of services in the schools that they don't tell us about. We have to find out word of mouth from a parent who has been through it."

It was clear that coordinating support for themselves and their families was central to the work of the mothers in my interviews. Whether it was ensuring children got home from school safely while they were at work, struggling to secure decent quality housing, coping with vermin, getting access to good after-school or holiday programming for their children, or finding financial help to bridge transitions, these mothers were actively working to meet their children's needs, sometimes, but not always, with help from CAS.

Some mothers had very positive experiences with CAS in this role of coordinating support. Saliha, for example, commented: "Now everything is stopped because they are not involved. I can't have anything free. Why are they not with me still?" Some had much less satisfactory experiences, like Melanie: "They have power, they have the ability to walk into my house and take my children at any time – without a judge, without the police – yet they don't have the ability to help me with a housing situation. You are complaining that my kids are living like that, but what are you doing? Their supervisors can't even get help for me."

Variable levels of support available from CAS reflect different factors: the intractability of the issues with which parents need support (zoo tickets are easier to provide than adequate public housing), the resources available in the community, the dynamics between mothers and workers, and of course, the framework of public responsibility.

Whatever the specifics of support provided, it is clear that the professionals with whom these mothers interact also see the parents as retaining full responsibility during the period of CAS involvement, notwithstanding potential concerns there may be about their capacity. A policy official from the Ontario Association of Children's Aid Societies (OACAS) explained, "Parental responsibilities should not change during the time a family is working with CAS. If you are doing good clinical work, you should be working to help them fulfil their responsibilities. You should keep as much responsibility with the family as possible. If the parent is doing things for themselves, it helps you to assess, to respond."

The notion of leaving parental responsibility intact can, however, lead to negative judgment on parents who require support over sustained periods of time. Delilah, a family service worker, seemed to see this paradox while still judging parents who are having trouble doing what is expected. Asked what a parent's responsibilities were (in the context of education), she answered:

The standard answer is that parents are responsible for getting the kid's education. Making sure their needs are met. The other side of it is some of our families can't. No matter how hard I try, as a worker, I can't make Mom do it. The kid's not going to school – we have had family support go in, but her daughter, she's not going to school. She looks at us now, *we're her crutch* – so she's depending on the society to do this. I say, it's not my job to get the kid to school. That's not my job.

For Delilah, if the child is not removed from home, then full responsibility to care for her remains with the mother. Where a short-term intervention is not successful, then public support becomes a "crutch"; meeting ongoing and significant needs that affect a child's well-being is not part of how she sees the role of child welfare authorities. Another family service worker, Mallory, expressed the same idea, perhaps even more directly: "Ultimately ... I hold parents responsible. I am not the parent. At some point I am going to be backing out, or I am taking your kids, right?"

Interviews with professionals tend to frame CAS as a "safety net" for children where there is a serious problem that threatens well-being or safety. However, even during the period of CAS involvement, where there were challenges in obtaining important supports, or where important service advocacy did not occur, the main safety net for the children actually remained family – mostly mothers – who were under the threat of a very sharp accountability system where serious failures of responsibility could lead to extreme consequences, including the removal of children. Beyond maintaining oversight, public support for children and families, by comparison, appears to be more discretionary – or at least, highly dependent on the availability of perennially scarce resources. When the state does not provide services and supports that may be necessary for well-being – or even protection – there is a much lower level of accountability that originates, in part, from a weak conception of public responsibility for these children.

Key Informants: "I don't think it is clear"

Interviews with leaders in the child welfare sector in Ontario suggest that there is considerable ambiguity about the scope of public responsibility for children who stay at home. Ambiguity is nothing new in public policy, and may even be useful (e.g., Stone, 2011), enabling compromise. The concern, in this case, is whether ambiguity about responsibility to children who remain in the community allows the state to maintain a broad mandate for children's well-being without necessarily providing the resources required to support it.

Perhaps the most expansive definition of responsibility to children being served in the community came from my interview with the Provincial Advocate for Children and Youth, though it was tempered by an acknowledgment that in practice there is little consensus. When asked about the distinct role of child welfare with children and youth who stay at home, he said: "I don't think it is clear ... If you were to ask me, I would say children are guaranteed rights under the UN Convention – once you have decided to intervene, because you want to see kids protected, you have the obligation to see that their rights in the Convention are being protected."

He acknowledged, however, that his office, while certainly having a mandate to serve these children under the Provincial Advocate for Children and Youth Act, 2007,[4] had not done any consultations with this group of children. Moreover, unlike the situation when children are in care, there is no requirement that these children or their families be informed about the advocacy services of his office. Not surprisingly, in these circumstances, the Provincial Advocate does not receive significant numbers of complaints from or on behalf of these children.

A service director at a large CAS took a similarly broad view from a personal perspective but in general, he thought that CAS responsibility for children in the community is "a weakness which is very evident." Looking at the record of his organization and others like it, he commented:

A CAS is primarily focused on safety, protection – often, workers don't see their work in the broader child welfare spectrum. When we get involved, we should be looking at the wellness of the child, not just protection. We have a huge role to play in the system – we know what is going on in the family, we could be helping teachers, educational social workers. I don't believe those children's educational needs are somebody else's business. I don't see the difference between those kids and children who are actually in care.

This service leader articulates a double perspective: while he doesn't see a theoretical difference between the kids based on their care status, in practice, his agency differentiates, like most agencies in the province.

This reality was also echoed by policy officials in the Ministry of Children and Youth Services. As one official said, "from a ministry perspective, the kids who are not in care – we don't meet them."

A policy leader from the provincial CAS organization saw a principled basis for differentiating between state responsibility for children in care and children receiving services who remain with their families. Based on his understanding of the legislative scheme, he suggested there is an appreciable normative difference. He explained:

> The day-to-day parental relationship with children is different. Once legal guardianship transfers, the game changes. We move to a place where we try to maximize potential. With a protection investigation, there is a minimum standard of safety and security you have to meet, then the case is closed. If the state was in the game of maximizing potential, things might be different.
>
> Sometimes kids leave care and go back to homes; they are not necessarily going to do better in those homes. But their parents have met the test and so kids are going home. When the state assumes parental responsibility, they take on the obligation to ensure potential is maximized.

In this view, the shift in guardianship represents a move from a narrow focus on protection and safety to a broader focus on well-being and maximizing potential. His position was not absolute; for example, he clarified later that addressing issues of well-being for a child or parent (e.g., a mother with mental health issues) may well be a necessary part of ensuring a safe and sustainable home for a child. The logic of this theory is that the initial justification for intervention is related to a child's need for protection – from some threat to their safety – and that intervention ought to be restricted to its initial scope. Furthermore, his position recognizes the reality that CAS involvement is involuntary and often unwelcome by parents, and that the involvement of CAS in a broader program of promoting well-being would not necessarily be perceived as supportive. Limiting the scope of child welfare involvement in order to respect the autonomy of parents, or the privacy of the family unit, insofar as possible, has been called the principle of minimal intrusion and is strongly linked to conceptions of parental rights that are sometimes understood as in opposition to children's rights (particularly in the United States, see Gelles, 1997).

A family service supervisor, Mary, expressed a similar view in stronger language and for different reasons. In her view, as she is particularly informed by front-line practice, the mandate is in fact a narrow one:

> A family service worker has a mandate to protect children – the CFSA [Child and Family Services Act] mandate. That role needs to be pure child protection ...

They ought to be doing protection. They try to delve into doing preventative work but they are not funded for preventative work. If it doesn't meet the eligibility line for protection, they are not even involved.
Doesn't CAS have a mandate around well-being?
It's different – it's around how people interpret the legislation. They do well-being stuff, through mostly community links at the intake level. [My agency] was looking at well-being, but the criticism from staff is, "Are you kidding? We're so busy. You haven't hired. How can we do new work?"

There are more serious protection cases, and less serious. Well-being cases can fit the mandate – well-being you refer more, it gives you an opportunity to do more of the clinical social work. But when push comes to shove, those cases are obviously not as critical ... you do more well-being once you have ironed out the more high-risk child protection needs.

Mary sees the focus on the protection mandate as primarily an outcome of scarce resources in the agencies and pressure on the workers to manage their time for maximum effect.

The wide array of views expressed makes it clear that there is a significant policy gap about the responsibility of CAS to these children. This gap reflects, to some extent, the legislation and regulations that govern social workers' practice. The main regulations under the CFSA, with respect to the duties of the CAS to provide services, supervision, or care, are the Child Protection Standards, which set out a series of mandatory minima for service, essentially operationalizing the requirements of the act. The standards are highly procedural, dictating what issues need to be considered by social workers, and when. They are a mirror for the reality that safety is the paramount concern, at least in the initial investigation and decision about whether to open a case. For example, the practice note accompanying Standard 5 states, "The development and implementation of a safety plan is likely the most significant intervention during the investigation phase of service." Standard 7 makes it clear that determination about whether to open a case for family services is based on the existence of protection concerns, as well as on the perceived level of risk according to the prescribed eligibility spectrum (Ministry of Children and Youth Services [Ontario], 2007 [February]). However, when a case passes investigation and is open for family service, a much broader set of social work tools (including a Child and Family Strengths and Needs Assessment and an overall service plan) structure the social workers' tasks and interactions with the family (Standard 9) alongside the safety plan. This is consistent with the language of well-being in the purposes of the act. Social workers are required to use the planning tools, but they are not necessarily required (or able) to ensure that the services contemplated are provided unless there is a concern about protection. Even in the area of safety and protection, as a policy official from the ministry remarked, "The legislation is not particularly clear about what is a mandated service and what is not. Everyone says protection is mandated, but different CASs operationalize protection differently."

The notion that the involvement of child welfare should be minimally intrusive and/or that workers should limit their mandate to safety is at odds with a fulsome interpretation of CAS's mandate to promote well-being, and not particularly consistent with the Child Protection Standards once a case has been opened for family service. All informants agree that the state has an obligation to ensure the safety of a child receiving services in the community. But beyond safety, in the broader area of well-being that is also a mandate under the Child and Family Services Act, there is even less clarity. Even informants who said that CASs should be taking active steps to promote well-being expressed doubts that this purpose is systematically implemented unless there is a specific protection concern.

Educational Supports: The Mandate to Support Well-Being in Action

In chapter 1, I reviewed policy efforts to improve coordination between education and child welfare. Until this year, only one initiative undertaken in the past decade focused on children in care. The exception is the Child Welfare Outcomes Expert Reference Group, which proposed a framework that tracks outcomes, including educational outcomes, for all children (2010); ultimately, however, the performance indicators being implemented by the ministry do not track well-being outcomes (including education) for children who are not in care. All other initiatives focus on the children in the care of the state, including:

- the Ontario Looking After Children Project (OnLAC), which tracks developmental outcomes including education (see Flynn & Byrne, 2005; Kufeldt, 2006)
- pilot efforts to share educational data between boards and CASs;
- the creation of scholarships and financial assistance programs for post-secondary education;

- an inter-ministerial working group on preventing school changes; and
- early efforts to develop and disseminate standardized protocols for joint working between boards and CASs.

In 2009, an official at the ministry who was deeply interested in closing achievement gaps for children in the child welfare system commented, "No part of the strategy deals with the needs of children involved with the child welfare system who are living at home. They are not really on the radar." In February 2015, however, the provincial template for the Joint Protocol for Student Achievement became the first major policy initiative that explicitly included children in the community. The protocols are meant to be signed by both CASs and school boards. As of this writing, more than half of Ontario's CASs have entered into the protocols (personal communication, OACAS, 2015). With the consent of parents, under the Joint Protocol, children receiving services are also supposed to have focused joint planning for student success, and this is not just for children in care. This development post-dates the research in this book; it will be interesting to see what, if anything, changes under the terms of the new protocol.

Casework and practice in individual agencies, it appears, show the same pattern of attention primarily to those "in care." The agencies – through their workers – face the challenge of ensuring that children in the care of child protection authorities have the types of educational supports that are "available to well-informed and adequately resourced parents in the community" (Jackson & Simon, 2006, p. 49). These types of support include setting high expectations, limiting instability arising from changes of school, providing positive role models, providing practical supports where necessary, and effective advocacy for appropriate services, and appropriate responses in the context of bullying and discipline (ibid.). The evidence suggests that high parental expectations are one of the most powerful ways in which parents positively influence their children's academic achievement (e.g., Jeynes, 2005); this critical form of support may be absent in the child welfare context. In the large Children's Aid Societies where I did my research, there is evidence that efforts are underway to provide supports of that nature for children in their care (although there continues to be a concern about a limited evidence base on effective educational interventions for children in out of home care; see Forsman & Vinnerljung, 2012). But on the whole, most informants agreed these efforts were only very occasionally extended to children receiving services from a CAS but living in the community.

There are considerable differences between the education advocacy practices at different CASs.[5] However, the education advocates at the three large CASs were unequivocal that a majority of their work was with children in foster care.

Proactive Interventions

Two of the CASs have developed systems to regularly review cases for educational issues. In both cases, the proactive review or tracking process was limited to children in care (as noted by two education advocates). In one CAS, the education advocate, Carla, was involved in reviewing all Individual Education Plans for students with special education needs arising out of mandatory Identification, Placement, and Review Committees (IPRCs) before the social worker signed. That advocate also met with all crown wards, social workers, and foster carers before the transition to high school. Carla explained the significance of these meetings in helping set high expectations and improving student motivation:

It really works. You can see it when you talk about kids' dreams. They say "But I'm not going to be able to do this." Then you plan with them, not only the educational but the financial aspects of making their dreams feel possible, like something they can accomplish. It makes a really big difference to children. We need to write them detailed educational plans. It might include big changes, like a transfer of schools – for example, to be at the school where a foster parent has good relationships, or a school that has the prerequisites. The plan has to set out the responsibilities for everyone – the kid, the foster parent, the social worker, the education advocate.

Another aspect of proactive support was the development of more positive relationships with school and (since CASs are repeat players) board personnel. Jane, another education advocate, described it as gradually improving trust between the institutions. These trust relationships could also be an asset for children in the community, but only if, as discussed in chapter 2, the CAS is actively involved with the school in the case of a child receiving services in the community.

In another example, a ministry official talked about how a consultant worked with a number of boards to deliver training sessions on education for foster parents at several different CASs. Those training sessions were not offered to parents of children being served in the community. Providing them was seen as logistically complicated and not necessarily of interest to those parents. A number of informants talked about the relative complexity of the educational needs of the children in the system and the relative lack of knowledge of social workers and foster care providers. Given this, it is hard to believe such training would not be equally relevant to the parents caring for their children, notwithstanding the challenges of engaging them.

Practical Supports

Several informants talked about CAS being able to obtain a psycho-educational assessment (a prerequisite for formal identification and placement in a special education program) much faster than would be possible through school boards. Many school boards routinely limit the numbers of assessments performed at a particular school in a year (People for Education, 2011, pp. 13–14). In this, the CAS is acting like many parents with adequate resources who try to help their children get the help they need without waiting for an overstretched system to provide it. Generally, informants agreed, this important practical support was not available to children served by CAS who are living in the community.

There is some evidence that other practical supports were provided to children in the community on a more episodic and exceptional basis. A resource that has been demonstrated to be of assistance to children in foster care (e.g., Flynn et al., 2012; Harper & Schmidt, 2012) is access to tutoring supports. One of the advocates, Jane, commented,

We have a number of workers who bring situations to our attention about kids who are not in care. We try to help them, but resources are limited, be it money for transportation, assessments, or tutoring.

It's not all the time, but sometimes, with the right resources, we can prevent kids from coming into care. Up until now, we have not approved tutoring for any child not in care being supervised by CAS. Maybe it is something to look at ... but then the question becomes, how do you prioritize?

Implicit in that analysis is the assumption that the existing priority is on children who are in care, or at least on children where there is some kind of heightened issue of risk or safety that could be ameliorated by exceptional educational support. Carla, the education advocate at a different agency, commented simply, "If a child is in care, we have more resources to support the child." The allocation of these resources is naturally political; the priorities in the system are a reflection of how the scope of responsibility is defined and the way in which the accountability system structures incentives.

Advocacy: Double-Edged Sword?

Research that shows high involvement of maltreated children in special education and discipline issues (e.g., Scherr, 2007) clearly implicates a need for educational advocacy and problem-solving at a relatively high level. There is considerable direct and indirect evidence that advocacy – usually led by parents – is an important factor in ensuring children get the placements and services they need in special education, and that they are able to challenge disciplinary actions by school and limit adverse consequences where there is a finding against them (e.g., Nespor & Hicks, 2010; Ong-Dean, 2009; Phillips, 2008; Sander, Sharkey, Olivarri, Tanigawa, & Mauseth, 2010; Skrtic, 2010). Advocacy in this sense can improve the material conditions of a child's schooling (keeping them in school, ensuring appropriate accommodations to permit learning) and is likely to contribute to children's sense of security in the world by ensuring they are listened to and that someone is sticking up for them. In other words, advocacy bridges both the parental and the professional tasks that may or may not be coordinated by a CAS working with a family.

At one of the CASs, an education advocate worked on an on-call basis; that advocate estimated a quarter of his cases involved support to children in the community or adoptive parents. As a former principal, this advocate, Mark, described his work as training staff or managing crises – issues of behaviour and exclusion from school, or obtaining appropriate special education placements. In Mark's view, children in care were at a disadvantage relative to those who remained with their parents:

You've got to be more like a parent and not a social worker when you are working with the school. When it is two professionals discussing a student – you don't have that intensity that a parent brings to the meeting. When you are working with a parent, you expect a parent to be very committed, very earnest, sometimes demanding – whereas worker to worker, it is more collegial. That can prevent things getting done that should be done, things that a parent should insist on.

This "professional perspective" in the negative sense was expressed by some of the social workers I talked to. For example, Mallory, the experienced social worker whose clients identified her as a real advocate, commented about a case she was handling:

I am working now with this one child that is eight years old and may have Asperger's. There is something amiss with him ... I've talked to the school social worker. We're going to try to keep in touch ... The school [social worker] says, you know they have assessments: psychological, or psychosocial, or education assessments through the school. He said this child isn't even on a list for an assessment because the resources are so few, and because he's not like two or three grades behind ... The mother says, "I don't want him to fall behind," but unless he's way behind, the other kids will take a priority. Generally you try and work with the school and try and find out what is their impression of the kid: Is the mother overreacting? Is this kid just an awkward and bumbly kid? Is there something there? With this one, maybe it is not that the school is laissez-faire, it's that they're limited in resources, so if this kid isn't the highest priority ... We know he's not taking knives to school, or beating up other kids ... we know what a priority could be in the school system.

Mallory had already gone beyond the school system to get a developmental assessment for this child from a hospital, but she expressed substantial deference to the position of the school in a way that can, and sometimes does, let schools off the hook. Her response suggests she puts more faith in the professional judgment of the school about the lack of urgency than the intuitive (and eminently reasonable) parental sense that it could be disastrous for a child to be falling behind for years before help became available. As another worker, Kavita, said, "as much as we try as a child's worker, nobody advocates better than their own parents. In terms of advocating for their child, a parent might bring a deeper passion I think." Ironically, however, she added as an afterthought, "But as professionals with less, maybe, passion, we are still able to effect more change than parents."

Overall, the social workers I interviewed tended to take a perspective that was relatively aligned with the school – they were inclined to recognize the challenges facing a teacher with a large number of students, and to understand and rationalize a lack of services based on overall resource shortages. As Mary, the family service supervisor put it, "I don't know that there is much criticism about what schools do."

However, Mary clearly recognized that there is a role for advocacy in dealing with schools, and that sometimes parents alone are not in a position to be effective in dealing with a school on a child's behalf:

> When the child is not in care, sometimes CAS workers will support families or advocate for or with them. The reality is we are all bureaucracies – sometimes the family has a great relationship with an FSW [family service worker], some workers will help advocate, go to a meeting, write letters – all done with parental consent. You are a parent and you don't know anything, really, and you are marginalized for whatever reasons ... you don't get the system, sometimes workers will act for you in those cases.

This quote confirms the obvious: many parents have difficulty coping with school issues for their children, particularly if their child is facing challenges, and social workers can be of considerable assistance in negotiating these challenges. It also makes it fairly clear that there is wide discretion about whether and how a social worker will get involved. In this case, Mary, as a supervisor, attributes a social worker's decision to get involved as being related to the strength of relationship with the family, rather than the level of educational need that arises.

Several educators talked about the power of CAS involvement and advocacy in situations where a child needs additional help. Some perceived CAS as helpful to the school, for example, by providing assistance in trying to shift a parent's decision about whether or not to consent to unwanted special education services for their child, or by facilitating a child's involvement in services that required active support from the parent, such as attending a children's mental health program. Others saw CAS as making a difference by getting the school system to produce resources. Jane, a school social worker, commented:

> I see them being able to move the education system to respond if they lobby hard enough ... If a CAS worker sees a kid who is having real difficulty with school work – they can advocate that that child needs an IPRC, an assessment or something ... Those are the kinds of things where advocacy really is the difference between getting help, and "it's going to take two years to do it, and then the horse is behind the barn." We'd be scrambling in grade four or five to get it done. For a list of twenty kids, there are another twenty who are fighting for priority.

Jane is describing a situation where CAS chooses to become involved. Melanie expressed frustration that CAS had not gotten involved with her children's serious school problems until her son was in middle school and she had managed to create positive relationships with the school on her own:

It's like I have always told my CAS worker and my [school] social worker: there are different rules for different people. When the school called, he came right in to the school. But when my son was having the crap beaten out of him every day, with bruises and all, he would never do anything. Look where he is: he's being bullied, now he is a bully. CAS has witnessed behaviour and still does nothing. Maybe if they had gotten involved earlier, way earlier, it might have been different.

These different perspectives help make clear the potential for CAS to make a significant difference for at least some kids in the community with respect to education.

"I'd rather just deal with things myself"

One of the factors that may make it more challenging to routinely expect social workers to become involved in supporting parents' educational advocacy is the inherently coercive nature of child protection. A policy official at the Ministry of Children and Youth Services who had considerable front-line experience explained:

As a system we need to turn our mind to those sorts of outcomes [outcomes related to well-being]. We need to have more conversations about "hey, how are you doing in school? What are you comfortable with? What makes you uncomfortable?" But there is a balance which workers often walk: it makes it hard to be there as an advocate for families. If you start asking a lot of questions about school, the family may look at you, "Oh no, now if my kid is doing badly in school, now they're going to take my kid away?"

This account returns to the theme of minimal intrusion; again, from the perspective of this official, there is limited room to work with families on issues that relate to well-being or are outside of the scope of the concern which brought them to the attention of child welfare in the first place.

At least some of the mothers I interviewed expressed the view that they would not want CAS involved in schooling issues for their child.

Anisha commented, "I don't think they need to have anything to do with the school – nor does anybody outside of myself and my family." Reflecting on her own experience, Anisha said she would not turn to CAS to help her with a (relatively minor) problem she was having at her son's school. "I was a Crown ward with Children's Aid myself. I feel like if I address stuff with them, they are going to take the side of the teacher. I don't like to go to them with anything. I'd rather just deal with things myself."

An education advocate, Carla, reported that there were extra challenges involved in doing advocacy work with children in the community. She said it was not generally the practice in the agency to have the education advocate get involved in those cases. Complexities can arise out of the sometimes-fraught relationships between particular parents and the school and also may arise out of parents retaining decision-making control.

With kids in the community, they are the most complex cases to be involved with ... Often, we need to work on the relationship with the school, which can be very frayed. The interactions are so difficult. A mother is so frustrated – she can't afford uniforms, or the right kinds of pencils. When a child is with their family, there is no accountability. Whenever I work with a family – we can decide on a strategy. But the parent can change her mind.

Carla went on to provide an example of a case where she had gotten involved in appealing a twenty-day suspension for a situation in which a youth had not removed his hat in class, which the teacher had interpreted as a threatening behaviour. She said, "I got involved. I explained that *this is not usually what I do for children in the community*, but the situation was so blatant" [italics added]. However, during the appeal meeting the mother changed her mind and agreed to the suspension because the principal had told her that if her son returned to school, she would call the police. From the advocate's perspective there was the issue that "everything in his life was so negative – and then the school became a part of that," *and* the issue of a disproportionate penalty that was part of a racialized pattern at the particular school. The mother's perspective was shaped by fear that if she and her son did not go along with the process, things would get even worse. This is a very interesting example of how, where a child is in care, the social work role of coordinating "professional" supports can be *less* problematic than where there is a parent who still holds onto the full bundle of parenting responsibilities, including decision-making.

The Imperative to Integrate Services:
No Time to Scale Back Advocacy

So we see it is the view of CAS workers that educational advocacy is sometimes necessary and often helpful, and that this support is provided much more frequently to those in care than to those living in the community. Those services can make a significant difference to children's well-being. In light of this, it is worrying to see the Commission to Promote Sustainable Child Welfare (Ontario) (2010) suggest that child welfare should consider a scale-back in this kind of activity. In a section titled, "Mainstream services not sufficiently responsive to the needs of CAS kids," the commission wrote:

> CASs invest considerable resources in advocating for access to services for the children and youth in their care. The Commission has heard many examples of children in care missing weeks of school while the CAS negotiates for their admission with a local school board and/or for appropriate supports for their special needs ... We must move from this reality of having to negotiate for access to services to a system in which resources are balanced and coordinated and able to be responsive to the needs of these vulnerable children and youth.

It is hard not to be frustrated by the utopianism of this vision in light of the political reality and clear evidence that mainstream services too often fail the most vulnerable children. Any suggestion that child protection should be scaling back its role in relation to advocacy for and within other public systems is inconsistent with a conscious effort to overcome the gaps in achievement and inferior educational experiences of children in care; indeed, these services should be extended to also serve children living at home who are abused and neglected.

A final note on the nature of education as an example of how the state deals with well-being: educational services are a very important component of well-being, and it makes sense to examine them to see how well-being is addressed. But there is a range of outcomes that are associated with well-being. Looking After Children tracks health, self-esteem, self-care, pro-social behaviour, and anxiety (e.g., Flynn & Byrne, 2005). In the United States, national targets for mandated Community and Family Service Reviews look at outcomes in terms of support for families, ensuring children's educational needs are met, and ensuring their physical and mental health needs are met. In the United States, where outcome tracking is mandated, child welfare agencies consistently have their highest scores in terms of meeting children's educational needs (see most recently Department of Health and Human Services/Administration for Children and Families [U.S.], 2010, p. 25). It is generally assumed that part of the reason for the relative success on educational outcomes is the more universal nature of the public education system, particularly in comparison with areas such as mental health. In areas where there is less universal coverage, the roles of advocacy and practical provision are likely even more important.

Accountability for Services to Children in the Community: Missing in Action

Policy leaders see public responsibility for supporting children who remain in the community as being unclear or ambiguous, which is significant in that there is serious resource scarcity in child welfare. Ill-defined responsibilities are much less likely to receive resources. The example of educational supports reveals patterns of non-support, or highly discretionary and occasional support, for educational needs of these children. Accordingly, if we turn to individual and systemic accountability for service provision by child welfare, it is unsurprising to find that there is very limited accountability for services provided to children in the community.

Individual Rights in Respect to Services under the Child and Family Service Act

The Child and Family Services Act reflects a progressive approach to intervention in the family. As the forms of intervention authorized by the act are intensified, there are more comprehensive obligations on the government. Accordingly, the government tends to have fewer legal obligations to the lower-risk families who receive services from Children's Aid Societies. The main focus of the formal protections in the act is individual children, and then their families. In general, section 2(2) provides children and their families with procedural rights in respect to services under the act, including the right to be heard and represented in decisions about service. Unless there is a court order, parents must consent to services (s.27). A person may complain about a service "sought or received by that person from the society," and has a right to have their complaint heard and finally determined by the society (s.68), through a mandatory Individual Complaints Review Panel. In certain, fairly limited, circumstances, the Child and Family Services Review Board will adjudicate complaints about a CAS. From the perspective of a parent or advocate trying to obtain services or challenge the quality of the services being delivered, there are very limited rights under the CFSA. Notably, it is also clearly the perspective of CASs that they face considerable and indeed overlapping demands for accountability (e.g., Ontario Association of Children's Aid Societies, 2014).

While a CAS is required to "provide the prescribed standard of services in its performance of its functions" and to follow prescribed procedures and practices (CFSA, s.15[4]), the act and the regulations are silent on substantive standards of service for developmental services, treatment services, and community support services or non-residential child welfare services. The expertise and judgment of a social worker (appropriately supervised), combined with the resources available in a particular community, governs determinations about a child and family's strengths and needs and the appropriateness and adequacy of services in the service plan. This contrasts with the language in the more adversarial parts of the act where the agency is required to demonstrate, for example, that a child cannot be supported in the home prior to a change in guardianship.

In the context of community services – particularly under the policy of differential response – the goal is both to prevent placements and to avoid being adversarial, particularly in court involvement, where possible. However, it is notable that under the CFSA, the main mechanism to force Children's Aid Societies to account for the adequacy of services provided to families is judicial oversight. But according to the CIS, the courts are involved in less than 5 per cent of cases (Public Health Agency of Canada, 2010). Very likely, most of those 5 per cent are the most adversarial cases in which a change of residence is required – in other words, the very opposite of a typical community service case of ongoing vulnerability. There is an unambiguous legislative preference for minimizing disruption and for leaving children in their own home where it is consistent with the best interests of the child to do so. This pressures the CAS to demonstrate that all reasonable measures have been taken – this pressure is strongest in the high conflict cases.[6] In a case that is highly adversarial, social workers consult regularly with in-house lawyers, and the need to meet judicial requirements clearly structures practice. But it is not clear what impact these standards have on social work practice in the lower-risk cases, or on the perceptions of mothers where the courts are not involved from an early stage.

It is obvious that the judicial process is extremely resource intensive for CASs, not to mention very stressful for the affected parties. Nevertheless, there is reason to be cautious that case management that is not operating "in the shadow of the law" (Mnookin & Kornhauser, 1979) does not sacrifice the regular interrogation about the adequacy of services provided as part of the judicial process. If judicial oversight is supposed to decrease, what is the tool by which families and the public can be reassured about the adequacy of service provision?

In summary, the scheme of the Children and Family Services Act, not unreasonably, reflects greatest concern with those over whom the state is exercising most power, particularly children in care in addition to families potentially facing a loss of custody of their children. Court-ordered supervision also attracts some duties on the part of the state. But people who are merely receiving services have far fewer rights, particularly if the services in question are being provided by third parties. Overall, the government's main obligations are procedural fairness in service decision-making. These weak individual accountability mechanisms underscore the importance of vigorous systemic measures of how well children and their families are being served by the child welfare system.

Systemic Measures: Service Reviews and Outcome Reporting

Unfortunately, however, there are very few systemic measures in place to ensure any kind of public accountability for the respective fate of children who are maltreated but remain at home, whether compared to the general population or to children in foster care.

The Child and Family Service Reviews in the United States may not be a policy tool that any Canadian jurisdiction would want to adopt, given their somewhat punitive nature, but they do provide important descriptive information about how the system is working for both groups of children.

As noted above, the Office of the Provincial Advocate for Children and Youth has a mandate to conduct systemic inquiries and now investigations (see the Public Sector and MPP Accountability and Transparency Act, 2014). The office could draw attention to the policy void around these children and what appears to be a relative lack of service, but they do not routinely inform children living with their families about their services, and they have not been receiving complaints. The government's latest effort to remake the child welfare system, the Commission to Promote Sustainable Child Welfare, has not identified issues relating to children who are not in the care of the state as being among its priorities as it looks to a reorganization of services.

There has been an ongoing discussion about regular reporting on child welfare outcomes, suggesting it would be a useful way to maintain focus on achievement or gaps in both protection and well-being for all children receiving child welfare services. Ideally, outcomes should be reported separately for groups receiving different kinds of services and compared to the general population. At least in principle, it is clear that the trend towards accountability in child welfare is to focus on child outcomes (e.g., Commission to Promote Sustainable Child Welfare, 2012b; Ministry of Children's Services, 2005; Ontario Child Welfare Outcomes Expert Reference Group, 2010). Key approaches are the National Outcomes Matrix (see Trocmé et al., 2009a) and the national and Ontario Looking After Children projects (see Flynn & Byrne, 2005; Kufeldt, 2006) and the ongoing effort to develop an agreed-upon list of child welfare Performance Indicators (OACAS, 2014).

Differential Response and Child Welfare Sustainability: Individualization and Flexibility without Accountability for Services

If overall, that parental responsibility underlies a patchy and inconsistent framework of public responsibility for a group of very vulnerable children, the latest waves of child welfare reform (without stronger accountability for services) has the potential to make these tendencies even more intense. In 2005, the Ontario government joined at least twenty North American jurisdictions when it committed to "differential response" as its latest direction for the reform of child welfare; the broad policy direction has been affirmed by more recent overall reviews (Commission to Promote Sustainable Child Welfare, 2012a). Differential response is as much a catchphrase or a philosophy as a service model. But the underlying prescription is that, as part of the initial investigation, and from time to time throughout the management of a case, child protection agencies should assess the level of risk to a child posed by a particular family situation (e.g., Shlonsky & Wagner, 2005). Services the child and family receive should be tailored accordingly. Child protection agencies need to be prepared to intervene dramatically, which should include a focus on gathering evidence and determining whether removal from the home is appropriate in high-risk cases. However, experience in the field suggests that these high-risk cases are a minority of the caseload at any time. In the majority of cases, which are lower risk, the child protection system may more usefully be involved by a process of family assessment and by linking families with services in the community. In most differential response models, (at least) one stream of cases is treated as requiring less adversarial involvement by child welfare than has traditionally been the case. Families streamed into the less adversarial stream may either have their cases closed, with or without community connections, or may have their cases open for family services. Some higher risk cases may also be in the family service stream – these concerns apply to them, too.

Differential response arose as an effort to handle a rapidly expanding system that was experiencing considerable strains, and in which overlapping, interconnected critique – for its under- and over-inclusion, lack of capacity and inadequate service delivery – were all framed by an inflexible and coercive service orientation (e.g. Waldfogel 1998, p.122). It was increasingly important to respond to significant overrepresentation of people of colour, Aboriginal families, and poor families, especially those headed by single mothers (in the ranks of those policed by the system) (Blackstock et al., 2006; Roberts, 2008; Swift, 1995; Trocmé, MacLaurin, et al., 2005; Trocmé, Knoke, & Blackstock, 2004), and to deal with burgeoning costs which had doubled over a 10-year period marked by cuts to other children's services (e.g., Ministry of Children and Youth Services, 2005). The approach appeared to address these major issues; however, the architects of differential response were always clear about one of its key limits: specifically, that children from families assessed as low risk on the basis of immediate safety concerns remain vulnerable (e.g., Ministry of Children and Youth Services, 2005, p. 9). The concern which flows from this continuing vulnerability is the significant risk that differential response could result in governments failing to fund the community services that are supposed to underlie the model. As one author put it, "a differential response does not guarantee that any needs identified are necessarily met. It is possible to identify needs through a child and family assessment ... and provide little or no service response to meet the needs" (Waldegrave & Coy, 2005, p. 34).

How differential response plays out in practice may vary considerably depending on the context. For example, in small Aboriginal communities where there may be fewer social services available, and where child welfare funding is actually lower on a per-child basis than child welfare funding averages nationally, workers and agencies have fewer mid-range options for services for families and children, which leads to a continuing pattern of removals and adversarialism (see generally, Blackstock, 2011).

Almost ten years into implementation, the impact of differential response is clearest in the area of curbing growth in the child protection system. The Commission to Promote Sustainable Child Welfare contrasts the period between 1998–1999 and 2003–2004 with the period between 2003–2004 and 2009–2010, and shows that the process around differential response has been effective at limiting the increase in the number of children going into care (from 46 per cent to 2 per cent) and at limiting cost increases from 97 per cent to 32 per cent, which is now in line with government-wide expenditures (Commission to Promote Sustainable Child Welfare [Ontario], 2010, pp. 10–11). However, information on child outcomes in the two timeframes is still not reported at the provincial level, and it is difficult to assess the impact on service provision or children's outcomes.

Even outside Ontario, there are only a few major evaluations of differential response published at this time, and the overall evidence is still inconclusive (for recent overviews, see Fluke et al., 2014 and Waldfogel, 2009). Ontario has not conducted a prospective evaluation of the impact of differential response. Considerable methodological challenges posed by the wide range of models and changes throughout the implementation process have made it difficult to draw any cumulative findings about key outcomes from the literature, which to date, does not address the relative well-being of children in the low risk categories.

Amorphous Public Responsibility and Weak Accountability: Changing the Cycle

There is little consensus on the scope of public responsibility towards children receiving care from child welfare authorities while living with their families, and public responsibility for the well-being of these children is particularly controversial. The scope of this responsibility is especially important in the context of reforms promoting "differential response," where "lower risk" cases are streamed into services on a non-adversarial basis. There is limited evidence (and none from Ontario at the provincial level) about the impact of differential response on services and supports for children in the low risk category. However, interview data suggests that in the area of education, children being served in the community receive fairly limited supports from CASs, which suggests a similarly limited practical institutional commitment to the well-being of these children. Even in the context of abuse and neglect, there is a strong presumption that families – overwhelmingly mothers – can, will, and should assume full responsibility for their children when they stay at home. Alongside a more discretionary support role, CAS has clear responsibility to police the adequacy of parenting, thus holding mothers accountable for the exercise of their family responsibilities. By contrast, CASs operate in the context of very limited individual or systemic accountability for the well-being of these children. This group of children remains vulnerable. They deserve a stronger, clearer statement of the state's responsibility both for their protection and for their well-being. A stronger accountability system – including public reporting on both sets of issues – is an essential part of clarifying this ambiguous area of public responsibility.

This chapter also contains a message for schools. As a whole, particularly where students need exceptional supports, the school system continues to rely upon parental advocacy of a very privileged kind to push to provide the supports and consideration that the students are theoretically entitled to. Where parenting is compromised, without strong CAS support, it is too often the case that educational services continue to underserve these vulnerable children.

Chapter Five

Regulating Aspirations: Teachers' Responsibility and "The Whole Child"

There are always some people who will not believe the obligation of a school is to provide the wraparound of support that will make it possible for all children to succeed.

– Policy official, Ministry of Education

Does the fact that schools – specifically teachers – have the potential to make a crucial difference in the lives of abused and neglected children make it their responsibility to do so? The next two chapters explore the question of teachers' responsibility for the success and well-being of their abused and neglected students. It looks at the legal and policy context – the explicit rules that govern teacher responsibility – and at interview data from parents and front-line and policy workers in the fields of education and child protection. There is significant ambiguity about the scope of professional responsibility for children's overall success and well-being that is consistent with the literature on teachers' work, in both the system of formal rules and the empirical accounts of lived experience. Teachers consistently confront a tension between minimal and maximal definitions of their responsibilities, which – though a reasonable response to the complexity and constraints faced by teachers in diverse classrooms and generally high aspirations for their work and students – renders significant challenges in terms of regulation.

The focus of these chapters is the responsibilities of teachers, specifically, rather than the responsibilities of the school or larger systems. There are several reasons for the focus on teachers. First, as Michael Fullan observed (2008), teachers are the determining factor of education reform. Any change in education depends on what teachers think and do. Second, the Education Act primarily allocates responsibilities to those in professional roles, not to the school as a whole; it prescribes the duty of a teacher or a principal, but not a school. (Boards have recently been given some explicit responsibilities.) Third, an important strand of thinking about the well-being of children experiencing significant challenges emphasizes resilience – the power of some children to do well in adverse circumstances. A key factor in resilience is one or more close relationships with an important person in a child's life (e.g., Howard, Dryden, & Johnson, 1999; Ferguson & Wolkow, 2012; Ungar, 2009). It is a truism that relationships are with people, not with institutions. Fourth, there is a compelling body of literature, looking at human service organizations such as schools, that emphasizes the experiences and pressures facing front-line workers, called "street-level bureaucrats." One of the key arguments of this literature, and of the broader literature on policy implementation, is that "the decisions of street-level bureaucrats, the routines they establish, and the devices they invent to cope with uncertainties and work pressures effectively become the public policies they carry out" (Lipsky, 1980, p. xii; see also McLaughlin, 1987; Maynard-Moody & Portillo, 2010). A focus on teachers does not, of course, mean that institutional context is irrelevant. Indeed, one of the main arguments in these chapters is that schools as workplaces, organizations, and sites for children's learning and development have significant potential to shape and either support or undermine teachers' exercise of responsibility.

There is a well-established body of research that emphasizes the (arguably growing) scope of teachers' responsibilities and the significant uncertainties inherent in their jobs. The literature on organizations, particularly, emphasizes the contradictions around the regulation of teachers' work in the context of these uncertainties. It is not surprising, in this context, that the responsibilities of teachers for children's educational success – let alone in the case of children experiencing abuse or neglect – is defined in conspicuously general ways in the legal and policy framework.[1] Their responsibilities are set out in an array of different sources. Legislation (the Education Act and other statutes), case law, professional conduct regulations of the Ontario College of Teachers, and collective agreements are the major formal sources of responsibility.

Teacher action is likely to be shaped not only by formal rules but also by the informal expectations that circulate as part of the culture of the school and the profession (e.g. Scott & Meyer, 1997; Tamanaha, 1995). Interview data – listening to how teachers and others talk about their responsibilities – is a useful lens on the cultural understandings about teachers' professional obligations. It is also clear that teachers do not work in a vacuum. To understand their responsibilities it is worth investigating the different perspectives of their colleagues within the school (administration and student support personnel), parents, and – for this purpose – child protection workers.

Teachers' responsibilities tend to be defined in one of two ways – either as a core of responsibilities that represent a minimum, below which teachers ought not fall (almost "do no harm"), or aspirationally in terms of teacher potential ("do it all"). I identified three core areas of teacher responsibility across the different groups – instruction, communicating with parents, and keeping children safe. Even within these core areas, however, participants clearly identified both minimal and maximal definitions of responsibility. Overall, this creates a potential conflict for regulation – exactly what it is that makes the work most meaningful is also difficult to reduce to well-defined obligations for which individuals can be held responsible.

Regulating Irregular Work: Teachers, Responsibility, and Endemic Uncertainties

There is extensive scholarship, which includes both sociological and policy research, on teachers' work that helps inform a discussion of teachers' responsibilities. One key issue – the subject of considerable debate – is the extent to which teachers' responsibilities are in fact subject to regulation and control, and if so, the means by which this control operates. The literature across several decades suggests that the very nature of teachers' work makes it extremely difficult (and not necessarily desirable) to define teachers' responsibilities in a way that is readily amenable to top-down regulation. In this chapter, I review both the literature on regulating teachers' work and the legislative framework in Ontario that governs' teachers' responsibilities. I then identify a tension between an idealized, holistic definition of teachers' responsibilities, and a more constrained core of responsibilities for instruction, communication, and safety. Notably, the well-being of children is not part of the core where schools or teachers will be judged to have fallen short. Yet even within the "core," elevated aspirations trump any clear articulation of responsibilities for which teachers may be held accountable. The scope of work that teachers – and parents, and social workers – identify as being among teachers' most important contributions to children's development and learning both inspires often exceptional commitment and resists prescription.

Dan C. Lortie's *Schoolteacher* (2002, first published in 1975) is considered a classic in the sociology of occupations for the comprehensive way in which it links research into teachers' attitudes and the structure of recruitment, formation, and promotion, with research into the challenges of the workplace. He emphasizes teachers' wide discretion in central aspects of their work. So, for example, in the context of a discussion of teacher co-operation, Lortie's data showed a wide range of teacher practice. He comments, "The reported differences, plus the comments of respondents, make it clear that norms are permissive, rather than mandatory ... Normative permissiveness has a self-evident function; it encourages individuals with different needs to satisfy themselves along lines they find most rewarding" (Lortie, 2002, p.194).

Lortie appears to see the utility of this type of permissive normativity – insofar as it enhances teacher autonomy and their ability to find psychic rewards in their work – but also views it as a natural outcropping of the "endemic uncertainties" of teachers' work itself. Describing the fundamental conditions of teachers' work, he argues sympathetically that "Endemic uncertainties complicate the teaching craft and hamper the earning of psychic rewards. Intangibility and complexity impose a toll; built-in difficulties include assessing performance, balancing demands and relationships, and managing the self under provocation. In each instance the technical culture falls short of resolving the issue; it is most unlikely that so many teachers would experience difficulty if effective solutions were at hand" (p. 159).

Lortie also posits that teachers' attitudes or sentiments – most important among them, "conservatism, individualism, and presentism" (p. 208) – are a rational response to the sometimes painful uncertainties of the job. However, at the same time, these sentiments actually contribute to what he describes as the "lack" of a strong technical culture. In his argument, an effective technical culture – norms and all – would tend to "raise the performance level of the group" and relieve an intensified and individualized "burden of failure" arising from what he identifies as a lack of "normal expectations within the occupation" (p. 81). Further attenuating the potential for a strong technical culture, Lortie emphasizes that the "global, even utopian" objectives of education further reinforce conservatism, individualism, presentism, and the profound challenges of regulation (p. 208).

By contrast, Richard Ingersoll, in *Who Controls Teachers' Work?* (2003), does not paint a picture of permissive norms where teachers exercise wide discretion. Instead, he portrays teachers constrained though "both formal and informal modes of workplace control." He argues that "a close look at the job of teaching reveals that teachers are pushed to accept a remarkable degree of personal accountability in the face of an equally remarkable lack of accountability on the part of the schools that employ them" (p. 13). With a particular focus on the socialization of children, Ingersoll uses large-scale survey and ethnographic evidence to show that teachers are indeed subject to rules, that teachers are overseen and supervised in many aspects of their jobs, and that rules for teachers are effectively enforced. This process is, to a greater or lesser degree, inherent in schooling as a democratic, publicly funded mass system. However, after 125 pages of demonstrating the extent to which teachers are controlled, Ingersoll points to the limits of what can be achieved through bureaucratic control (in language that echoes Lortie's) in light of the "particular character of the clients, objectives, processes and products of schooling." He summarizes that "regulations often don't work well for irregular work" (p.142).

Almost a decade later, the Organisation for Economic Co-operation and Development (OECD, 2005) released a major cross-national study of the teaching profession, reflecting concerns that teachers too often suffer from low status and insufficient formation, induction, and professional development. In the course of the review, the OECD articulated a wide range of roles that are expected of a teacher in the twenty-first century – roles spanning classroom, school, and community (p. 97–8), and a commensurately large range of competencies required of expert teachers (p. 100). In terms of policy, however, the OECD's major recommendation appears to be a backhanded acknowledgment of the ongoing difficulties in defining – let alone enforcing, or supporting the exercise of – teachers' responsibility:

> The overarching priority is for countries to have in place a clear and concise statement or profile of what teachers are expected to know and be able to do. This is necessary to provide the framework to guide initial teacher education, teacher certification, teachers' ongoing professional development and career advancement, and to assess the extent to which these different elements are being effective. A fundamental precondition for the preparation of a profile of teacher competencies is a clear statement of objectives for student learning ...
>
> The teacher profile must reflect the broad range of competencies that teachers require to be effective practitioners in modern schools. It should

encompass strong subject matter knowledge, pedagogical skills, the capacity to work effectively with a wide range of students and colleagues, contribution to the school and the wider profession, and the teacher's capacity to continue developing. (p. 131)

In other words, thirty years after Lortie, there is a lingering ambiguity about what teachers are supposed to be doing and how they are supposed to be doing it. Student learning is identified as the core of professional competency, but the objectives for it are defined as being external to particular relationships between teacher and student and, often, defined in largely content-based ways.

The uncertainty about teachers' work has been identified as a cause of its relative lack of status. Further, the supposed lack of a defined area of specialized knowledge (alongside a lack of control over working conditions), has been one of the key factors that, in some views, makes tenuous the claims to professional status by teachers as a group (e.g., Etzioni, 1969 on "semi-professionals" such as teachers and social workers, and see Biklen, 1995 for a critique). Ingersoll sees the concept of professionalism as one of the key organizational resources used by schools to overcome the difficulties with bureaucratic control. He argues that the extra-contractual work teachers suspend in work-to-rule campaigns is not just beneficial but essential to the functioning of schools (Ingersoll, 2003, p. 177). From his perspective, it is striking how, through conceptions of individual responsibility and professionalization, teachers have internalized the idea that "these kinds of tasks [those withheld in work-to-rule] are not extra efforts to be rewarded, but obligations to be expected. The assumption is that it is teachers, not the organization or the community, who are primarily responsible for the social growth and the well-being of students while they are in school" (p. 177–8).

For Ingersoll, the discretionary nature of "extra efforts" (Lortie's "normative permissiveness") "should not be confused with power." He goes on to observe that "in struggling to successfully balance their mix of demands and constraints, employees can end up easily co-opted – by working hard to make things work in an organization that may have denied them the power, autonomy, and resources to accomplish their tasks adequately in the first place" (p. 182). In seeking to be identified as professionals, but without control over the conditions of their work, Ingersoll suggests that teachers' claims to professionalism are primarily attitudinal and, in fact, operationalized through taking on extra responsibility. This analysis is consistent with a growing literature on "organizational citizenship behaviour" – work not formally prescribed in an employment contract that is "highly desirable if not essential for the effective functioning of almost all organizations" (Leithwood & Beatty, 2008, p. 17). This literature documents a very similar phenomenon (e.g., Belogolovsky & Somech, 2010; Jimmieson, Hannam, & Yeo, 2010).

The Legal and Policy Framework of Teacher Responsibility for Student Success

The legal framework of teacher professional responsibility consists of an interlocking network of legislation, regulation, case law, and collective agreements. Depending on the source, teachers' responsibilities are sometimes seen as being very broad and focused on positive relationships and the long-term, holistic success of the child, or narrowly in terms of duties of instruction and avoidance of harm.

The Education Act

The recently adopted preamble of the Education Act declares that all partners in the education system – including the minister, the ministry, and the boards – have a role to play in enhancing student achievement and well-being, closing achievement gaps, and maintaining confidence in the province's publicly funded education system (s.0.1[3]). Responsibility for promoting achievement and well-being is also allocated to the board (s.169.1[a]; 218[1][g]). Historically and today, a key function of the Education Act is to set out the duties of a teacher: to teach assigned classes or subjects, encourage pupils, inculcate key (specifically Judeo-Christian) values, co-operate as a member of a staff team, and maintain order and discipline.[2] Principals have all the duties of teachers (s.265). In addition, they have numerous administrative duties ranging from timetabling to the reporting of communicable diseases; determining student promotion and access to class or school; ensuring discipline and co-operation and coordination of the staff; and giving "assiduous attention to the health and comfort of the pupils, to the cleanliness, temperature and ventilation of the school, to the care of all teaching materials and other school property, and to the condition and appearance of the school buildings and grounds."

Common Law and Constitutional Law

In common law, the responsibility of the teacher towards his or her pupil is defined as that of a "careful and prudent parent towards his or her child" (*Williams* v. *Eady* [1893]; see also Brown & Zuker, 2007, p. 6). This expansive standard of care was developed in the field of negligence where the broad language of parental responsibility was contextually limited to preventing risk of foreseeable harm rather than meeting a child's full needs. The Supreme Court of Canada has also defined the responsibility of teachers and principals very broadly:

> Teachers and principals are placed in a position of trust that carries with it onerous responsibilities. When children attend school or school functions, it is they who must care for the children's safety and well-being. It is they who must carry out the fundamentally important task of teaching children so that they can function in our society and fulfill their potential. In order to teach, school officials must provide an atmosphere that encourages learning. During the school day they must protect and teach our children. In no small way, teachers and principals are responsible for the future of the country. (R. v. M. (M.R.), (1998), para. 35)

The language is quite comprehensive, emphasizing caring for children's well-being and teaching children so they can function in society and fulfil their potential. But the scope of the analysis, again, limits the significance of the responsibilities enunciated there. Despite the expansive language, the aspect of teachers' responsibilities that are actually given effect in this decision are very much concerned with maintaining order and safety (for example, by enabling searches for suspected drugs) – responsibilities which map tightly onto the narrow duties enumerated in the Education Act.

Professional Regulation and Professional Ethics

In addition to the Education Act and common law, the Ontario College of Teachers Act[3] also sets out a legal framework for understanding teachers' responsibilities. Teachers wishing to practice in Ontario are required to be members,[4] and the College has among its objectives to establish and enforce professional standards. It has the power to investigate and discipline members as part of policing fitness to practice. Professional misconduct is defined by regulation[5] as any one of a range of unacceptable behaviours, such as abusing a student or falsifying information. Professional misconduct also includes failure to maintain the standards of the profession, which articulate an expectation that "Members are dedicated in their care and commitment to students. They treat students equitably and with respect and are sensitive to factors that influence individual student learning. Members facilitate the development of students as contributing citizens of Canadian society."[6]

This commitment is buttressed by standards calling for appropriate professional knowledge and participation/leadership in learning communities. The Standards of Practice were developed in conjunction with a set of ethical standards for the teaching profession, which the College identifies as "vision" to "inspire" members, guide decision-making, and foster public respect.[7] This ethical code is quite different from the content of ethics programs in the classic professions, which operate as a list of fairly specific and highly enforceable prohibitions (e.g., a lawyer may not allow a witness to knowingly mislead the court and has quite precise obligations in handling other people's money).[8] By contrast, teachers' ethical standards are framed in terms of values – care, trust, respect, integrity – rather than responsibilities. Standards of Practice are enforceable through the discipline process of the College. However, a review of the summaries of the discipline cases[9] reveals, unsurprisingly, that the more positive responsibilities set out in the Standards of Practice – demonstrated care, equitable treatment, response to factors affecting individual learning – operate largely outside the realm of supervision by the College. The College's Manager of Standards described the standards as intentionally "descriptive not prescriptive" and "aspirational," arguing that their power is a basis for individual and collective reflection and critique in local educational sites, such as schools, boards, and faculties of education. She explained, "The standards also communicate to the public the values and dispositions that exemplary teachers in the province demonstrate and the skills and knowledge that teachers need to possess."

Regulation as Employees

In addition to being regulated professionals, teachers are, of course, employees, and have responsibilities as such. The collective agreements prescribe teachers' rights and aspects of their working conditions, but they are silent in terms of what is expected of teachers' practice beyond meeting the requirements of the Education Act and following principal direction.[10] As one union representative told me, "you are not going to get disciplined if you are not promoting well-being."

There is a provincially regulated system of teacher performance appraisal that is required of all teachers employed by public boards every five years (and every six months for new teachers who are required to demonstrate "satisfactory" performance twice before being treated as an experienced teacher). Performance appraisals are conducted by principals and require teachers to demonstrate "competencies" in sixteen domains, grouped (as is the principal's feedback) under commitment to students and student learning, professional knowledge, teaching practice, and leadership and community.[11] The teacher evaluation program is characterized by a low possibility of failure, highly intermittent observations, limited follow up (except as a best practice), and wide discretion in terms of what is observed or reported on by the principal (see more generally, Kennedy, 2010).

In sum, the legal and policy framework of teacher responsibility vests primary responsibility for the relationship with students in teachers. The Education Act prescribes basic duties of instructing pupils and contributing to the school through maintaining order and co-operation with colleagues. Common law defines the responsibility of teachers expansively, even as being "like a parent," but only in the context of avoiding negligence or establishing parameters of safety. Teacher professional standards and performance appraisal documents emphasize teachers' caring and commitment to student well-being, alongside their responsibility for students' learning, as among the finest qualities of the profession – an ethical commitment. Prescribed forms for teacher evaluation include an emphasis on commitment to students, though there is considerable breadth in terms of the attributes that can be evaluated. In the context of this sort of generality and mixed messages of the policy framework, it is useful to go beyond what official documents have to say to look at the way teachers – and the adults around them – see as their responsibilities.

Understandings of Responsibility in Practice: A Minimum and an Expansive Maximum

Many Messengers, Same Mix of Messages

As one would expect from a group of interviewees that included marginalized women, front-line workers in two different sectors, and policy workers within and outside government, there were many differing opinions about how to improve educational outcomes for children in care. It is noteworthy, however, that when it came to the question of teachers' responsibilities, there were very limited differences between participants' opinions. With one exception, responsibility for attendance,[12] differences in opinion on this topic were not clearly related to differing backgrounds.

Responsible for the Whole Child

The most striking aspect of the discourse around teachers' responsibilities for students experiencing abuse and neglect was the tendency for participants – like the courts – to define teachers' responsibilities comprehensively, in very elevated terms, and with a strong focus on the whole child. It was relatively difficult to get any of the research participants – especially teachers – to identify particular areas of responsibility. At least some of these teachers saw their stance as a bit subversive of a more explicitly academic orthodoxy. But based on what they told me, the starting point for almost all of these educators is clearly a responsibility to teach and support the whole child, and success is seen in those terms.

Dana is a veteran teacher with experience in both special education and classroom teaching. For her, a holistic sense of responsibility flows from her definition of success:

Success would be to holistically help to develop lifelong learners. The success would be that a child would be able to learn for themselves in their day-to-day life – not necessarily your three R's, but including health, social management, and emotional health as well – being a learner of themselves and of the world around them, and even at this young age, to have the confidence that they can do and be who they have been created to be.

Flowing from that, her definition of her own responsibility to ensure student success was similarly broad:

I probably will come at this from a different angle than others – it means really looking at where they are coming from, really looking at social emotional issues – in order for them to be as successful as they can academically. I try as a classroom teacher to create an environment of trust. I really try to create a classroom that is about helping a holistic child – parent connections, building team within a classroom and within a school. I try to assess things, not as my teaching, but as their learning – are they learning, are they socially-emotionally adapting or learning?

Although Dana saw herself as having a fairly unusual vision of success and responsibility, in fact, her views were quite typical of my interviewees.

Antonio, for example, talked about his responsibility "to make sure all students understand what respect is" by showing them respect and teaching them how to interact with each other. "It is so important. They'll take that with them through life. It's more than math or something," he explained. Particularly in the setting of a behaviour class, he saw his main role as "teaching them values and things in life that they will really need just to get along." Another teacher, Kanti, saw success as seeing a child working to the best of their ability, "having a vision for their future, having some ambition for themselves ... they need to feel they have something of value to contribute."

The adults around them also define the responsibility of teachers comprehensively. As Rachel, a mother, noted, "They are given a mind, I mean, in their job as a teacher, they are given these empty minds at a young age. They [teachers] need to nurture them and try to teach them to the best of their ability how to come out and become productive members of society, and not foster any negativity and make kids feel less than they are." Another mother, Ruby, talked about teachers' responsibilities in terms of children's learning:

Learning, they're learning to know left and right. At the same time, to do good things, because the teacher, they can teach that too, because they know some people do bad stuff. So they can teach you do this, do this, you're not allowed to do this, you are not allowed to do this. I know the teachers know everything. And they know more than me. So if you give them time, they can teach you more.

Family service workers recognize that teachers are often involved in trying to foster and support the whole person, particularly if they recognize a child or parent is struggling. Kavita talked about how a middle school homeroom teacher working with one of the children she serves has become "an advocate for the child in terms of the school in general." She explained: "A lot of her other teachers have been sending [this child] to the principal whenever they can; she's been an advocate in terms of helping them connect with the child in a different way, encourages the child to get into extracurriculars – it's a bit more than just the straight imparting knowledge."

Despite this holistic focus, three focused areas emerged where there was broad consensus that teachers have particular responsibility: to ensure their students receive effective instruction, especially in "the basics"; to communicate with parents, especially when there is a problem; and to ensure children's safety and freedom from abuse at school.

Responsibility for Instruction: "Teach my child what they are supposed to teach them"

Central to the unique professional responsibilities of the teacher is the responsibility for instruction based on the curriculum. Even where the challenges of working with particular learners are recognized, most people in and out of the system place responsibility for ensuring children learn the key requirements of the curriculum at the centre of what is expected from teachers. This is likely why the OECD describes "responsibility for student learning" as being at the heart of teachers' professional profile. It is also part of the intuitive salience of test-based accountability regimes (e.g., Elmore, Abelmann, & Fuhrman, 1996; Hunt & Levin, 2012). That responsibility can be quite general. Asked what a teacher's responsibility is, one mother, Melanie, said simply, "Teach my child what they are supposed to teach them." Deborah was looking forward to a future where her son would be successful as a musician or performer. Asked what the school could do to help him, she responded, "Just getting the reading and math into his head, because wherever he is going to go, he's going to need it." Another mother, Anisha, explained that "the school's responsibility is to educate my child – educate them about the courses they are taking, if you are teaching him math, the basic things you need to know in math." Later, in regards to any changes she thought the school could make to support her child's learning, Anisha expressed concern about high and consistent academic standards. "Do I have a wish list? Sometimes, when I look at his work, I wish the teacher would give him less of a mark because of how he wrote it. I guess it's the teacher's judgment, and every teacher is different." For Saliha, as a mother, "education is the first thing." She describes her frustration at being unable to help her children with homework because of language barriers and how she wants help because she doesn't know how schooling works here.

She looks for assistance from the teacher to provide extra support to ensure her children learn at a high level: "I always say to the teacher, can you give me something, this, that, extra help. I always go after school [and ask], 'can you give me extra work?' [and] 'he doesn't understand.'"

Social workers from CAS also clearly identified the teacher's central responsibility, the one by which they will be judged as having succeeded or failed, as academic. As one family service supervisor, Mary – who also had experience as a school social worker – explained, "The teacher needs to focus on the child's education – that very specifically needs to be their primary focus. If there are impediments, there are support services within the school board to meet those needs." Later in the interview, when asked about a teacher's ongoing responsibility where they are aware of children's aid involvement, she reiterated that the main way teachers should deal with child protection issues was through the ongoing duty to report. "If they observe and feel a kid is not doing as well, they can always refer for social work, a CYW [child and youth worker], guidance. The teacher's role is to teach ... they need to do what they are the experts at doing. If they need support around things – that's why there are other supports in the school system."

Another social worker, Delilah, talked about her frustration working with a child who had just started high school. "What I hate is when they are just trying to get them through the system. They move them on. I wish you could interview my fourteen year old. He has not learned anything." For this social worker, the school should be ensuring that all children are actually learning. What she observed, however, was that both the school and CAS often frame graduation – "getting the piece of paper" – as a goal, and push for that without necessarily emphasizing learning. She went on:

He would say, school's a farce, everything is a farce. He doesn't get it, he doesn't understand why ... he wasn't going to school, and I was concerned about his marks. I knew he's not going to school, he's not doing his work. He was in a behavioural class. He's saying, "we have to do the same thing again and again." I was thinking he would fail. But the school says, "we can work something out."

Why are they passing this kid on, when he doesn't know anything? He went on, he went on to grade 9, and now, he doesn't do anything in class ... he just disrupts. I don't get it. I don't think he can write a letter to save his life. I guarantee grammar, spelling ... I don't think he could do it. And yet – give me

a break ... The teachers told me he's capable. I know the reason for this is that this kid is difficult ... Oh my god, this poor teacher ... But part of it is, I think the work he's doing is not very challenging. He's going to graduate with a piece of paper and not know anything.
That is not your definition of educational success?
No, that is not education, and that is not success!

This social worker was hugely frustrated with the child's experience of being in school without learning. While acknowledging the challenges faced by individual teachers, she is indicting the school as having given up on both achievement and well-being for this difficult student.

As these quotes illustrate, family service workers could be quite critical of teachers where they observed significant unaddressed issues with academic performance. At least some social workers (though few of those I talked to) could also be critical if there was too much focus on academics. An education advocate, Mark, commented that too often there is an adversarial relationship between CAS workers and teachers, with each group saying the other is not doing enough. He commented, "I have heard social workers say, 'all the teacher's concerned about is math.' Well, I know teachers – most are concerned about kids."

A few teachers expressed a focus on academics expressly in terms of contributing to children's holistic well-being. Clearly, a concern with effectively teaching math, or other parts of the curriculum, can be a powerful manifestation of a concern for children and a commitment to their future. For example, Vizheh talked about the responsibility to help children achieve academically. A first-generation Canadian herself, she teaches in an extremely diverse school serving a largely low-income, immigrant population. For her, supporting academic achievement was crucial because "Their parents have given up everything to come here – for their kids. They don't have resources, they can't be going out and doing enrichment activities, so I need to give them tools to help their children. I send homework, even though the board says I should not, because that is how I help these families realize their dreams. They have sacrificed so much."

Another teacher, Kanti, identified her responsibility to be an intellectual force in her students' lives, explaining that, for her, "the teacher is the child's interpreter of the world – they come and they discuss issues – for some kids, this is their chance to talk about what is going on in the world. So the teacher helps form their perspective."

Parent Communication

There was strong consensus among all participants that teachers have a responsibility to communicate with parents about their children's educational successes or challenges. Communication may not be enough to overcome problems at school, but parents need to know what is going on, and, in fact, teachers should work to engage them. Many of my respondents identified communicating with the school as the key thing a mother could do to support her child's educational success.[13] However, there is a corresponding responsibility for teachers – and others in the school administration – to maintain communication.

There is a set of specific legal requirements for communication: report cards must be issued and acknowledged by guardians and teachers are required to participate in regular meetings with parents/guardians;[14] guardians must be notified by a principal if a child is harmed by an activity that leads, or can lead, to a suspension, including bullying,[15] or if they face serious disciplinary consequences such as suspension or expulsion.[16] In special education, parents must consent to and be invited to participate in significant processes such as the Identification, Placement, and Review Committee (IPRC) meetings.[17] But the duty to communicate goes beyond these formal requirements, as we see in comments from mothers, educators, and social workers.

Mothers in my study were very emphatic about a duty to communicate on the part of teachers and the administration, particularly if their kids were struggling. Situations in which there was a failure of communication were identified as a serious breach of responsibility on the part of the teacher and the school. Deborah talked about a situation that had happened several years before about which she was still extremely angry:

The vice-principal never approached me for things because I apparently looked too grumpy. And when my daughter was having problems she would never talk to me. Months went by before a serious problem was discussed with me because they said I looked upset every time they saw me. This was the principal and the vice-principal. So I said to them, you are going to tell me that my daughter fell behind – it was during the Gulf [Iraq] War, she started freaking out because they kept announcing the war, and she was fighting and beating up her teachers, you know, because they scared her – I had no idea. So I said, "You're going to tell me that my daughter fell behind three months because you didn't want to speak to me because I happened to be grumpy-looking?"

It was clear that Deborah had a strong expectation that a serious concern would be communicated with her. She was actually more upset about the school's failure to communicate this problem – something that was happening at school – than she was when the school reported her for suspected neglect. She had, however, made her feelings about the reporting clear to her child's teacher, and said she had "just blasted them" for calling CAS instead of her when they observed a problem.

A common concern among the mothers in my study was that no one at school would communicate if a child were falling behind. Caroline explained, "The school's responsibility is to tell me what's going on with my kids and keep me in the loop." She gave the negative example of her older children who had made it into high school with a very limited ability to write or do math. Although she was concerned about her children's lack of basic skills, she seemed to feel that a particularly serious part of the problem was that nobody had communicated with her about their progress. She said, "The school never told me there was this much of a problem. The report cards seemed always pretty good." Now, she sees her own involvement with the school as a way to ensure the same thing doesn't happen with her younger children. She speculates that things had gotten out of hand with her older children because she was working and not close to the teachers.

Another mother, Saliha, had extremely positive relationships with her child's teachers – her son's grade 1 teacher, Vizheh, identified her as one of the most supportive parents she had ever worked with. Saliha still expressed concern that her child's teacher would fail to communicate important information about her children's progress. While she had been happy with her sons' experience with Vizheh, Saliha was concerned that her daughter's kindergarten teacher was not adequately preparing her for grade 1. "She says they are very young, in kindergarten. But after that, when they attack them with other things, then you can easily see, 'Oh, your child is far behind.' But first they say, 'Oh, don't worry about it.'" She was also concerned when she did not know what was happening in her children's new classroom.

Melanie was also happy with her children's school, and particularly with her youngest son's (behaviour) class where she was able to spend a few minutes each morning to see him get settled and have a quick conversation with his teacher. According to her, an important part of the school's job is to communicate, both through planning ("my kids have always been in certain classes where they have charts and stuff") and ongoing monitoring, saying, "If the child's having a hard time, they have to call me, and we have to figure out together what we can do with my child."

Teachers, too, talk about their responsibility to connect with parents and build a relationship, even when it's difficult. Dana, for example, identified relationships with families as the starting point of her responsibilities as a classroom teacher: "Connecting and focusing on family is really important – getting to know parents, making sure communication has happened." For her, communication with parents helps her assess a child's learning and make suggestions about educational testing or programs where there is a need. Evelyn, another experienced teacher, also emphasized the importance of building a relationship with families:

Usually a kid that gets called to CAS is a fair bit of trouble in the class – I try to phone home to give positive calls rather than just negative calls. Sometimes I am successful at that, and sometimes I am not. If I do see [the parents] in school, I will go and talk to them ... obviously if it is something really severe, like a kid punched a kid and lost a few teeth, then I would make that phone call, but I really try not to. I would try to build a relationship: sometimes it works and sometimes it doesn't.

Antonio, teaching in a behaviour class, commented, "the big thing is the parents – so I make sure that I have constant and direct communication with parents at all times. They call me freely – we're communicating every day." Through regular communication, he believes that he creates the trusting relationships he needs in order to challenge parents where necessary. "When something goes on at home, I call and say, 'This is going on and what are you doing about it?'" He identifies this as the kind of communication that contributes to children's safety and connection to school.

Administrators also identified communication as key, particularly in the context of work with child protection. Simon, a principal in a large suburban school with a diverse, mostly low-income population, said simply, "Our role is open and clear communication and transparency – having parents understand what we're doing and why." He also said that where CAS was involved, school administration has a role in explaining to parents that child protection didn't necessarily mean taking children away. Fernanda, another principal, explained, "We're trying to get them to build relationships of trust with us. We always hope that by some of the conversations we have to hurdle, we'll get the trusting relationship we need to have with parents and children to build in the kinds of supports that we know need to be there."

The school social workers were particularly emphatic about the need for teachers to stay in touch with parents. Social worker Carol identified a communication log with parents as part of a teacher's assessment of how kids were managing, particularly if there were concerns about neglect. Another social worker, Cory, talked about communication in terms of engaging parents. After acknowledging the many challenges of being a classroom teacher, she said:

It's as difficult for parents. They feel like they don't know what is going on in the classroom. Teachers want to help but they have their own constraints. I try and support [teachers and parents] in dealing with each other – it's just a social skills issue …That happens a lot at one of the schools I work at – at one school, especially, there is a lot of difficulty in helping parents being comfortable, helping them be engaged in the process of their kids being educated.

The perspective of the school social workers is particularly interesting because they were working directly with families where there were, by definition, issues beyond what a classroom teacher could reasonably be expected to handle alone. Even where someone else from school was supporting the family, the school social workers saw it as the duty of a teacher to actively maintain communication about what was going on in the classroom as well as what was happening with a particular child, and to actively work to make parents comfortable. They identified this active work at engagement as very important to help children thrive at school.

For the CAS workers, too, direct communication with parents was a very important aspect of teacher responsibility. Several of the workers expressed frustration when teachers would contact CAS rather than talking to a mother directly. One reason CAS workers hesitate to get involved with schools is that they hope to empower parents to deal directly with their child's teacher. A few expressed the view that teachers who went around the parent to deal with a worker were shirking their responsibility to engage the parents. Kavita, for example, talked about working with a family: "Unfortunately, the teacher would call me when there are issues at school, instead of calling the parent. It can really negatively impact the relationship between school and the parent when they go through us. Mom felt, I think rightly so, that she was being excluded from decisions about her child's education."

Sheylinn, a family service worker who had worked in schools before she went to CAS, was scathing about schools, "calling about everything," using CAS as a "crutch" to avoid dealing with parents. She gave an example of a child having a meltdown. "They will call us. We say, 'Well, call Mom, have you talked to Mom about it?' They aren't playing that role that they are supposed to have – engaging parents." Sheylinn saw engaging parents as being central to a teacher's responsibility:

What is a teacher's responsibility?
I think about it a lot. Growing up in inner-city schools – sometimes you are stigmatized even by the area you come from. Teachers are more invested in kids they know are going to university. Sometimes, the kids are falling between the cracks because people aren't investing as much. If a child is acting up, coming to school not well dressed, not warm enough, no lunch, you know... the teacher has to really engage the parent. If you just send a letter, that's not enough. You have to really reach out. If parents are really not responding, that's where we start. The teacher has to really get a sense of what the child needs.

Other family service workers echoed the view that persistence was required to fulfil the responsibility to communicate. Merely leaving a recording where there was a problem, like a child regularly missing school, did not meet the standard. As Delilah commented, "It would be helpful, if the kid is really not showing up, to actually contact the parent – one on one, not just the recordings."

Safety and Avoiding Harm

A third core area of teacher and school responsibility, widely agreed upon by research participants of all backgrounds (and very prominent in the legal framework of responsibilities), was ensuring that children be kept free from harm at school. While an emphasis on safety initially appeared relatively minimal – ensuring the child didn't experience abuse at school – in fact, the implications articulated by participants were broad. Most participants defined safety in very expansive terms that seemed to amount to a kind of emotional comfort-zone. While safety was considered a responsibility of the teacher, it was clear that most of the participants saw responsibility for safety as being school-wide, with particular emphasis on the principal. However, when participants referred to the more socio-emotional aspects of safety, the teacher's role became pre-eminent.

Mothers and school personnel emphasized school should be a safe place. As Anisha said, "The school's responsibility? The safety of my child." Another mother, Rachel, who was a domestic violence survivor suffering from depression, answered that the school's responsibility for well-being means children need to be free from abusive treatment by teachers:

Does school have a responsibility for his well-being?
What kind of well-being?
   You tell me. (pause)
Yes and no. I mean they have to make sure he's safe, number one, and I think that his well-being in terms of self-esteem needs to be nurtured, so they can't be abusive in any way. The teachers, even if it is saying something simple like you are dumb or stupid or ... that can be a problem.

While freedom from verbal abuse may seem like a low minimum, other mothers who identified safety as a primary responsibility of schools clearly defined safety in both physical and emotional terms. Deborah – a survivor of abuse, in her case, childhood sexual abuse – said her school's responsibility for helping her kids was "that it's a safe place. Safety is a humungous issue for me, and trust ... Because we have been there a long time, that's why I like it there, I trust them with my kids, and I don't trust very many people, anybody, with my kids."

A broader version of safety is evident when others talked about safety in terms of protecting children from bullying and from racism. Melanie described significant, recurring conflict she had with her children's former school, ultimately leading to her being banned from the school property because the principal "couldn't stop the bullying." She explained, "I did what I had to do to protect my kids." For Melanie, the principal's disregard of the specifically racist nature of some of the bullying her children were experiencing was of particular concern. She explained, "He was fighting a lot. Kids would call him the N word every day. The principal would say, 'tell him it's just a word.' I'd say, 'You tell that to his black family!'"

Several educators identified the child's safety as being a crucial priority in their work with abused and neglected children. While many of them emphasized physical safety, their responses suggested that the focus on safety was, again, considerably broader. Antonio, for example, explained that in his class, where students have been identified with behaviour issues that "they are coming in with difficult experiences. They are often not feeling good about themselves. We have to give them that feeling that they want to be at school, and that school is safe for them." Another teacher in a regular class, Kanti, commented, in her judgment, when she was working with children who had experiences of abuse and neglect that "for example, sometimes you might need to not push the academics as much, to start with the behavioural things, help them remaining calm, getting homework done – that child needs to feel like there is a safe place at school and someone they can talk to there. That is the first priority."

A guidance counsellor, Gabriella, talked about providing safety in the context of defining educational success, saying the school has succeeded if it provides safety and a separate life from children's home life. Dana, a teacher, expressed a related idea in a child-centred way. Noting that children who have been involved with CAS have often had "huge challenges, which really affects their learning," she suggested that some of the kids she had taught were "just trying to be secure and survive" when they came to school. For her, students' needs for security fit at the base of Mazlow's hierarchy of needs: without safety, learning was not going to be possible. Interestingly, when educators talked about safety, very few of them talked about the reporting process – or even their own vigilance about abuse or neglect – as part of the safety they hoped to provide for a child.

The Paradox of Regulating High Ideals

There is a strong parallel between the legal framework for professional responsibility of teachers, and the ways in which teachers, mothers, and social workers articulate their responsibilities. In both sources of understanding, one is struck by how often a tremendously broad set of responsibilities is articulated. In legislation and common law, we learn that "In no small way, teachers and principals are responsible for the future of the country," (R. v. M. [M.R.] [1998], paragraph 35) and they are expected to be dedicated in their care and commitment, to provide inspiration, to inculcate values through example and teaching, and generally to "help students fulfill their potential" (ibid.). From teachers we hear these aspirations have been internalized, where their goals are to develop lifelong learners, who, in addition to the curriculum, have what they need to succeed in terms of health, social emotional development, world view, and attitudes. Teachers' responsibility for achieving these ideals – the way teachers and regulators articulate their responsibilities – are manifestly challenging to prescribe, and indeed, what is clear from the regulatory framework is that mandatory aspects of the job seem disconnected from the high aspirations.

With probing, it is possible to identify three areas of responsibility that may represent a core, or apparently minimal, definition of teacher responsibility: instruction, communication with parents, and students' safety. The particular salience of these "core" areas is that – unlike the broadest definitions of teacher responsibility – teachers and schools will be judged to have failed if they fall short on these fronts. However, analysis in each case shows also how each of these relatively simple-sounding areas in fact includes significant breadth and ambiguity. There was a tendency for teachers and others in these interviews to start from fairly concrete ideas and then import elevated aspirations for practice. As Lortie (2002) remarked, teachers routinely "dignify and elaborate the significance of the tasks they perform to earn a living ... high ideals are not, after all, without significance in the affairs of men and women" (p. 111).

It is clear that high ideals contribute to teachers' motivation and often performance, including their willingness to undertake the taken-for-granted work of organizational citizenship in schools through extra-curricular activities, trips, planning, and above all, student support. Yet the aspirational discourse also contributes to professional and regulatory challenges. The status of the profession is more tenuous without a clear articulation of distinctive expertise and contribution (exacerbated no doubt by the fact that the vast majority of teachers, especially elementary teachers, are women [Biklen, 1995; Casey & Apple, 1989]). The discourse also weakens the capacity of educators and regulators to establish clear norms for the work and butts up against the push to develop a stronger technical culture, which has been identified as a key aspect of both professional development and school improvement more generally. In the next chapter, we will look in depth at one aspect of the high ideals and maximal definition of teachers' responsibilities – the specific responsibility of care for students.

Chapter Six

Between Labour and Love: Individualizing Teachers' Responsibility for the Work of Care

Can you tell me a story in your experience about how a school made a difference for one of the children you worked with?
I would say it is not the school, it's the teacher. In working in child protection, the main difference that would make or break a child's success in life is connecting to a person. The education system has the opportunity to put someone in this child's life who can make a difference, whether they do it or not.

Sheylinn, family service worker

Holistic definitions of student success and teacher responsibility are an important – if lightly regulated – aspect of a strong school system that can meet children's and society's needs. In this chapter, the focus is on one particular element of the holistic set of responsibilities articulated by so many teachers (and by official statements of the ideals of the profession): the work of care. The significance of the work of care and its positioning between private and public, has been articulated by generations of feminists, and yet it is consistently absent in the major accounts of teachers' work. When teachers, parents, and social workers are asked what matters for vulnerable children, however, they clearly identify care, as does the major research about powerful teaching and learning for all students. There is a paradox: the responsibility to care is treated as an individual and personal undertaking rather than a part of the job, even though it is also seen as a prerequisite for effective work. Because care exists in a shadow land of professional expectations, it raises real issues of teacher burnout resulting from a lack of support, a lack of systematic improvement or planning in this area, and real challenges of interagency co-operation arising from uncertain expectations.

Care has not only been invisible in defining teachers' work. Rather, the inevitability of caring and relational aspects of the work have been a key battle in the struggle to define teaching as a profession, as Sandra Acker (1999) reflected:

> [There are] pervasive conceptions of teaching as a calling, and of teachers as adults who do what they do mostly because they care so deeply about children. The association of such images with women is important in shaping the occupational culture and the approaches of scholars. Thus, an emphasis on teaching as "work" serves not only to highlight the tension between "work" and "profession," but also speaks to the difference between work and non-work, the latter associated with the notion of doing "natural," quasi-maternal "caring." (p. 19)

Acker's critique points to particularly gendered "social expectations that women's caring work should blur the distinctions between labour and love" (Acker, 1999, p. 105). This blurring contributes, in turn, to the invisibility of "caring work" or "emotional labour" (Hochschild, 1983).

The Work of Care

The larger research on "caring as work" predicts a pattern of inattention to caring as part of the work of teachers. Most of this literature has been developed in the context of household work (e.g., Eichler & Albanese, 2007). A subset of the literature, however, looks at caring in the context of paid work, most clearly in the professions most associated with women (Folbre, 2001): teaching (e.g., Gannerud, 2001), nursing (e.g., Staden, 1998), and social work (e.g., Freedberg, 1993). Feminist social theorists have argued that care operates as the largely devalued but completely essential substructure of society as we know it, even in the "public sphere" of paid work. Social theorist Carol Pateman, for example, notes that "the welfare state has always depended on a good deal of social care being provided, unpaid" (Pateman, 1997, p. 5). Mary Daly and Jane Lewis (2000) point to key role of social care, noting it "lies at the intersection of public and private (in the sense of both state/family and state/market provision); formal and informal; paid and unpaid" (p. 282). They argue that "Care is more than just unpaid personal services but is inherently defined by the relations within which it is carried out, relations that tended to be characterized by personal ties of obligation, commitment, trust and loyalty. The process of care is emphasized, explored in terms of 'loving, thinking and doing'" (p. 283).

In this argument, the work of care crosses the boundary between home and workplace, and it is undervalued and under-examined in each setting. The state has a role in "policing the boundary" between the extent to which care work falls within the private or public sphere. The sources of obligation for caring work are important: they frequently arise in the context of social relations of dependency, and within an ethical or normative context (e.g., Carol Gilligan's "ethic of responsibility," [1982]; or Noddings, 1983) that can be observed in discourses around the work – discourses which may support, marginalize, or undermine it. Caring work has costs, but where it is privatized, these costs are usually borne by those providing care.

A Blind Spot in Understanding and Regulating Teachers' Work

The canonical accounts of teachers' work – even Richard Ingersoll, with the explicit attention to socialization in *Who Controls Teachers' Work?* (2003) – have a consistent blind spot for the work of caring, particularly for children in the classroom. In *Schoolteacher,* Daniel C. Lortie observes that "the self is implicated" in teaching work, and he argues that teachers gain much of the satisfaction and sense of meaning from their work through relationships with their students; they choose "people work" (2002, p.230). But he does not talk about how that reality affects the work teachers do or the inadequacy of a "technical culture" as a solution to the challenges of this particular kind of work. *Teachers Matter*, the OECD's survey of teachers' expanded roles, notably makes no reference to the work of building and maintaining relationships, attentiveness, providing support for children's physical and mental well-being, conflict resolution, and crisis management (see Organisation for Economic Co-operation and Development, 2005, pp. 99–100). The profiles of what teachers are expected to know and be able to do that the OECD selected as exemplars (including one from Quebec) are notably without reference to the interpersonal aspects of the work.

This omission is particularly striking in light of the strong research suggesting that teachers' relationships with students are not only inevitable but an essential aspect of effective teaching and learning, alongside high expectations and academic press (Lee & Smith, 1999; McLaughlin, 1993; National Research Council Institute of Medicine [U.S.], 2004;

Pianta & Walsh, 1996). The core notion of an instructional triangle at the heart of schooling (e.g., Cohen, Raudenbush, & Ball, 2003) emphasizes interactions and relationships between teacher, learner, and content in environments. Yet major school improvement efforts – the push for a technical culture, or an OECD-approvable description of what teachers should be able to accomplish – focus primarily on cognitive or organizational goals.

Similarly, in the regulatory framework, the work of care occupies a peripheral place. Care for students is referenced only in the ethical standards developed by the Ontario College of Teachers, which are explicitly intended as a "vision" to "inspire." Among the values (not responsibilities) articulated in the standards is "care," which "includes compassion, acceptance, interest and insight for developing students' potential. Members express their commitment to students' well-being and learning through positive influence, professional judgment and empathy in practice."[1]

Other aspects of the ethical standards included supporting student wellness and dignity, openness and honesty, and moral action. As discussed in chapter 6, care – along with support for students' wellness generally – is seen as an aspect of exemplary practice, rather than something prescribed as a routine duty required of all teachers.

The ethical standards are an interesting example of the way the state has to some degree explicitly embraced the importance of caring work and simultaneously left it as a matter of private concern. By articulating and taking seriously the "ethical" aspects of the standards, I argue that the College effectively places them in the zone of moral or personal responsibility, in a tangential relationship with the zone of professional responsibility. Lyse Langlois, an academic whose work influenced the College in the use of ethical standards, specifically differentiates between ethics and law. While both are based in values, she argued that "Ethics are therefore an autoregulatory process ... Autoregulation signifies that the regulation comes from within us in our choices and actions and calls for personal effort. Ethics call for self-control and the ability to act freely and responsibly" (Langlois & Lapointe, 2010, p. 149).

According to the Manager of Standards, consultations have shown that teachers have been extremely responsive to the approach, and have found it "empowering" as a tool that is responsive both to the complexity of the teachers' role and the diversity of contexts in which they work. Yet while it may feel empowering to be free of external control or accountability, the relegation of care to ethics also limits institutional responsibility or support.

In the last chapter, we found that both legislatively and in the discourse around teachers' work, there is a tendency to articulate both success and responsibility for students in very holistic ways, and that even where teachers and others pointed to more concrete responsibilities (instruction, communication, and safety), there is an elevated or aspirational aspect to the description of expectations. A key element of the consistently holistic view of educators' responsibility is the responsibility of care for their students. Looking at the interview data, it is quickly apparent that when teachers are asked to talk about what they do, the significance of caring emerges very clearly. Parents and social workers also consider this aspect of what teachers do as critically important, but neither group consistently defines this important contribution as "work."

"Like a second family"

Very often professionals will articulate the role and responsibilities of schools and, above all, teachers, as being "like a family" in their relationship to their students. This simile reflects both teachers' contributions to their students' holistic development and the lastingly gendered nature of teachers' work, the tendency to "blur the distinctions between labour and love" (Acker, 1999, p. 105). As Margaret, a very insightful and practical principal, commented, "It's loco parentis – I've often said to kids, I'm your mom when you are at school."

Caroline, another principal, looked back on her own experience as a teacher and reflected, "Our students are like your own children – you expect to not have anybody damage them emotionally or physically. When I was a teacher, my principal mentioned that I was like a mother duck, with all my ducklings: 'You are very protective of your students. You feel very responsible for their well-being.'" Delilah, a family service worker, commented:

For me, because school is such a big part of our kids' lives – it's huge, they spend so much time in school – it becomes their second family. So we need to work together, collaboratively, thinking about what is good for this kid. Kids don't want to be talked down to, analysed, but we need more creative ways of getting them to talk about what is going on so we can identify what is going on, really early on. [Teachers] need to be attentive, proactive.

If they see behavioural stuff, they need to jump on it right away. It's not going to go away – we sometimes think it's going to go away. Kids are stressed, anxious. We need to pay much more attention to children's mental health.

Melanie, the mother who had had such difficulty with her former school, appeared to see the school like a specifically patriarchal family. When her older son in middle school was having difficulties, she consistently opted to speak to the principal: "I like to talk to the principal, because the VP has told me I am a rotten parent – not in so many words, but she called me to tell me about something that happened, and she tells me I should watch Supernanny ... It is more work on him, but he's the father in the school, he runs everything. It is his responsibility to know what's happening, everything, all the time."

Fernanda is another principal who highlighted the educator's duty to be "in loco parentis." She explained, "When they are here, they are our children ... It is far more than teaching them to read and write – they need to learn conflict, conflict resolution, social engagement, how to make friends, how to lose them – the caring domain."

This work in the "caring domain" often falls on the classroom teacher, although many people also pointed to the ways in which principals also contributed to care for vulnerable students. Teachers I interviewed identified caring as a key source of their responsibility for children, particularly where they felt there was something wrong at home. For example, Evelyn was able to describe a number of occasions when she had become significantly involved in advocating for services with CAS – for example, waiting with a child in the CAS office on a Friday night until a social worker promised to investigate:

How do you see your job?
If I suspect strongly that a kid is being abused I feel like I need to follow it until – not necessarily something is resolved satisfactorily – but at least until I know there is someone looking out for him.
Where does that sense of responsibility come from?
Ultimately we see kids more than their parents see them during the school year and on some level, if we're in tune with our kids, we know more, even more than their parents might know. I guess ... I just feel responsible for them. I care about them quite a lot. If some harm is coming to them, I can't come and take the child away from their parents, and I know that the kids don't even want to be taken away ... so you have to do something.

This quote shows both how her sense of care motivated a very powerful response on the part of the teacher, and it also shows how her sense of duty was informed, in part, by concern about parental failure to protect a child. She literally sees herself stepping into the breach.

Another teacher, Kanti, described her work with a child who had a recent history of abuse by his mother, and who had been acting out in her class, being "pretty violent," and bullying younger children. She maintained regular contact with the child's father (who had custody). Recognizing that the child "didn't want to deal with women," she had matched him with a male support teacher for when he started "melting down and self-destructing." She made significant efforts to be visibly even-handed in discipline "so he would not feel picked on." Slowly, she was able to build trust and get the child talking to her. Asked about her approach, Kanti explained, "Well, I like to think I would have been so caring for any child in his situation – I just *liked* the child, you know."

Educators recognize that "the caring domain" is an important part of positive relationships with children and families, and it's an important part of the learning process for all children. Caroline, the principal who remembers being called a "mother duck" as a teacher, reflects on her experience as a parent to inform her sense of teachers' responsibility and student success:

As a parent I was more concerned that the teacher cared about my child, that they liked them and kept their self-esteem intact. I wanted my child to enjoy going to school, that they felt safe and cared for to the point that they were willing to take risks in their learning, for example, by answering questions. This is something that I share with staff. The curriculum is very important, but it is a must that children feel cared for, feel safe, and that we are there for them. That's what I want for the kids here – I want them to be the best they potentially can be. I want them to find coming to school an enjoyable experience.

Like her, many of the mothers in my study talked about the importance of knowing that teachers care. When asked whether there was something her children's school could provide to help her family, Deborah immediately identified the emotional connection:

I don't know, it's just I can say that they care. I know other people, they say, "Oh, I hate that teacher," or whatever ... but even my troublesome kid there, while he was there, he wound up going other places, going into care, he was a whole different story – they always looked after my kids. Other parents would always complain about this one teacher who was my daughter's favourite teacher. What am I going to say? They really loved my kids. They really like us. It was [pause] something that was there when we were going through so much hell ... it was, these strangers, basically, but I didn't have to worry about them.

Another mother feels confident about the education her younger children are receiving:

For some reason the school loves my kids. They really seem to have taken to my children. No matter what teacher. Teachers that I don't even know. "Oh you're Angela's mom. She's such a beautiful little girl." Or something like that ... so I know that my children are well liked at the school and that they're cared for.

For both of these women, the school has effectively anchored them – and provided a safety net for their children – through hard times. In both cases it is teachers working as a team at the school, rather than as individuals, that has contributed to the sense of safety and the sense that kids are fully cared for there.

Responding to the Need that is Right in Your Face: Context

The sense of responsibility to care for children expressed by these educators arises both out of the teacher's role and out of the contexts in which they find themselves. As Milbrey McLaughlin (1993) argued decades ago, students themselves are teachers' most important context. Many of the participants I interviewed emphasized the demands made on teachers because of the challenges of the classroom, particularly, but not exclusively, in high poverty contexts. Key aspects of context were the large number of children (teachers rarely have the luxury of dealing with students one at a time), and how often many of the children had high needs. Another critical aspect of context is the nature of public education as compulsory and local: "come as you are." So schools are different from many helping agencies, which are forced to ration their services by using waiting lists, and which enrol for the most part clients/families who are sufficiently motivated to be able to participate in a fairly demanding program. Ingersoll (2003) describes public education as a "dual captivity" for both teacher and student. As one of the education advocates, Jane, commented ruefully, "it's public education you know ... you have to take the good with the bad and always make the child's success the priority."

One school social worker, Cory, explicitly contrasted teachers' contexts with those of workers in the mental health centres for which the same children were on waiting lists: "In a school, the need is right in your face. Teachers see that too – they do what they can. They just do their best for the kids they are working with. By and large, they are able to do that in a way that's seen as helpful and respectful."

Both school social workers and CAS workers were frustrated by how difficult it is to access more specialized services, resulting in their own caseloads being full of people with significant needs who were waiting for months for needed help from specialist mental health agencies. Child protection staff readily acknowledged the demands faced by teachers. A family service worker, Sheylinn, after expressing frustration with teachers who let students slip through the cracks and failed to engage parents, conditioned her comments by noting, "I think teachers are very overwhelmed to be engaging parents like they should be. They often have a hard time engaging with thirty kids in their class let alone the five families of those children that probably need support." Mary, a supervisor with experience at several CASs, commented that there is relatively little criticism of schools by those in child welfare because "the reality is, it is difficult for a teacher to manage a class with twenty to twenty-eight kids. It's really hard with a kid who is acting out. Oftentimes it's going to be 'get out, go to the office.' It is not always realistic for teacher to go over and deescalate situation, work it through." A front-line family service worker, Mallory, hesitated even to define school responsibility for children's educational success, explaining:

That's a tough one because I know some of the schools they take an enormous amount of responsibility for ensuring the well-being of kids. Some of these schools, I stand back in awe at these schools. Working with some of the inner-city schools, if they call, you know they've done everything in their power to work with the parent, with the family, work with the kid ... Could schools be doing more? It's all time and resources, isn't it – it's all time and resources. How much time can you put in when you've got twenty-five students in your class?

While the social workers were quick to identify aspects of context that limit what teachers can do, most of the educators I interviewed studiously avoided any reference to it. This is consistent with what legal theory describes as a "dilemma of difference" (Minow, 1990). References to challenging contexts by educators are often considered suspect in an organizational culture of "no excuses" for teachers and schools – just an excuse. However, failure to acknowledge the challenges of a context can also lead to an individualization of responsibility for dealing with it, and an even more heightened emotional burden for teachers working in situations where there are fewer resources to support children's well-being (e.g., Rothstein, 2008).

In the cultural context of "no excuses" (and perhaps reflecting sample bias), perhaps it is not entirely surprising that only one of the teachers I interviewed identified challenges arising from her context. Marika was, however, passionate in her articulation of the demands of her context and the expectations that seemed to flow from it: "I don't know what people think about teachers. It's as if they are superhumans. Most of us are normal human beings – I don't know where we get the energy and the talent to deal with an incredible complex environment – what the board forces upon us and what the kids bring to us in the class."

Shortly afterwards, Marika resisted a question about whether there was anything schools could do differently to improve support to children experiencing abuse and neglect, explaining:

I don't want to put more on the teachers ... I don't want to say something that will mean ... a report comes down to say teachers should do *this* too. I don't know what else we can do. There is only one person for twenty or more often emotionally or physically sick kids. The board could stop asking us to do all the extra things so we could just teach and be a person – so maybe I would not be so stressed. The best would be if the kids would be taken more and some talented ... ed assistants, I don't know who ... would talk to them, play with them. In a class we don't have much time for them.

And they also take us away from the rest of the class. It is very unfair for the other children – and then you are just there with them, and your son or my daughter would have to sit there and wait while the poor teacher figures out something until the screaming, object-throwing kid calms down. The poor six- and seven-year kids with a child popping up and screaming – you have to show them it's OK, it's normal. You have to be very good at being calm, teaching the other kids so that they can just tune it out. It scares them and scars them. But at inner-city schools, nobody will line up and complain.

Many, if not most, educators work from the assumption that the demands placed on them by context are a given, but not all respond to them the same way.

The combination of a challenging context and the commitment to caring and support for holistic child development identified in the last chapter adds up to a very expansive set of responsibilities, one that far surpasses what could be asked of an employee on a routine basis. Instead, what is revealed in the interviews is that many educators (and others) see the basis for teachers' responsibilities as existing beyond the job.

"Teaching is not a job: it is a vocation."

A strikingly wide range of participants defined teachers' responsibilities as having a source that goes beyond their job and into the moral and personal realm. Asked where teachers' responsibility for well-being arises from, Caroline, a principal of a large school who consistently emphasized the importance of caring relationships with students, answered: "Teaching is not a job: it is a vocation. You go into teaching because you want to share your knowledge with others. You enjoy working with students and watching their learning develop. We are very proud of our profession and feel strongly about the impact we make on society ... The children are our future. The responsibility would be our commitment to society."

Many of the participants in the research acknowledged that teachers often have to go beyond their "job" in order to meet the needs of the children in front of them. Antonio, for example, describes his extensive work with parents, saying, "So many times we play psychologist and social worker and sometimes I feel like you are their only friend, the only person who is there for them ... I don't mind doing it, *it's not my job*, but what I get out of it is their support for the program and what we do here." An education advocate, Jane, asked what schools' responsibilities are, responded, "I can name some principals who go *way beyond the call of duty*, do everything for the child, take time to hear the stories, have the kid under their wing and give them their support, for example, to be in their office for half a day, keep things moving" [italics added]. A family service worker who had grown up in poverty herself, Sheylinn, pointed to an example of a teacher with whom she worked who "really reached out" to a child, spending an hour and half after school several days a week to help a child with an intellectual disability with math homework.

Do you think that's part of her professional responsibility, or part of being a good person?
I think it's her responsibility – but I know teachers would try. But with a huge class, what can you do?

Sheylinn recognizes the constraints that would limit a teacher's ability to offer this level of support to many children, but nonetheless, sees it as part of the teacher's responsibility to do so. Mary, the family service supervisor who emphasized that teachers' main duty around abuse and neglect is ongoing reporting – and who specifically maintained that teachers ought to be relying on out-of-class supports to help with the social implications of abuse and neglect – reiterated: "The teacher's role is to teach. I think they can do it in a good way – lend an ear. If child has disclosed [abuse or neglect to a teacher], they need to support child, listen to child and that sort of thing ... They need to teach, and to be human, receptive, able to listen, do what any normal, reasonable person can do."

In other words, the good teacher brings her personal self into the interaction, supporting a child disclosing abuse or neglect by listening and being receptive. In this view, in doing so, she is not acting as a professional but as "any normal reasonable person."

At the same time, though, and paradoxically, several participants talked about how merely fulfilling legal requirements – or "just teaching" – is inconsistent with doing teachers' job well. Fernanda is a principal who was often frustrated with a policy context that she saw as limiting her ability to be responsive to the needs of her students. She remarked, "Once we've made the call, we've fulfilled our legal obligations, but it doesn't alter the fact that we still want to do what we can for the child without exhausting ourselves." A very experienced school social worker, Carol, commented:

Good teachers intrinsically always have radar for knowing when a kid is maybe not doing so well at home, and they pick it up in all sorts of overt and covert ways ... A good teacher always has antennae up – she will pursue a conversation with a kid that may be a throwaway, or they can sit down in a one on one for ten minutes to find out what is going on ... You can do this job to the letter of the law and be doing your job fine and be minimally effective.

In this part of the interview, she recognized that "doing your job to the letter of the law" is inconsistent with being "a good teacher." Another school social worker, Cory, remarking on the challenges of teachers' jobs, commented, "Every teacher's different, you know. I recall one teacher saying to me, 'You'll do the most social work in the classroom as a teacher.' Some really embrace that, and others just want to plan their lessons for the next day. They don't feel prepared to handle it and manage all that."

Sarah, a teacher in a solidly upper-middle class school (a school that was chosen by a mother I interviewed because she thought it would provide better opportunities for her son) was a fairly extreme example of the minimalist approach. Sarah had noted a serious pattern of absences and some evidence that all was not well at home, and she reflected "it's going to be a real hard long road for him." But she could not identify any supports that would be available for such a child at school. She saw the idea of taking any particular responsibility for a child she had identified as struggling as risky, possibly even forbidden:

You know, our hands are tied. Without something actionable – you know, some reasonable sign, or the child saying something to us ... we can't do anything.
What do you mean by doing something? Are you talking about a call to CAS, or something else?
Well, of course we have a legal duty to call.
Are there any supports the school can provide?
Well, schools cannot and do not provide these services. We generally do, informally, as human beings and responsible adults. Generally, there is someone, usually a principal or a vice-principal if there is one, who will look out for the child, make sure someone is informed when he moves along. But our hands are tied, both under the Education Act, and union-wise.
What is the role of the union here?
Well, it's not the union so much, it's our vulnerability. If we get in trouble because we spoke to someone we shouldn't have, something like that, the union is there to defend us.

I didn't ask what the problem with the Education Act was – I suspect Sarah's concern was rooted in confidentiality of the Ontario Student Record (OSR, the record of a child's educational progress through school in the province). Nevertheless, it is striking that she identifies the only basis for action in a case like this – even to pass along information to a child's next teachers – as being the "informal" response of "human beings and responsible adults."

These responses suggest that one key way teachers rationalize the inevitable conflict between an expansive definition of their responsibilities and a significant set of contextual challenges is to see it in terms of a personal responsibility – intertwined with, but not the same as, their responsibility as an employee or a professional. Strikingly, however, most participants in this study also identify the exercise of this personal responsibility as the difference between a teacher who responds effectively to the needs of a child experiencing abuse and neglect and one who simply shows up for work.

The Impact of Individualizing Responsibility to Care

The potential impact of individualizing teachers' responsibility to provide effective support to children experiencing abuse and neglect is significant. It can lead to a lack of necessary supports for the teacher, it is removed from oversight or systematic improvement, and it is difficult for external partners to effectively coordinate services if responsibility is heavily personalized.

Minimizing the Contribution

Many of the administrators and student support staff I interviewed expressed concern that teachers might get too involved in focusing on students' social needs and lose an emphasis on their academic role (see chapter 2). Over-involvement was viewed pejoratively by at least some principals: teachers were not to "play social worker" (in the words of Fernanda), or "try to parent children" (as Simon commented). Meeting students' pressing social needs is seen as more appropriately the role for specialist agencies and, where possible, their own families.[2]

School leaders, of course, have reasons for concern. Signals sent by the educational system – particularly, measuring the success of schools exclusively by narrow academic measures – create incentives on the academic side and leave the "caring" side in the shadows. Moreover, the challenges of finding a balance between the pastoral and academic mission of schools gives rise to one of education's persistent dilemmas of practice. Children can't learn without having their basic socio-emotional needs met, but nor are they likely to learn without consistent academic press and challenge (Lee & Smith, 1999). Particularly for children facing relatively high levels of disadvantage, there is strong systemic evidence and there are powerful arguments that care for the social mission can overwhelm the academic mission and be a factor in limiting the opportunity for disadvantaged children to learn (Guiton & Oakes, 1995; National Research Council [U.S.], 2002). But a response to this evidence that concludes teachers should only focus on academic content is simply reactionary. Without laying responsibility for solving all of society's problems at the foot of the classroom teacher, evidence suggests that a complementarity between an academic focus and social support – at the school and classroom level – produces the best academic and social outcomes. At the National Research Council, a gold ribbon panel concluded that in the context of urban schools, those serving children facing different forms of disadvantage, "Evidence suggests that schools need to convey a clearly articulated and coherent set of values that focus on learning and achievement in the context of close and caring relationships with adults and peers" (National Research Council Institute of Medicine [U.S.], 2004, p. 105).

If a very significant and challenging aspect of teachers' work is minimized and even disparaged by some administrators and the system, I would hypothesize that it leads to a greater sense of alienation from the purposes of the school on the part of teachers, a heightened sense of conflict about what is to be accomplished, and a greater likelihood of burnout. These are not good outcomes for the system, and an approach likely to lead to them needs to be confronted.

Beyond Supervision or Support

A perhaps more challenging problem in dealing with the caring work of schools is a sense that it is not a fair or reasonable expectation to impose on teachers. As discussed in chapter 2, many teachers are unprepared and perhaps even unwilling to handle the non-academic aspects of the teaching responsibility. John, a school social worker, commented rather harshly that "Generally, teachers are not trained in mental health. They don't want the responsibility. Occasionally a teacher will be more involved, meddling, interested in the information, but by and large dealing with kids' abuse and neglect flatly depresses them. They just want to teach."

This quote not only reinforces the point that teachers' personal involvement and concern for children may well be disparaged by those in administration, but it also shows how caring work in schools largely falls into the zone of "organizational citizenship behaviour," something teachers shouldn't *have* to do. Inherent in the definition of caring work is that it emerges out of a sense of obligation developed through personal ties. Accordingly, administrators are unlikely to be comfortable requiring that teachers work on their caring relationships with vulnerable students. And at the systemic level, the danger in framing caring work more specifically as work is to risk commodifying it, which can also be disadvantageous. First, commodities need to be paid for, and in times of relentless pressure to contain public expenditures, paying for things that are already taken for granted is an unlikely political "win." Second, the literature on emotions and work emphasizes the psychic cost of having to "mask and manage" the emotions for the benefit of the employer or consumer (e.g., Hochschild, 1983). Even if many teachers willingly do this work for their students, there is a discomfort inherent in requiring anyone to care. Moreover, to commodify emotions runs the risk of taking something powerful away from them – the importance of "authenticity" in teacher talk is undeniable. Hargreaves (2000) argues, for example, "emotions should not be reduced to technical competences," and he expresses suspicion of efforts to embed them as another zone of teacher development (p. 814).

As a middle ground, however, the system should ensure that teachers have a developed vocabulary and have received some direct instruction in a range of skills and resources to handle the emotionally demanding parts of their work: for example, by recognizing and understanding the implications of mental health issues in the classroom (such as "mental health first aid" programs endorsed by the Canadian Mental Health Commission), and by helping to develop boundaries and tools to strengthen community and family involvement, even in challenging circumstances. Minimally, there should be an investment in supports for teachers in doing this work. Recall Mark, the education advocate, speaking out for teachers to have routine opportunities to debrief the emotionally challenging encounters that are a predictable part of the kind of caring engagement that makes a difference for children. Teachers, too, need care.

A Basis for Collaboration

Finally, leaving the work of care to teachers' personal discretion poses real challenges in relationships with external agencies. As outsiders looking in to schools, social workers (and others) don't have clear expectations about what they can ask of teachers. And so – as we saw in chapter 2 – they usually don't ask, which is a pity and could represent a major loss to a vulnerable group of children. Long-standing evidence suggests specific invitations make a difference promoting change in teachers' practice (e.g., McLaughlin & Marsh, 1978; Reed et al., 2000). Often this missed opportunity may deprive a child of some day-to-day supports that might well be available and extremely useful. Further, at this point the structure of interagency working is set up so that most dealings are with principals, not teachers, even though in the context of child welfare, most people will identify the teacher as the person who has the most opportunities to make a difference and who has the greatest knowledge of the child.

In the relatively rare instances where there are formal interagency meetings or connections, the emphasis is far more likely to be on formal programs, interventions, and supports than on day-to-day classroom practices and interactions. Yet if you ask either teachers or social workers what matters most for these vulnerable students, they emphasize day-to-day support and consistent relationships. There are very limited resources for teachers around best practices for connecting with and supporting these children as part of a school team (a recent exception is Ministry of Education, 2014b).

Collaborative work between teachers and front-line social workers should work from a starting point that both groups of professionals have responsibilities that encompass well-being. As an intermediate goal, they might use their joint professional expertise to develop toolkits to support teachers in intervening positively, which would set reasonable expectations that social workers and teachers who work with the same children would have of each other. Social workers in Children's Aid Societies have many demands on their time, but their direct interactions with teachers of specific children have the potential to be incredibly salient opportunities to mobilize a key support for those students. If social workers have access to carefully constructed tools to emphasize key messages and strategies to support the children and an understanding of key issues where advocacy within the school system can make a difference, they can be especially supportive. Those tools do not yet exist. Moreover, current efforts to spotlight the needs of children who are actually in the system of foster care will be much more likely to be beneficial to children living in the community if there is some effort to talk about their distinct situation and how teachers' strategies for this group may be similar to – or different from – strategies developed to support kids in foster care.

Conclusion

Faced with the challenge of improving outcomes for maltreated children, it is hard to avoid the conclusion that schools will have to change. And teachers are essential, both for system or school change, and for students' learning and relationships. A serious approach to improving outcomes must include not only removing administrative barriers between child welfare and school authorities and ensuring that children get the necessary material and program supports but also, and above all, building strong supportive relationships in the classroom.

Evidence on what actually helps maltreated children do better in school is exceedingly thin, but the broader literature points to positive relationships with a caring adult as a crucial asset that helps tip the balance towards children's resilience and the possibility of better outcomes despite hardships. A teacher can be, and sometimes (more often than many other occupational groups) is the person who makes a difference for children, one child at a time. To improve system-level outcomes requires an approach that is a bit less hit-and-miss, yet this approach poses a puzzle: How can the system do more to ensure caring relationships flourish around these vulnerable children?

Can you regulate caring relationships? The review of the literature and legislation around teachers work in chapter 5 showed that teachers are subject to multiple layers of regulation, but also that teachers' "irregular work" is in fact highly resistant to prescriptive regulation – not just in the caring domain, but overall, due to its complexity and ambiguity about goals and processes. In this chapter, I have argued that teachers' caring work, in particular, tends to be overlooked and taken for granted as a natural outcropping of a love of children, being a good person, or being driven by a sense of vocation rather than seeing teachers' work as "just a job." From the point of view of regulation, there is a conundrum, in that teachers swing between a minimal and maximal definition of their responsibilities. The former is basically insufficient for effective teaching, and the latter sometimes seems unattainable, particularly in the non-voluntary, large-group context of public education. Teachers manage the contradiction partially by resisting prescription and often by individualizing their sense of responsibility for the well-being of children as part of being a good person. This approach, while understandable and often compassionate, creates several problems in the design of a systemic response to maltreatment where teachers' potential contribution is maximized. Teachers' individualized responsibilities receive little institutional support or development; teachers' caring is not really available "on demand" where need may be greatest, and staff at other agencies are uncertain about what is reasonable to ask.

This is not a problem susceptible to a quick fix. Joint professional working and better-developed knowledge about what effectively supports children through hard times like abuse and neglect would certainly help. These external approaches would help both legitimize the contribution teachers do make in this area and help develop their capacity to provide it in ways that are less likely to lead to burnout. Just as acknowledgment of social context does not necessarily take anything away from schools' responsibility to help children learn, explicitly valuing the importance of caring work and relationships alongside academic press is part of a holistic approach to ensure that children have their best opportunity to learn.

Conclusion

Revisiting the Dilemmas of Collective Responsibility: Implications for Research, Practice, and Policy

> In contrast to the deep love we feel and express in private, we lack any sense of "public love" for children, and we are unwilling to make public commitments to them except where we believe the commitments will pay off.
>
> Grubb & Lazerson, 1982, p. 52

In this book, I have looked at the exercise of collective responsibility for children's well-being by focusing on how schools and child welfare authorities work, together and apart, to respond to the needs of abused or neglected children who remain at home with their parents. While the data and details of the regulatory scheme in this book are drawn from one province, there are substantial similarities in the administration of child welfare and schools across North America and Great Britain, and the lessons learned in this book have application far beyond Ontario's borders.

The topic is an important one, both practically and in terms of principled development of public policy. Practically, most children in the child welfare system – 92 per cent – are never removed from their parents' care. While they may not face immediate safety concerns warranting removal, they remain extremely vulnerable. As a group they struggle in school. Education is widely recognized to be an extremely important developmental asset and a key determinant of health – one for which there are a basket of policy tools.

At the level of principled policy development, the response to these children's needs raises significant theoretical and political issues, because effective responses to their situation straddle the border of public and private responsibility. The involvement of child welfare is not only a reflection of the children's vulnerability it also represents a judgment that there is a need for public intervention to ensure protection and well-being. As such, their situation explicitly challenges the dominant narrative in which families are assumed to have, and capably exercise, comprehensive responsibility for their children. In this situation, strong, proactive, and coordinated support by governmental institutions – such as child protection agencies and schools – should follow. Unfortunately, the evidence in this study suggests that there is very limited proactive support, let alone coordination, in place for these children outside of mechanisms directed towards safety concerns. The fact that these children stay at home means responsibility continues to lie primarily with parents, however overextended or even compromised they may be. Meanwhile, silos of professional responsibility built around narrowly defined priorities dominate the work and planning of both schools and child welfare, while lower-priority goals, where government bodies have overlapping interests – children's well-being, in particular – fall outside those silos.

Linked and additional unlinked accounts from participants in different locations in the system – mothers and professionals, front-line workers, and policy officials – combined with a description of the framework of formal law, regulation, and policy, contribute to a multilayered picture of interactions between the child welfare and education systems. While the small number of linked cases allowed some additional insight – for example, seeing that many teachers were unaware of child welfare's involvement – the analysis in this book was not mostly of specific cases but patterns that emerged across the data from all participants.

Ultimately, in a book that started out looking at issues of coordination, the key issues that emerge relate to strengthening public commitment to, and accountability for, issues of well-being within systems of schools and child welfare.

Revisiting the Dilemmas of Collective Responsibility

A key theoretical framework for this analysis is Martha Fineman's concept of "collective responsibility for dependency" (2005). This concept is an effort to develop a stronger entitlement or claim to support on the part of caregivers – a lens that recognizes both the value and the burden of their work and provides a standard by which to assess the adequacy of the public response to the needs of dependent children. To the extent that public policy reflects a recognition of this collective responsibility for dependency (of vulnerable children, in this case, but also of the frail elderly, those with certain categories of disability, etc.), those who need or want help with this essential caregiving work should be able to get it from potentially diverse public sources. A person needing support should not have to concede the right to individual, intimate decision-making in order to obtain that support.

This book has shown that public responsibility towards these vulnerable children is ambiguous and highly discretionary – the opposite of a meaningful entitlement to support on the part of some of the more vulnerable children and youth in society, and/or their caregivers. Where supports for parenting were made available through child welfare, it was very clear that control over decision-making lay with the authorities, not caregivers. For example, while some participants appreciated the support they received, most expressed wariness and frustration with their experience and a distinct lack of control over the terms of the interaction. These concerns are not baseless. Perhaps the most explicit articulation of the lack of control attached to support came from Mallory, a family service worker who was described to me by her former client as effective and compassionate. She holds the parents she works with fully responsible for the well-being of their children: "At some point I am going to be backing out, or I am taking your kids, right?" It is hard to imagine a situation of less control for the primary caregivers handling their boundless responsibilities. Where it comes to support, particularly at school, many mothers had positive experiences to relate. At the same time, they viewed that support from the school as a matter or luck or kindness on the part of a teacher or staff, not a matter of the system providing supports on which they could rely.

There are clear examples throughout the text of mothers who valued concrete, effective support they received from social workers and teachers: where teachers followed up on educational concerns, or made the whole family feel cared for, or where social workers "did everything for us," or contributed to material supports, for example. But interviews with front-line workers also revealed examples of missed opportunities for advocacy, occasional apathy, and a widespread sense of helplessness or resignation in the face of a large set of needs and limited resources. Until the introduction of the Joint Protocol for Student Achievement in 2015, there was no plan to effectively address the educational needs of this vulnerable group of children on the part of authorities. Still less is there a system of accountability for these children's outcomes that reflected a sense of collective responsibility, despite the children's recognized vulnerability or dependency. Instead, the children's educational well-being is left to individual responses by teachers and social workers. Indeed, it seems that those on the front lines are left to improvise or "go beyond the call of duty" without clear mandates or access to resources, supports, or information likely to make their work more effective. This paucity of public responsibility for vulnerable children is also reflected in persistent narratives in education and child welfare that continue to individualize responsibility in ways that are both decontextualized and highly gendered. Mothers, particularly, feel a sense of comprehensive responsibility. The interviews confirmed that mothers are held responsible for meeting standards of parenting, while the role of the state is to provide finite supports based on availability of resources; mothers felt subject to sharp blame for their children's problems and an ongoing threat of removal from the home, with limited acknowledgment of the challenges they faced.

At the start of the book, I identified another key complication that affects the public response to the situation of these children on the borderlands of private and public: not only is there a lack of a robust sense of public responsibility for meeting their needs and supporting their caregivers but there is also the "problem of many hands" (Bovens, 1998; Thompson, 1980). As this book makes clear, the educational success of these children requires the active participation of a range of interdependent actors, and, indeed, the participation of different branches of the state. Under the status quo, schools and child welfare operate separately and in accordance with different imperatives. The involvement of schools does not obviate the need for the work of child welfare (and vice versa). Neither entity can effectively fulfil their responsibilities without the other, and indeed, they cannot accomplish their work without the support of the families. So there is very limited accountability or credit for success in the areas of joint concern. Both education and child welfare agencies as institutions benefit from the success of the other – children are more able to learn where child welfare has marshalled effective support and protection; children are better protected and more likely to thrive when they are engaged and learning at school. But the areas of overlapping responsibility are exactly those where there is the least policy attention internally.

Indeed, too often the "problem of many hands" seems to produce wishful thinking on the part of public administration. A striking example of this perspective was the Commission to Promote Sustainable Child Welfare's vision that child welfare could "move beyond a reality where CASs default into the role of advocates or gatekeepers facilitating access to services that are intended to be universal" (2010, p. 14).

They specifically cited difficulties, for example, registering students at schools when they had to move because of a change of placements. Child welfare would work better if, in other parts of the system of public services for children, "resources [were] balanced and coordinated and able to be responsive to the needs of these vulnerable children and youth" (2010, p. 14). Unfortunately, that possibility seems like a far-fetched basis on which to scale back advocacy and gatekeeping activities, even if they are resource intensive. Certainly, based on the concerns expressed by child welfare workers in this study, the resources in schools are not currently balanced, coordinated, and responsive. Workers expressed concern, for example, about discrimination or stigma because of their involvement with child welfare or because of their race; they expressed concern that schools often wait until a child falls years behind before intervening, and concerns that schools "just pass along" difficult students or worry more about graduation rates than whether children are learning. Generally, child welfare workers were not confident that teachers juggling the demands of many children were always able to meet the needs of the children served in the child welfare system and their families. Concerns of this type require advocacy, even in the context of universal services. It verges on unconscionable for public authorities in child welfare – supposedly, acting in place of a parent – to expect the inequities and gaps within the school system to be addressed through internal "balance and coordination" without pressure from those with parental responsibilities.

Another non-solution to the problem of many hands is blame-shifting, as we see when educators wish child welfare were doing more for children and criticize non-communication by Children's Aid, without routinely following up to find out what has happened or to discover whether additional supports from the school may be useful. Even more worrying is when non-communication by CAS is assumed by educators to mean inaction which in turn contributes to educators' failure to report the next time they see a problem with the same child or another one.

To address the problem of many hands requires a two-pronged strategy to be embraced by the different arms of government. Agencies working collaboratively must actively embrace the fuller scope of their own responsibilities, including areas where they overlap with others (here, their responsibilities for the well-being of the children they serve). They must *also* seek appropriate opportunities to actively leverage the resources of other arms of government to help achieve those aims.

Achieving improved coordination and leverage likely requires both improved trust relationships – across silos – and a shared understanding of the key processes that help contribute to better outcomes for children across the different arms of government.

In the area of reporting suspected child abuse and neglect, there is extensive formal coordination and explicit, detailed law and policy. Social workers are also required to contact knowledgeable "collaterals" like teachers as part of their casework. Teachers are expected to know and share information about what is observed at school and to rely on the knowledge and oversight of child protection in the home domain. This model, which I have described as "complementary scrutiny," is clearly articulated by front-line workers in both schools and child welfare agencies, and both groups express support for the model. Yet the research, both in this study and the wider literature, reveals significant limits to the sharing of information between schools and child welfare. It reveals significant distrust on both sides. In practice, teachers often hesitate to report and child welfare workers have significant reservations about involving school personnel in child welfare matters. Not only does this distrust and non-communication leave gaps in the protection of children, but the model itself focuses the attention of both groups on possible shortcomings or strengths of families to the exclusion of a focus on the actions the other public institution may or may not be taking to promote children's well-being.

An example of how this advocacy work between institutions might be useful emerged from my data. In light of the significant data around the overrepresentation of racialized groups in the child welfare system, it was worrying to see the frequency with which educators in my study perceived the socialization of immigrant families as a key role for child welfare agencies, based on a stereotype that abuse is more common and condoned in those families. Large-scale data shows that, while rates of physical harm suffered by children is consistent across demographic groups, professional reporters – such as educators or police – are more likely to report visible minority children to child welfare on a suspicion of abuse than white children (Lavergne, Dufour, Trocmé, & Larrivée, 2008). No child welfare workers in the study talked about working more with groups from particular cultures. But, because they rely on potentially biased professional reporting, this data suggests that educators' beliefs may well affect the demographics of child welfare and the perception of those services in the broader community. These findings suggest a role for advocacy on the part of child welfare workers in schools to try to challenge stereotypes about abuse among cultural groups.

Beyond issues of coordination and interdependence, each sector has internal issues that have a significant impact on their ability to work together to support children experiencing abuse and neglect.

In child welfare, a particularly acute issue is the ambiguity around appropriate responsibility – and ultimately, accountability – for services for children in the community. Where children are "in care," the model of corporate parenthood suggests that the state will exercise comprehensive responsibility both through substitute care arrangements and "organizing support" for children. When they remain with their own parents, even though children may have comparable needs, it is not at all clear whether child welfare has the responsibility to organize support for these children. The research undertaken here, on educational supports, shows that the needs of these children are significantly deprioritized by child welfare agencies as a matter of both policy and practice; this situation is exacerbated by a lack of individual or systemic accountability measures that take into account children's needs or outcomes in the area of well-being.

On the school side, there are critical challenges in developing a system of regulation that is able to handle the "endemic uncertainties" faced by educators. Indeed, it is striking that in both formal regulation and the discourse of teachers, parents, and social workers, the responsibilities of teachers swing from maximum – acknowledged to be aspirational – and minimum standards that most agree are insufficient for effective work with children. There is a significant disconnect between mandatory aspects of teachers work and teachers' aspirations for the job, which tend to emphasize the holistic development of a child alongside building the child's skills as a lifelong learner and each child's command of "the basics." Holistic aspirations and high ideals are critical for a strong system and a motivated teacher workforce, yet they are all but unenforceable, creating a contradictory regulatory environment.

A key aspect of teachers' expressed sense of responsibility for the overall development of their students is the work of care. Conventional wisdom tells us that teachers are among those with the greatest opportunity to make a difference for vulnerable students, especially through caring relationships. Yet the work is ultimately treated as voluntary, a matter of ethics, and a natural outcome of being a good person, rather than being incorporated into a formal system of professional responsibility. The impact of personalizing or privatizing this set of responsibilities is that they are not supported, not demanded, and not planned for, which makes interagency co-operation more challenging and contributes perniciously to teacher burnout. Ultimately, children's access to these important supports is hit and miss.

In summary, an effective state response to improving the educational outcomes of this group of abused or neglected children who live with their families requires not only improved coordination and communication but, more fundamentally, an active embrace by both sectors of their common responsibility for the well-being of the children they serve. This responsibility goes to the heart of the mandate of both schools and the child welfare sector, yet there is a profound policy vacuum in terms of action, knowledge, and accountability. This vacuum likely reflects a deep resistance to the notion of collective responsibility for dependency. Relying on comprehensive familial responsibility is a much easier and more familiar default, but it is not always sufficient to meet the challenges of raising healthy and resilient children, particularly those facing exceptional circumstances such as abuse and neglect. At the same time, this lack of policy attention is perpetuated by "the problem of many hands" where, despite the fact that both arms of government are essential to the success of students, neither "owns" the challenge of helping them succeed.

The persistence of individualized and subdivided responsibility may go some way towards explaining the persistent problem of improving the integration of services across different agencies of government. There will always be a range of causes, such as different organizational and professional cultures and priorities and practical obstacles (e.g., teacher schedules) that make it difficult for different agencies to work together. In the social service sector there is often frustration about the challenge of collaborating with "fortress schools," which seem to actively resist engagement with the community. Indeed, even building collaboration within schools is a major focus for school improvement efforts. Shared goals, increased interactions leading to trust, and a shared understanding of the key points in each others' systems must underlie improved working relationships with the community (e.g., Dryfoos & Quinn, 2005). A starting point for establishing these goals – a way of creating priority for the needs of these children on an institutional level, not merely counting on ethical individuals – is the acknowledgment of common responsibility for these children.

Recommendations for Future Research

This study was a small-scale exploratory work with a strong emphasis on theory. The subject deserves further research.

The very process of research for this book suggests that there will continue to be a discomfort about research, particularly among schools. The relative vulnerability of mothers – and the potential of conflict with the school system – should not be a reason to limit research about schools and social agencies. It is a great concern when gatekeeping by public institutions (beyond the claims of equity or resources) creates a barrier to research, particularly when the refusal to grant permission is based on stereotypes about vulnerable groups or discomfort with scrutiny. As noted in Appendix 2, these issues of research gatekeeping shaped my research. It was impossible to do focus groups in schools, which may have reduced the number of linked cases in my sample and reflected a great deal on the capacity of schools as institutions to be open to co-operation with external groups where it may entail scrutiny or discomfort.

The findings of this research suggest that it would be useful to review a randomized selection of cases in number of CASs to interrogate the patterns of communication and co-operation with schools. In how many cases open for services has the worker sought consent to contact the school? Have they actually done so? Has there been an identification of any education issues, and has there been a plan to address them? Has there been follow up on that plan? Has the worker identified any educational interventions that might be useful, and are they in place? A quantitative assessment of practice would help target areas for improvement.

There should be more systematic research on the nature of educational supports received by maltreated children staying at home and their educational outcomes. This research should look at supports and outcomes relative to the general population and to children in the care of the state. The obvious tools for this assessment are the educational measures from the Canadian Looking After Children Project (Flynn, Ghazal, & Legault, 2006; Vincent, Moffat, Paquet, & Flynn, 2010). It would be possible to use these measures to track a matched comparison group of children who stay at home and compare the supports they receive, and their outcomes, with the population of children in care and with the general population. This assessment should be conducted in a number of CASs across the province, including at least one CAS that has a strong record of services for children who are being served in the community, in order to compare both service provision and outcomes. Researchers at Western University and University of Ottawa have taken a key step in this direction in their review of the outcomes of children in care as compared to those in the community at eight CASs in Ontario, but the focus of this work was on overall outcomes (not services), and information about services received was too general to help understand children's educational issues and supports specifically (den Dunnen, Drouillard, & Lescheid, 2014; Lescheid & den Dunnen, 2015). Research underway at Queen's University has begun to look at the impact of Crown Ward Championship Teams and the Joint Protocol for Student Achievement; this is anticipated to be an important contribution to the evidence base in this growing area, and hopefully the Joint Protocol research will look at both children in care and children in the community.

Child welfare touches the lives of one group of children in schools in an important way, but it is not the only bureaucracy that can have significant impact on both children and their schools. It would be fruitful to explore the overlapping responsibilities of schools with parents and other public agencies – from welfare and disability administration, to mental health or settlement services – to understand how they work together.

Finally, it is very important to see further educationally informed research on the types of supports and interventions – especially those in the regular classroom – that have the potential to improve the well-being and learning of children who have experienced abuse and neglect. As noted in the introduction, although there is growing research on moving towards positive systems of child welfare generally (e.g., Cameron, Coady, & Adams, 2007), the social work literature has identified a hole in research on effective educational interventions (e.g., Forsman & Vinnerljung, 2012; Liabo, Gray, & Mulcahy, 2013). There is, in addition, a key role for educational researchers (and leaders) to help improve the transparency of the core processes of schooling to help social workers and families better understand whether the students they are supporting are in fact getting what experts would consider a good quality education. Are they getting the assessments and services they need? Are they receiving relevant academic supports and appropriate challenging, culturally relevant curriculum that provides them with rich opportunities to learn? Are they in a school with a constructive approach to discipline and an inclusive climate? How are they affected by school processes such as streaming, where students learn different curricula, in different classes, based on perceptions of ability or future prospects? These are not necessarily questions about specific interventions but about how well schools are working for vulnerable children. There is a relatively strong basis in the education literature on school quality. Yet there needs to be a better focus in helping child welfare and families understand factors that contribute to better educational experiences for students, including those who are abused or neglected, and how to assess them. The focus of this study was responsibility, but the exercise of responsibility also requires a better knowledge of effective tools and the ability to ask good questions about context, rather than taking what happens within school walls as a given or a matter of chance.

Recommendations for Practice

There are a number of recommendations for practice that flow from this study. Most fundamentally, schools and CASs need to broaden the scope of existing efforts around co-operation. This is of course easier said than done. Efforts to improve formal structures around co-operation between schools and CASs and to set in place scholarship support for foster children are important. But genuine success at meeting children's needs requires improved front-line co-operation between the most important parts of each system. The front-line workers – teachers and social workers – are the people, other than parents, who work most closely with these vulnerable children.

There are a number of more specific recommendations for working together that flow directly from the findings in this study that go beyond teachers and social workers more explicitly embracing their roles as advocates in each other's systems and building relationships of trust and ongoing communication. In particular, child welfare workers should be required to routinely seek parental consent to contact schools and should work actively with educators to overcome stereotypes about patterns of abuse in certain cultural groups. Educators should routinely follow up after making a report, seeking, if not the particulars of an investigation, basic information about whether children are or are not receiving services. Services that have been made available to children in foster care, such as advocacy in school processes, educational planning, or tutoring, should also be made available to children receiving community support in the community. Teachers facing heavy responsibilities of care should expect to have time and competent help debriefing the emotionally demanding aspects of their work with these vulnerable children, and they should receive support and recognition for their work of care alongside their work of academic transmission.

The new Joint Protocol for Student Achievement templates that the Ministry of Education and the Children's Aid Societies have implemented are an important framework for ongoing co-operation. It is hopeful to see policy prescribing routine structures for joint planning and a much stronger expectation of communication. These protocols have the potential to lead to improved trust relationships between social workers and educators, improving teachers' willingness to engage child protection services and creating a clearer sense, on the part of family service workers, that engagement with the school could provide meaningful benefits to the children they are serving. The protocols should promote two-way sharing of information about children's educational needs and goals, key safety plan issues, and strategies that promote resilience. They could support explicit plans for ongoing communication, for example, on which signs of ongoing abuse or neglect may require follow up; academic or disciplinary issues should be discussed with both parents and CAS. Furthermore, parents may be more likely to consent to information sharing with the school if they understand that significant benefits and additional supports for their child could flow from this co-operation. At the time this research took place, most of the family service workers I interviewed did not see particular benefits to engaging with the school except to gather information. This perspective may partially explain why many workers did not seek consent, and it may have contributed to parents' reluctance to consent to information sharing. Given all these potentially significant impacts, it would be highly appropriate to develop an evidence base on the Protocol through rigorous evaluation to help contribute to the larger global discussion about schools and child welfare's joint efforts. Currently, most evaluation research in the field is focused on particular programs rather than systems issues.

At this point the Joint Protocol calls for the appointment of a staff member in the school to take lead responsibility for coordinating with CAS for each child. This research suggests that both schools and CAS recognize the importance of engaging teachers specifically, not just principals and social workers. Teachers should be released from classroom duties as required to enable them to participate routinely in these meetings and the planning that flows from them. At the same time, the school should be aware of the differing capacity of teachers in the exercise of their caring responsibilities, and the school should be prepared to supplement where necessary. More formal and explicit attention to students' need for care, and teachers' capacity deliver it, should inform decisions about where the child will be placed the following year. Efforts should be made to find a suitable advocate/mentor/supporter elsewhere on the staff if a particular teacher does not have a strong relationship with the child and the child cannot be moved. Furthermore, the school needs to ensure it is supporting teachers' work of care, whether it be through training in positive mental health strategies, explicit recognition of their contributions in this area, or quick responses to requests for additional supports or links to additional services.

These recommendations have resource implications for overstretched bureaucracies and front-line staff. As Sheylinn, the family service worker, ironically remarked, "the bigger the list of collaterals you get, the more you risk someone being unhappy." However, as the research on parent advocacy in education makes clear, sometimes children receive significant benefits when they have "a squeaky wheel" on their team, where parents or others push for better responses from bureaucracies. This research points to the largely unrealized potential for educators and family service workers to more effectively advocate for the children they serve, not only within their own systems but also across systems. In particular, family service workers can advocate for better learning opportunities for the children for whom they have responsibilities, and teachers can advocate for enough knowledge about the work of Children's Aid to be more confident in the supports being provided to promote the safety and well-being of the children they serve.

Child welfare workers – either through outreach activities, intake, or ongoing family service – should also be prepared to address the impact of stereotypes about physical abuse associated with certain ethnic groups when they work with educators. This should aim to address what appeared in this research to be fairly widespread efforts to use child welfare as a tool for disciplining parents and addressing cultural difference.

More routine two-way communication, extending to advocacy, has significant potential benefits. It can lead to improved understanding of the work of both agencies, shared goals, and more human resources – people already working with the child, newly attuned to a child's needs and opportunities – in the lives of vulnerable children.

Recommendations for Policy

There are a number of legislative changes that should receive serious policy consideration. In the introduction I surveyed efforts underway in England and the United States, including efforts to improve integration of children's services in England ("Every Child Matters"), system-wide child and family services reviews (Department of Health and Human Services/Administration for Children and Families [U.S.], 2010), and the efforts to build a focus on well-being in the United States (Biglan, 2014).

Some elements of England's "Every Child Matters" reforms (2004) should be considered seriously, particularly the explicit, reciprocal duty of schools and child welfare to co-operate. Ontario has continued to reaffirm its commitment to a consent-driven approach to the sharing of personal information between public bodies with overlapping responsibilities for child well-being (Ministry of Children and Youth Services, 2015). Currently, the only disclosure allowed under the Freedom of Information and Protection of Privacy Act and the Municipal Freedom of Information and Protection of Privacy Act is for purposes of reporting and investigation. The evidence elicited in my research suggests that concerns about parental privacy and reluctance to even seek consent to share information are significant barriers to information sharing on the part of CAS, and I believe that there ought to be explicit consideration of the conditions under which an approach like England's, which allows information to be shared where it is in the best interests of the child, (e.g., Department of Children, Families and Schools [England], 2008) could be implemented. There are genuine concerns about stigma. However, to paraphrase Michael Kirby, saying there is a problem with stigma is a nice way of saying we aren't doing anything about discrimination against a group.[1] The existence of stigma is a reason to improve communication and advocacy for children and families, not to avoid it. The current regime around protection of privacy, in my view, arises out of a rights framework and not from a "best interests of the child" framework. Sometimes these privacy rights provide a very convenient excuse for routine failures of information sharing that is in the best interests of children.

Transparency and communication are an important part of an accountability framework, but by themselves they are not enough. There are a number of areas in which accountability within these public agencies regarding the well-being of this group of vulnerable children could be improved.

On the child welfare side, a relatively simple change would be to amend the Provincial Advocate for Children and Youth Act (Ontario) to require that all children receiving services from a CAS – not just those in care – and their parents, be informed about the Provincial Advocate for Children and Youth office and the services available. This should occur on the same regular basis as for children in care, and children receiving services should have the same rights to meet privately with a Child and Youth Advocate.[2] The Child and Youth Advocate has the capacity to conduct systematic reviews, inquiries, and investigations into the adequacy and appropriateness of service provision; it would be at least one tool to allow children or parents who need help and aren't getting it to seek recourse. As a matter of policy, the Child and Youth Advocate should conduct at least one consultation annually with children in the child protection system who stay with their parents to help develop and maintain a better understanding of the unique issues that this underserved group face.

More generally, it is of critical importance that Ontario's Ministry of Children and Youth Services and Children's Aid Societies clearly articulate the scope of their responsibilities towards children who receive services in the community. There is no doubt that this group of children is vulnerable. The evidence available on their outcomes, educational and otherwise, suggests a need for intervention. The evidence in this study suggests they are underserved relative to children who are in foster care. In my view, the involvement of child protection should trigger a responsibility on the part of agencies to "coordinate the supports" required to set a child on the path for well-being, even while the parent continues to hold primary responsibility. There should be accountability for these activities. For example, the performance indicators being implemented by Children's Aid Societies must include children receiving services in the area of well-being as well as safety.

A key facet of the Joint Protocol for Student Achievement is that it addresses one of the key issues underlying a "problem of many hands" by changing amorphous responsibilities into better-defined ones with clearer process benchmarks. For example, it is the responsibility of the school to ensure that each student receiving services has an Educational Success Plan developed in consultation with parents and the student. Ensuring that is the case, and that relevant social work factors have been considered, is the responsibility of Children's Aid (which is an organization that may also be able to identify additional resources outside of what a school could generally offer: for example, tutoring programs or short-cuts to assessments). The experience of services for students with special education needs tells us that mere process requirements are no guarantee of a good result for all and can be perceived as burdensome or mere paperwork. But at this point, in the area of abused and neglected children's educational success, the addition of some process benchmarks represents considerable progress and creates a platform for substantive discussions about better and worse educational choices and supports.

Finally, an overarching measure that may contribute to improved accountability – and therefore, hopefully, a more fulsome exercise of responsibility – for the group of children in my study is the development of an integrated set of indicators for well-being for all children's services, including but not limited to education and child protection (see also McMurtry & Curling, 2008). For at least two decades there has been a growing focus on outcomes as drivers of public policy (e.g., Barber, 2004; Ben-Arieh and Goerge, 2006; Corbett, 2006). In education, an emphasis on outcomes has been heavily institutionalized with almost ubiquitous test-based accountability systems operating at the level of schools, districts and provinces, states or countries, as well as internationally. In child protection, the move to outcomes-based accountability is relatively new, and Ontario child welfare officials describe themselves as "catching up" with areas like education and health by introducing system-wide Performance Indicators. The experience in education suggests that while outcomes are important, the most useful indicators should also cover the provision of educational opportunities (Hamilton, Stetcher & Yuan, 2005). The advantages of including information about these factors (what the program evaluation literature would describe as "outputs" or units of service), helps to ensure that accountability measures are focused on the system rather than finger-pointing at front-line service providers or those who appear to be struggling to achieve the desired outcomes (e.g., Guiton & Oakes, 1995). The new performance indicators focus on meaningful service targets (inputs) except in a few areas – safety (although the exact measure has not been finalized) and education. Any indicators being used should be analysed in terms of outcomes for subgroups, such as children in the child protection system, children from different racial groups, or Aboriginal children.

The Ontario Ministry of Education, working with boards of education, is overdue to develop a set of indicators that goes beyond achievement to well-being, and to incorporate measures that take into account the opportunity to learn (see People for Education, 2013). There are school boards that have experimented with relatively simple measures of student experience by asking students whether there is an adult in the school they feel they can ask for help. Many schools work on measuring school climate and students' physical and psychological health. Researchers have developed numerous measures that could be employed to track students' social emotional learning and their physical or mental health. There are tools to assess students' opportunities for creativity or citizenship. Health, social-emotional skills, creativity, and citizenship are key aspects of the curriculum, which provide positive student engagement and successful adulthood (e.g., Ferguson, 2014; Sears, 2014; Shanker, 2014; Upitis, 2014). "Publicly understandable and educationally useful" measures have the potential to be helpful to child welfare as well as educators and the general public alongside more basic student outcome data.

Integrated measures that include information about key opportunities and supports have the potential to improve the way bureaucracies work together in a number of ways. To the extent that the measures chosen are appropriate and useful, they can improve transparency of what "should be" happening in schools or child welfare, which helps those on the outside make judgments and enables them to focus their advocacy. In addition, by breaking the elements of appropriate responsibility down into component parts, it is easier to avoid some of the worst of the "problems of many hands" because it is easier to identify concrete areas where success is considered the responsibility of one group or another. One of the historic reasons schools have resisted mandates around students' well-being is to avoid inevitable pressure to "do it all." For this reason, working with other children's service sectors may help make it clear that the responsibility for "doing it all" is in fact shared – in understandable, concrete ways – across public agencies, and with families and communities.

Well-being will remain an unattainable goal that doesn't get attention in the stretched everyday environment of schools and child protection unless there is a significant institutional effort to make it a concrete and measurable priority. This work must accompany ongoing efforts to improve coordination and communication across sectors and with families. If well-being is left as an aspiration, then it is much harder for those on the front-lines to frame tangible expectations for each other, and too often they are left unsupported and under-resourced in areas of work that are important for children's healthy development. Strengthening a system to work towards children's well-being (with a focus similar to that we employ to develop their achievement and safety) is a key element in embracing collective responsibility for these children who are, ultimately dependent on our collective capacity to provide a strong network of support for them and their families.

Appendix One

Notes on Methodology and Methods

The key methodological issue in this study is how to meaningfully connect micro-level, narrative data about the perceptions and experiences of parents, social workers, and teachers with macro issues of context and institutions which constrain and constitute the interactions of role-defined individuals. Looking at the modern state, Julia Black (2002) asked which methodologies assist in better understanding a particular regulatory process. She noted: "Understanding such a process requires an understanding of the detailed level of its operation, the perceptions of its participants, and how those 'internal' processes interact with a broader context. Thus a combination of micro and macro, of linguistic base and social scientific concerns may be a fruitful one to follow" (p. 196).

A well-established approach to these micro–macro connections is institutional ethnography. Institutional ethnography – "looking out beyond the everyday to discover how it came to happen as it does" (Smith, 2006b) – has been used in a number of studies of the operation of the child welfare system (e.g., Brown, 2006; Swift, 1995), schools (e.g., Griffith & Smith, 2005), and families (e.g., DeVault, 1991). As a methodology, it presupposes a diversity of methods including in-depth interviews (DeVault, 2006). It focuses particularly on texts and discourse as the links to processes and relationships of power, which, operating outside the local, define experience (Smith, 2006a).

Overview of Research Design and Participants

To understand what drives the responses of schools and child protection at the day-to-day level as experienced by mothers and children, I clearly needed to talk to mothers, but I also needed to talk to teachers and child protection workers. As the standpoints of these front-line workers became better defined, they began to represent distinct starting points from which to work outward into the regulatory regime. At the same time, the key challenge for research design was how to get the clearest picture of the interactions between the different institutions, as understood and constituted by the people working within them. A case study method allowed me to look at the perspectives of different adults in the lives of particular children to construct an account of how the relationships between these adults unfolded, and how they articulated explanations for different actions or inaction. Linked interviews about the specific cases "tell a story" about how the different parts of the system work together to affect particular children. I sought out the narratives of individuals from different institutional positions, all of whom were working with serious constraints on their ability to provide optimal support. By looking at the experience of several separate groups of parents, workers, and teachers, I hoped, without making a claim to being representative, to be sensitive to some of the variation in possible interactions and within institutional regimes (e.g., different school boards or Children's Aid Societies). After some discussions with the researchers in a highly facilitative Children's Aid Society, I settled on eight sets of interviews. In order to protect the privacy and autonomy interests of mothers and children, each set of interviews would begin with a mother. My plan was to obtain the mother's consent, then interview the family service worker and teacher who had worked with her child while the case was open.

At the same time, in an institutional ethnography, one "looks up" to understand the ruling relations that explain why things operate as they do. Accordingly, in addition to the front-line workers I identified policy leaders from different points in the structures of CAS and school systems to interview – the individuals identified as the lead on coordination between schools and CAS at both the Ministry of Education and the Ministry of Children and Youth Services, staff in provincial organizations representing CASs and school boards, and CAS management and supervisory-level school board employees. The advocates were particularly important: the Provincial Advocate who has, among other things, the responsibility to advocate for children in the child welfare system; the director of an educational advocacy program; and educational advocates (working on staff or on contract, in different cases) within a number of CASs.

Criteria for Research Participants

The focus of my study was on children in elementary school. Rates of abuse and neglect are higher for younger children, and elementary school is the point where education and care begin to be offered on a universal basis, so it represents a point of relatively early intervention. My interest in the gendered nature of the work meant that elementary teachers – historically a much more feminized workforce than secondary teachers – were an obvious choice. The nature of the parenting work, too, is much more hands-on in the earlier years. At a pragmatic level, given my difficulties in getting permission to speak to different people, it was unlikely I would get permission to interview children or youth for the study. The omission of children's voices becomes more and more problematic as the children age. I would not have been comfortable doing a study on secondary school experiences without including the voices of youth.

To limit the vulnerability of the mothers in the study, they could no longer be working with CAS; to ensure the events were relatively fresh in the minds of participants, however, recruitment was limited to mothers who had had open cases with CAS in the past year. The other major identifying criterion for the study was that children lived with at least one parent throughout the time the case was open. In one case, the child lived with both parents; in another, the mother whom I interviewed moved away from the children, leaving them with their father. If there was a brief temporary removal – up to six weeks – the mother could still be included in the study. Further, the case had to have been open for family service, not just an initial investigation. Mothers were interviewed by me and asked (at the end of the interview) to formally consent to my following up and asking their child's teacher and family service worker for an interview.

Over an extended period of time, I was able to recruit eight mothers for the research, all of whom agreed to allow the triangulated interviews. I used a range of ways to contact the mothers: putting up posters (one participant), using personal contacts with social service agencies (three participants), obtaining a referral from a school social worker (one participant), obtaining a referral from another graduate student (one participant), and asking CAS workers if they would contact anyone (I spoke to 40 workers in three sessions, resulting in two contacts with mothers, both of whom consented to be interviewed).

Fully triangulated case studies were extremely hard to gather. Basic principles of ethics require that each individual consent to participate individually. Approximately half of the linked professionals (the minority of teachers, and the majority of family service workers) could not be reached or did not consent to be interviewed. In total, I was able to conduct only two fully triangulated interviews. Only two linked CAS workers agreed to participate. Five linked teachers and one linked school social worker agreed to participate. I interviewed a mother alone in only one case (arguably one of the most difficult) – a woman with mental illness whose children's case had been opened because of exposure to domestic violence, and who explained that she had ultimately left the home so CAS would stop being involved with her family.

In my study, because I primarily recruited the mothers through community sources, four different Children's Aid Societies in the Greater Toronto Area had served the families, and their children attended schools in three different school boards. I interviewed workers from three different agencies and educators from five different boards.

The table on the facing page summarizes the roles of all participants in the research, and the table on pages 164–5 summarizes key information about the mothers in my study.

Data from the Canadian Incidence Study of Reported Abuse and Neglect (Public Health Agency of Canada, 2010) suggests that, while not representative, this group includes a reasonable cross-section of characteristics that are relevant to an understanding of maltreatment.

By contrast, it was relatively easy to recruit participants from "upward" in the policy formation process – government, board and CAS organizations, and advocates. Informants were chosen based on recognized leadership roles in working to improve the interactions between schools and child welfare. All participants – who are anonymous – were responsive to questions and were generous with their time and insights.

The formation of my front-line sample was affected by a number of forces outside my direct control, particularly, gatekeeping within some school boards and CASs (see Appendix 2). Ultimately, my sample reflects mothers who are no less disadvantaged than those in the general child welfare population – indeed, perhaps more so. Based on their willingness to talk to me and to permit me to talk to professionals with whom they worked, it is safe to assume they are probably not those who have experienced the most conflict in their dealings with both schools and child protection. They provide insight into how the system "usually works." Similarly, recruiting teachers through the mothers helped ensure a breadth of perspectives. It provided some insight

Research Participants

Role	Number of participants	Role	Number of participants
Mothers	8	Linked teachers	5
Linked family service workers	2	Unlinked teachers	5
Unlinked family service workers	6	School principals (all unlinked)	6
Student support workers in schools	6	CAS education advocates	4
Ministry of Children and Youth Services employees	2	Ministry of Education employees	1
Staff members at provincial CAS organization	1	Provincial public school board organization employees	1
Management level employees – CAS	4	Community agency social workers	2
Provincial Child and Youth Advocates	2	Non-profit educational advocacy organization employee	1
School board trustee	1		
		TOTAL	**57**

not only into those teachers who saw themselves as particularly interested in issues of child welfare but also into those who happened to come upon it during work as usual.

Collection and Analysis of Data

The interview protocols for different groups of participants "mirrored" each other. All participants were asked about the same basic issues – definitions of success, how they see their responsibilities, how they see the responsibilities of the other groups, and whether they could identify ways to improve the system. The "linked interviews" were focused on the experience with a particular child. Each interview was recorded in detailed, typed notes that were sent to the interviewee to review. Interviewees were invited to change anything they thought was necessary to accurately reflect their views. The vast majority of participants wrote back to say the notes were acceptable; some expressed some surprise at seeing the record of the conversation. Two interviewees changed the transcripts to better reflect how they would like ideas expressed, not for reasons of

Research Participants – Mothers: Linkages and Key Characteristics

Name	Worker	Educator	Income source	Employment/ Student	Number of kids
Saliha	Mallory	Vizheh (teacher)	Social assistance	College student	2
Melanie	No permission	Cory (school social worker) / no callback from teacher	Husband's income	Homemaker	4 (1 in care)
Caroline	Mallory	Marika (teacher)	Disability	Homemaker	5
Rachel	No callback	Sarah (teacher)	Disability	Homemaker	1
Ruby	No callback	Antonio (teacher)	Social assistance	ESL student	3
Hua	Left agency	Wendy (teacher, no consent)	Disability	Worked in a salon	3
Deborah	No permission	No callback from teacher or vice principal	Work	Receptionist	3
Anisha	Left agency	Sabine (teacher)	Unknown		3; pregnant at time of study

accuracy. The transcripts were coded manually. For institutional ethnography, Smith argued against line-by-line coding in favour of organizing data into broader conceptual chunks, akin to indexing a book (DeVault, 2006, p. 39). Accordingly, I looked at the data under broad headings – surveillance, support, and responsibility. Within those headings, I was able to see fairly distinct subthemes (e.g., reasons why CAS workers didn't communicate with schools, teachers' responsibility to communicate with parents). I organized the data by subtheme and by the background of participants. I worked in a manner that was consistent with the constant comparison approach in grounded theory (e.g., Charmaz, 2000), and I began coding and re-coding the data while still conducting interviews. There are some themes – for example, whether or not CAS workers obtained parental consent to talk to schools – that emerged from the data and I followed up with more specificity in later interviews.

Marital status	Ground	Background	Child's father's background	School knowledge/Report
Divorced	Neglect (domestic violence)	Both parents Bangladeshi / 5 years in Canada		None / no report
Married	Neglect	White	Black Canadian	Yes / school reported
Separated – non-resident boyfriend	Abuse	White	Black Canadian	Yes / school reported
Divorced	Domestic violence	White	Latino	Yes (principal had knowledge, not teacher) / no report
Divorced	Domestic violence	Both parents African / 3 years in Canada		Teacher reports no knowledge, Mom says school knows / no report
Separated (not living with kids)	Domestic violence	Chinese / 2nd generation	Middle Eastern, English-language learner	Yes / unknown report
Single (not clear whether separated or never lived together)	Neglect	Cree / 1st generation off-reserve	No info	Yes / school reported
Single	Neglect	Caribbean / 2nd generation	No info	Yes / likely school reported

I spent quite a bit of time working with the front-line interview data before I began the legal and policy analysis. This approach was consistent with institutional ethnography, which questions how ruling relations become evident in everyday life. It is also a basic approach of socio-legal analysis, where efforts are made to understand how regulation actually affects actions by looking at how participants explain decisions that may be subject to a legal regime. This approach allows researchers to see how, if at all, participants invoke the legal regime to explain their actions (e.g., Engel & Munger, 2003). I analysed the legal regimes in terms of the same broad themes I had identified in the data – surveillance (including duties to report, protocols upon reporting, and duties to contact collaterals), CAS responsibility for educational supports, and educator responsibility for children's well-being. Finally, I looked at the diverse and overlapping ways professional responsibility is defined. The process of moving between the analysis of the legal and policy regime (including interview data with policy actors) and the front-line interviews was an iterative one. I found resonances between the legal regime and some of the interview data that considerably sharpened some of the themes that emerged from the interviews (e.g., the complementarity of surveillance responsibilities between schools and CASs).

Conclusions on Methodology and Methods

This study uses the analytical tools of institutional ethnography to start from the experiences of those on the front-lines of the interaction between families, child protection, and schools: mothers, child welfare workers, and teachers. Partial triangulation of accounts between specific mothers and the professionals who worked with them and their children allowed insight into the interaction between different families and the different institutions. A key factor in the development of the research was the role of institutional gatekeepers who were extremely apprehensive about critical academic work in this area (see Appendix 2), and in many cases actively prevented efforts to communicate with potential participants. Ultimately, by adding a significant number of unlinked interviews with teachers and child welfare workers, I was able to obtain a robust set of accounts of how workers, families, and schools worked together. The mothers I interviewed were not selected to be a representative sample. They did, however, broadly mirror the wider population of those involved with child welfare in a large urban centre in Canada in terms of the types of maltreatment for which their cases were opened and for their demographic characteristics. It is likely that those who consented to be interviewed and had their child welfare workers and their children's teachers interviewed were not high-conflict cases; the methodology and sample are both likely to provide information about processes and understandings representative of "the usual kind" of interactions between schools and child protection where children stay at home. The front-line accounts provided a starting point for a legal and policy analysis that worked from the participants' understandings. The analysis was sensitive both to the points at which the legal regime was invoked to explain what had happened, and to points at which the legal regime appeared to be relevant but was not invoked in on-the-ground accounts. This approach underscores the basic law and society insight that we cannot understand a legal regime without understanding how it plays out in the day-to-day interactions of those whose actions are supposed to be subject to it.

Appendix Two

For Whose Protection? Gatekeeping, Ethics, Research Review, and Access in Studies of the Front Line

A key element that shaped my study was the extensive process of both ethical review and institutional gatekeeping required to be able to interview mothers in the child welfare system, and particularly, to undertake a series of linked interviews. The research raised real ethical issues, which were addressed (over considerable time) through negotiation and elaborate procedures of consent. It appears that the research also raised questions about how the institutions under study might appear, which resulted in considerable challenges not with ethical review but with the granting of permission from the institutions under study. As this appendix illustrates, the process of institutional gatekeeping by schools and some elements of the children's services sector both reflects their beliefs about clients and workers and provides information about their capacity to work with external actors – a key subject of this book.

Ethical review is an essential aspect of university-based research today. Pressures for transparency and the protection of human dignity – not to mention the requirements for public research funding – have led to the development of elaborate ethical review procedures in all universities. High levels of procedure and a strong focus on individual rights characterize the existing university ethical review process through mechanisms such as informed consent. Both the procedures and the individualism have been the subject of what is now a substantial body of scathing academic critique, particularly from qualitative researchers (e.g., American Association of University Professors, 2006; Haggerty, 2004; Halse & Honey, 2005; Shea, 2000). Others have been critical of delay, arbitrariness, cost, and a lack of data on the level of effectiveness of research review in actually protecting human subjects (e.g., Fost & Levine, 2007; Upshur, 2009). Others argue that the primary purpose of these processes is to limit risk not only to participants but also to research institutions (e.g. Apple, 2005; Lincoln & Tierney, 2004). Nevertheless, university-based ethical review boards are generally committed to the potential of research to expand knowledge and contribute to social change, and they recognize that participation in research can offer benefits to participants as well as risks.

Ethical Issues Arising in My Study

The university ethics process is particularly concerned with issues of risk and vulnerability. There are three main groups of front-line informants in this study: mothers, teachers, and family service workers. As detailed below, the mothers in my study are clearly a "vulnerable population." Most parents involved with CAS are disadvantaged, frequently poor, and disproportionately members of racialized or Aboriginal groups (e.g., Children's Aid Society of Toronto, 2008). They often face significant personal issues, most commonly domestic violence, lack of social supports, or mental health issues, in addition to issues relating to their children.[1] Moreover, involvement with child welfare itself represents a form of vulnerability for the mothers, as most mothers experience it as frightening, intrusive, and coercive, and they operate with at least some fear of removal of their children (e.g., Brown, 2006; Swift, 1995). These overlapping characteristics are not incidental to my decision to put their experiences at the heart of my study, nor are these characteristics incidental to the nature of their involvement with school or child welfare. It was specifically to understand institutional responses to the situations of mothers with these kinds of vulnerabilities that I initiated this research.

Participating in the study had the potential to increase the vulnerability of these mothers. By sharing their views on their child's schooling, or their experience with CAS, there was a possibility of damaging relationships with people at their child's school or even bringing themselves back to the attention of CAS. There was a possibility that, in the course of our interviews, a mother might say something that I would have to report to CAS.

When I began my study, I did not see the teachers or family service workers as being particularly vulnerable – and indeed, I believe that relatively few of my professional informants *did* feel particularly vulnerable. However, I came to understand that participating in the interviews might pose some risk or difficulties for these professionals, too.

Some workers might be uncomfortable sharing their professional practice and possibly being judged upon it. One teacher, for example, was concerned about what would be appropriate to tell me; she had a conscious strategy of positive communication with parents, and she had some doubts about the parenting of the mother who gave me permission to speak to her. We agreed that I would not include certain information that would be identifiable to the mother. I suspected the teacher may have additionally protected herself by responding that she "didn't recall" whether or not she had reported the parent for suspected neglect or abuse. Another teacher, Wendy, who did not consent to participate in the study, said, "I do not want to deal with that family again." It was clear from our conversation – without getting into any details – that her relationship with the child and/or her parents had been stressful or upsetting, and that participating in the research would have entailed re-opening a relationship that she preferred to leave in the past.

Principles Governing University-Based Ethical Review

Review for research ethics is based on relatively well-defined principles. At the time my research was approved, there was a list of eight principles that governed the review process, including promoting and protecting human dignity, doing no harm, minimizing risk, and maximizing benefit (Interagency Secretariat on Research Ethics, 2005). Since then, there have been multiple revisions (the latest version is Panel on Research Ethics, 2014) and the process now focuses on three basic principles: concern for welfare, respect for autonomy, and respect for the equal moral status of all persons. Concern for welfare includes not only respectful interaction with research participants but also concern for the community, which for my purposes means making every effort to do high quality work that is in dialogue with active concerns of public policy. Participants' autonomy should be respected. They should have as much control as possible over how what they share is used. For example, I have allowed participants to change transcripts of their interviews to better reflect their views. Their autonomy is also respected by ensuring that they understand enough about what I am doing and how I am doing it to feel that they are participating in something useful. Equal moral status of persons was respected by using the same consent procedure for all participants, and by helping each person to participate on a substantively equal basis. In the case of the mothers, many of whom are unwaged, I also felt it was important that they be paid for their time. Of course the wage also operated as an incentive to participate. Mothers were paid at the rate of graduate research assistants in my faculty, though the value of their work in sharing their experience far exceeded the hourly wage. I don't believe the amount was sufficiently large to motivate someone to participate against their sense of their best interests; since I am aware of a number of women who declined to participate, this is likely a correct assumption.

The default position for research ethics is confidentiality. If nobody knows who said something, the possibility of someone being harmed or even embarrassed is substantially reduced. However, there are many common research designs in which complete confidentiality is not possible. For example, in an ethnography of a school community, even one that uses pseudonyms, other members of the school community will be able to recognize particular individuals or interactions and may learn something unexpected about their colleagues. Similarly, in my research design, linked interviews between participants concerned with a single child also limited confidentiality. For all public purposes, their interview data was anonymous. Participants' interview transcripts are completely confidential. The linked interview design, however, meant that something referred to in the triangulated case study might be identifiable to others. Participants were exposed to the risk of learning about the perspectives of others on their own actions, and to possible reactions arising from the new knowledge.

All participants are identified by pseudonym. Particular schools, boards, and agencies are not identified. In my legal review, it was necessary to refer to particular documents, which had the indirect effect of identifying at least one of the boards and one of the agencies involved. However, my informants were involved with multiple school boards and multiple CASs, so particular comments about operations of different agencies are not necessarily attributable to any one agency or board. I do not believe the schools can be identified in any way from the data. One participant was concerned that a particular incident that had occurred at her school would make both her and the school identifiable. Even though the information was highly relevant, I excluded it from the study.

In a context of limited confidentiality, the main protection for interview participants is the procedure for informed consent, which is intended to protect the autonomy of research participants. Participants can consent to have their confidentiality limited. The procedure needs to ensure that participants are fully informed of all possible risks as well as of the conditions of the research: that they have options to withdraw from participation or not to answer questions and that they are aware of those options; that they have a way to contact the researcher if they have any concerns; and that they have a point of contact at the university, beyond the researcher, if they want to express any further concerns. In my case, that translated into very detailed consent letters that were developed through several rounds of feedback over a period of eight months, with the assistance of different research ethics personnel in my department and at the university level. These letters demonstrated my seriousness as a researcher and commitment to the importance of participants' act of consent, but I am not convinced the final version actually was useful to participants as it was extremely dense. The letter only came alive in the informed consent procedure during interviews, where it served as a prompt for discussion and as a record of what had been discussed. For the mothers, it was my unvarying pattern to leave empty the part of the letter where they permitted me to talk to their child's teacher and social worker until the end of the interview, to ensure they still felt comfortable with that choice after talking to me for between 90 minutes and two hours. I think this procedure was reassuring, and it increased participants' control of the practice.

After significant dialogue with representatives of the Research Ethics Office at the University of Toronto, the design of my research was approved on the basis that it provided adequate protections for the mothers and other participants, based on the principle of informed consent. Like other observer–participants in university ethical review, I am "not convinced that the solution to reviewing a methodologically-complex study ... [is] to demand more administrative, contractually-based documentation; in short, to create more bureaucratic red tape for the researchers and our participants to navigate" (Rivière, 2011, p. 3). Nevertheless, my interchange with the university research office was, in my view, principled and helpful.

Research Approval in Other Public Institutions

Beyond the university, an ever-widening array of organizations – school boards, community agencies, hospitals, CASs, and others – have research approval processes. These processes are often, but not always or exclusively, framed around issues of ethics such as consent and confidentiality, autonomy and welfare, or the protection of vulnerable persons. In my view, research review processes often operate under "cover" of the formal ethical review process at universities as if they served similar functions and operate under similar rules. This is problematic. Institutional research review procedures in public institutions have distinct functions since they need to directly address the resource implications of a given research project – something that is usually outside the scope of a university ethics review. Research review processes may also address issues of "fit" between a research agenda and the overall agenda of a particular organization. Where an organization is a public agency, there may be more or less explicit public interest criteria.

There appears to be considerably less research or critique about these research review bodies, but in fact they play a very significant role in curbing or enabling research activity. Anecdotally, a manager at the University Research Ethics Board at the University of Toronto (UT) observed, "Regarding research ethics review and school board research review, I sometimes tell researchers that UT's rejection rate is about one in a thousand, whereas my understanding is that school boards' rejection rates can be more like fifty percent" (email to author, Dean Sharpe, June 28, 2011). In the case of my research, a succession of public institutions created a string of obstacles to access that were far more intrusive and serious than those encountered in the context of even a fairly arduous process of institutional review by the university. Many of the institutions used research approval processes both to control research on their institutions and as a measure of control over potential participants. This section is, in effect, a story of seeking access and a story about how public institutions may use research review procedures to protect themselves from external scrutiny.

My first experience with the research gatekeeping role in public institutions is a clear example of how the role can enable research and align it to better reflect needs in the field. I had a very positive interaction with the research department at one CAS. In an interesting shift of perspective, in their view, the research was relatively "low risk." I was only speaking to adults with closed cases and, by their standards, education was not a particularly sensitive topic. Our dialogue was useful, starting with the design stage of the research. The Director of Research encouraged me to expand the empirical base of the analysis by increasing the scope of my research from three case studies to eight. She helped me develop sharper parameters for inclusion in the study, and she suggested additional kinds of diversity to be represented. The office was also helpful with ethical review: the director required me to do more to identify potential risks to family service workers. The CAS research office also had practical concerns about the amount of worker time required, concerns that had to be addressed while still ensuring that the study was of sufficient rigour to be useful to them when completed. The process of permission seeking at that CAS was professional, transparent, and helpful. I should also note that this CAS actively supported this research at the institutional level, developing a randomized list of cases for a proposed worker survey (the response rate was so low that I omitted this data collection), sending out emails encouraging participation, and allowing me to speak to groups of family service workers to try to recruit participants.

By contrast, the research review process at a large urban school board was opaque and actively obstructive, and our interactions differed considerably in tone and result. There was no upfront dialogue, and no possibility of getting input prior to review. There are no published criteria for research review at the school board other than the requirement that university-based researchers have already obtained ethical review approval from their institution. The school board rejected my research project. The decision, from which there is no appeal, was conveyed in a letter that read (in full):

> The [Research Review Committee] of the [Urban School Board] considered the above-mentioned proposal at its meeting on April 16th, 2009 and has decided not to approve the direct participation of [School Board] teachers in these case studies.
>
> Please note that because the Parents and Family Service Workers are being recruited externally to the Board, we limited our review to the teacher-related components.
>
> The main concerns of committee members, and this was corroborated by feedback from central [School Board] Social Work staff, were related to the lack of confidentiality within each case study triad; and the possible ethical, practical and/or legal implications of sharing personal information or opinions about a student's family.
>
> More specifically, a sampling of comments related to:
> - The sharing of the final case study write-up with each of the case study participants, so that absolute anonymity or confidentiality of anecdotal comments *vis-a-vis* each other is not possible.
> - Potential discomfort or tensions in the relationships among these participants because of the level or intrusiveness of the personal information

being requested (e.g., discussing the extent of communications between the school and CAS; teachers making judgments about a family's functioning and/or challenging parenting strategies; personal assessments and/or potential criticisms of each other's roles and responsibilities; etc.).
- Potential liability concerns and/or the slight possibility that raw data could be subject to subpoena in some future legal action.
- Questioning a parent's underlying motivation to participate in such a study, raising the possibility of a skewed sample of volunteers.

Given the above issues, and in concurrence with central staff recommendation, we regret that we are unable to support this request.

As a researcher, this letter and rejection raised a number of concerns and was, in my view, inconsistent with the principles of autonomy and respect for the equal moral status of all persons. The image of the parents in the letter was extremely negative and reflects a clear bias against them. The board treated absolute confidentiality as a prerequisite for permission, notwithstanding the approval of a specialized ethics body to limit confidentiality under particular conditions. The image of teachers was infantilizing, as it disregarded their ability to judge whether or not to participate and what to share. The notion that it is the board's role to prevent uncomfortable discussions – combined with the wide array of discussions they perceive as potentially uncomfortable – exemplifies the climate that had been described shortly before, in a highly publicized review of one board involved in my study: "A 'culture of fear' or 'culture of silence' permeates through every level at the TDSB ... a palpable defensiveness and fear about anything being discussed that could reflect negatively on the TDSB" (Falconer, Edwards, & MacKinnon, 2008, p. 415).

A culture of silence maintained within a bureaucracy is particularly problematic for vulnerable groups who may be critical, perhaps justifiably, of authority. The arguments in favour of supporting research to help understand the experience of these groups and how the institution articulates and manages its responsibilities to them are particularly compelling.

Fortunately, with support from numerous faculty members, I was able to return to the ethics department at my university and amend my protocol so that I would not have to seek permission from a board of education. The summary rationale for my successful request to proceed without school board support, as set out in the Amendment Form, was that:

> First, under the Tri-Council Policy Statement 1998, as amended, (s.2), institutions such as corporations or government are not required to consent to research about them, nor should they be given the right to veto research. Second, the informed consent mechanisms contemplated in this proposal adequately "protect and promote human dignity" on the part of research participants. Third, the research is in the public interest, and the institution in question (the [School Board]) has been widely criticized for its "code of silence," particularly in respect of sensitive issues and highly marginalized groups.

Although this request was successful and the research was approved with modifications to reflect the board's position, the board's effort to block it had considerable practical impact on my research. Their refusal was clearly a factor that at least one teacher used in making her decision not to consent. It was much more difficult to recruit unlinked teachers without being able to go into schools and ask for permission to talk to them as a group to see if anyone was interested; indeed, it became impractical to conduct focus groups as originally contemplated in my research proposal. I did not feel I could put posters up on bulletin boards or approach family support personnel in any school-linked programs to see if they would help me recruit participants. One social worker who worked with that board was made to feel uncomfortable about her participation when she mentioned it in a working group. (I had disclosed that the board did not support the research, but apparently she forgot until her supervisor asked her about it.) It also affected the decision of other agencies as to whether they would participate.

The problem with the school board was not, however, the last gatekeeping obstacle. My initial idea for recruitment was to put up posters in "high-risk neighbourhoods," and to identify intermediaries in community agencies who might be willing to pass along the recruitment materials. There are many, many public institutions that will not allow you to put up a poster to contact adults. Hospitals and mental health clinics, for example, though affiliated with the university that had already granted ethical approval, required a full ethics application (with the attendant delays) before permitting posters to be hung. A sympathetic clinician at one clinic explained in an email that, "I think the theory is that patients of a hospital will be protected against being contacted by anyone outside of their care facility (sort of like having one's email given out to companies, etc.)."

Large public housing units have their own restrictions – locked bulletin boards – so you can put up a poster only if you can find the caretaker and she or he helps you. Areas one might poster outside these and other large apartment buildings have "no postering" signage and visible evidence of posters being regularly removed.

A number of organizations that serve parents and families specifically declined to assist with recruitment by putting up posters or by other means. I had identified one large community agency that runs parenting groups as potentially very useful in recruitment. In response to a written application for permission, its Director of Evaluation wrote:

> As you know, I had not received a lot of response internally to my early requests to assist you in recruiting research participants. As a result, when the Research and Evaluation Committee last met I asked them to review and discuss your request. A number of questions and concerns were expressed about the project. Especially concerning was the use of the linked interview design where the CAS worker, teacher and mothers would get to review the case study that emerges from the interviews with these three individuals. As a result, there was concern that the mothers would be vulnerable and that there may be unanticipated negative consequences of the interviews, particularly if the mothers are not complimentary about the role that the school and/or CAS played in the situation. Other issues raised included the fact that the focus of the research is mothers (as opposed to parents), that the consent doesn't detail in sufficient detail the potential risks to the mothers and concern about the decision of the [School Board] not to approve direct participation of teachers in the project.
>
> As a result of these concerns, the Research and Evaluation Committee made the recommendation to the senior management that [Agency] not assist you in recruiting participants and the senior management team agreed with this recommendation.

This agency at least acknowledged that there was an informed consent process, but it was nervous about its adequacy. Their view raises questions once again about respect for the autonomy of participants, as represented by the protective urge to prevent clients from making their own informed decisions. Notably, their response was influenced by knowledge of the board's decision.

For Whose Protection? 177

In the effort to recruit unlinked family service workers, I asked some colleagues at the Faculty of Social Work if they knew anyone who would be willing to talk to me. One person was interested but decided to check with her supervisor first. The supervisor went to a staff member in her agency with research and evaluation responsibilities and the staff member wrote to me directly:

> Your research sounds interesting. Our agency is currently involved in a number of system level projects that address the issue of educational outcomes for children and youth in care. As well, we have a number of targeted in-house strategies in place. It is encouraging to see that this issue is finally starting to garner significant attention and action. At this time, though I *feel it may be premature to see evidence of these efforts at the front-line level.* [Italics added]
>
> As far as the participation in your project goes, after consulting with [Director of Evaluation], I am sorry to inform you that [CAS] will not be able to participate in your research at this time. We are currently addressing a number of workload concerns in the agency and feel we need to be extremely careful about asking our staff to take on additional projects or activities [CAS Research Staff].

This response, like the school board's, confounds "permitting" a staff member to speak to a researcher at her own request, and committing agency resources to a task. I had not asked anyone to talk to me on work time, except at the one CAS where the research was supported. I had in fact interviewed senior management (this staff member's supervisor) and education advocates at that agency. Moreover, we see the same anxiety that was present in the board's response, that allowing front-line personnel to participate in research will somehow expose the agency to embarrassment or unwelcome scrutiny.

There was a final challenge of gatekeeping that adversely affected recruitment. At a less formal level, the perceived stigma associated with child welfare involvement affected some individuals' willingness to pass along recruitment materials to specific families, even where those families were known to fit the profile. On more than one occasion, educators I chatted with informally told me they knew of a child who had been involved in child welfare where the school had taken a very active role that was visible to the parents during a period of fairly intense crisis. However, those educators were unwilling to pass on a recruitment flyer to these individuals. As one principal, Abigail, noted, "I could never, ever do anything that would refer to their child welfare involvement. The relationship is already a difficult one. Referring to it [CAS involvement] would just single them out. I wouldn't want to do it." This perspective, while understandable and motivated by the importance of maintaining a working relationship with a parent, is absolutely indicative of the level of stigma associated with child welfare involvement in the school system.

Conclusions on Ethics and Access

In sum, the level of institutional defensiveness that arose in the context of seeking permission to conduct my research became, in essence, a chapter of the research. The underlying paradigm for the research ethics process is one of liberal individualism that is grounded in notions of consent and providing at least some protections for free expression, both on the part of the researcher and the research participants. Commitments to autonomy and equal moral value of persons map very clearly onto broader concepts of liberty and equality of subjects. Within this paradigm, there is a notion that free expression, wide participation, and open communication actually strengthen public institutions (Mill, 1956). By contrast, the responses of many – though not all – of the agencies which I encountered were marked by a high level of paternalism, efforts to control access, and a real defensiveness at even the possibility of external scrutiny. It was striking that many agencies even sought to control passive means of communication with their clients, in the form of putting up posters. The majority of institutions I dealt with seemed to see the mothers as too vulnerable to consent, or they saw the topic as too sensitive to raise directly with parents, or they saw parents as too likely to possess questionable motives to be allowed to comment on the institution. Cumulatively, these responses reflect and define the mothers' status as "dangerous subjects," both at risk in, and posing risk to, the existing order.

Moreover, the decision of the school board and one CAS to not allow me to speak with their employees again reflected both paternalism and a high degree of distrust. Employees, presumably trusted in their more important role of enacting/implementing the policies of the agency on a daily basis, were not to be relied upon to describe their job or articulate their understandings to an unknown, but not particularly high status, interviewer.

Ultimately, the position taken by many of the organizations approached in this study illustrates the ways in which these public organizations perceive the role of external scrutiny. Their responses may be somewhat specific to the process of being researched – perhaps reflecting a wariness of potential scandal or a general concern about gaps between prescription and practice being exposed. However, their positions also have significant implications for the potential of these institutions to work with individuals and groups from outside, which is one of the prerequisites of multi-agency working and part of ensuring a more integrated policy and front-line response to the interconnected needs of these children. An institutional starting point of defensiveness, suspicion of clients, and limited trust in front-line staff is not one that supports collaboration and the development of integrated, asset-based approaches to supporting vulnerable children and their families.

Appendix Three

Regulation of Teachers' Work: Sources and Responsibilities

Source of regulation	Scope of regulation	Responsibilities
Education Act and regulations under it, e.g. R.R.O. 1990, Reg. 298 as am; O.Reg. 181/98	Teachers assigned a role in the functioning of education system.	Teach assigned subjects, encourage pursuit of learning, inculcate morality by precept and example, co-operate as a staff member, and maintain order and discipline.
Common law	Responsibility for negligence in context of social role.	Fulfil "duty of a careful and prudent parent."
Constitutional law	Constitutional duties as part of state.	Treat students as rights-holders, except as justifiable in free and democratic society.
Professional Standards (regulations) under the College of Teachers Act	Maintain the standards of the profession through setting of expectations and policing professional misconduct.	Orient practice towards expectations: e.g., show care for and commitment to students, help develop citizens. Comply with prohibitions on abuse, dishonesty, etc.
Ethical standards under the College of Teachers Act	Inspire members, guide decision-making, foster public respect.	No responsibilities. Statement of values, including care, commitment to well-being and learning, and moral action.
Collective Agreements	Sets basic terms and conditions of employment.	Sets out hours of work, etc. Responsibilities as prescribed by Education Act and principal. The focus of the agreements is on teachers' rights.
Teacher performance appraisal (O.Reg. 99/02; O.Reg. 266/06)	Light accountability mechanism for employees; primarily qualitative feedback on work.	In induction period, teachers screened for "satisfactory" performance. Teachers required to take feedback into account.

Notes

1 Collective Responsibility for Maltreated Children and Its Dilemmas

1 The study is based on 15,980 child welfare investigations over a three-month period from a representative sample of 112 child welfare service organizations across Canada. It reports on the outcomes of investigations approximately six weeks after the initial report. The CIS is a study of initial investigations and dispositions. Events occurring afterwards are not included in the study.
2 Education Act, R.S.O. 1990, c. E.2, as am., s.169.1(1)(a) (hereinafter, Education Act).
3 Child and Family Services Act, R.S.O. 1990, c.C.11, as am., s.1. (hereinafter, CFSA).
4 She makes this argument both in *Manufacturing Bad Mothers* and more recent work which queries the continued overshadowing of child welfare's ameliorative role (Swift, 2011) and the evolving forms of authority, particularly risk assessment and management (e.g., Swift & Callahan, 2009).
5 CFSA, s.1.
6 Overall responsibility for child protection in Ontario rests with the Ministry of Children and Youth Services. The Minister appoints a Director of Child Welfare and authorizes forty-six Children's Aid Societies to investigate abuse or neglect and to protect children where necessary. In pursuit of those aims, the society may provide guidance, counselling, and other services to families, provide care for children assigned or committed to state care, and supervise children where there is a supervision order (CFSA, s.15(3)). "Service" is a defined term in the act (s.3), and it means a child development service (for children with disabilities and their families), a child treatment service (for children with mental or psychiatric

disorders and their families), a child welfare service (broadly defined as including anything from case management to residential services to adoption services or counselling), a community support service, or a youth justice service. Community support services are any services – including prevention services – provided in the community. Examples of community support services would likely include daycare, a tutoring or mentorship program, a women's shelter, or a drug treatment program. The definition of "service provider" is broad, including the government, societies, licensees, and contractors (but not including foster parents).
7 Every Canadian province except Prince Edward Island has a child advocate position.
8 The situation is worse in the foster care context, due to the greater availability of foster homes outside large urban centres, which often results in a switch of board and CAS for a child placed in care.
9 See http://reescentre.education.ox.ac.uk/.
10 The *Tri-Council Policy Statement: Ethical conduct for research involving humans* has since been updated and replaced since the time this research was conducted. The current version, TCPS-2 (2014), also includes provisions that limit corporate consent. See http://www.pre.ethics.gc.ca/pdf/eng/tcps2-2014/TCPS_2_FINAL_Web.pdf, and also Appendix 2.
11 There is a detailed discussion of recruitment efforts in my dissertation: *Schools, Child Welfare, and Well-Being: Dimensions of Collective Responsibility for Maltreated Children Living at Home*. Ontario Institute for Studies in Education, 2011.
12 Unpublished data from CIS 2008 shows that 90.2 per cent of primary caregivers are women.
13 At the last census, in Canada, 81 per cent of elementary school and kindergarten teachers, and 76 per cent of social workers are women. See http://www.statcan.gc.ca/c1996-r1996/mar17-17mar/occupation-profession/t1/4185895-eng.htm.

2 Separate Spheres and Closed Systems: Reporting and Communication between Schools and Child Protection

1 For example, in Toronto, the Toronto District School Board has P.045 SCH, Dealing with Abuse and Neglect of Students, and P.071 on Gender-based Violence, in addition to P.R.560 which is a detailed operational guideline. All four boards in the Toronto area have entered into a detailed protocol

with the Toronto Police Services (see http://www.torontopolice.on.ca/publications/files/misc/schoolprotocol.pdf).
2. See extensive discussion in chapter 5.
3. See "Transfer of Cases from Intake to Family Services," Service Manual, Child Protection Services, Children's Aid Society of Toronto.
4. In Ontario, sharing of information without consent of the individual or parent is prohibited under the Freedom of Information and Protection of Privacy Act (FIPPA) and the Municipal Freedom of Information and Protection of Privacy Act (MFIPPA), with a narrow exception for the duty to report suspected abuse, neglect, or risk thereof in the Child and Family Services Act. See FIPPA, R.S.O. 1990, c.F-31, as amended, Part III. Section 42e provides for exceptions in accordance with other statutes; and MFIPPA, R.S.O. 1990, c.M.56, as amended, Part II. Section 32 provides for disclosure in narrow circumstances, including in accordance with other statutes.
5. This is the puzzling case where the mother says the workers were at the school talking to teachers, and the teacher was very surprised to learn the family had been receiving services from a CAS. The CAS did not return calls.
6. I am not sure whether this means that those are the cases where a teacher is most often aware of CAS involvement. While teachers are the second most common source of reports about abuse and neglect, their reports make up approximately one-third of all calls, which suggests to me that dealings with parents in the context of CAS involvement ought to come up in a variety of ways. But in the context of my study, it seemed that the main context for these conversations was always teacher reporting.
7. In the same study cited above (Hill, 2009), 87 per cent of administrators reported that they contacted CAS to make a report and to seek informal advice, while only 43 per cent reported contact with a specific CAS worker because of ongoing issues. Ten per cent reported they contacted CAS to seek resources for diverse groups in their community. See Hill, ibid. The survey did not ask under what circumstances CAS would contact the school.
8. This is the clearest legal distinction between a child who is a society ward (temporary care) or a Crown ward (permanent care) and children who have open files with CAS but remain in the community with their parents. See chapter 4 for a discussion of the difference in CAS responsibility to these children.
9. R.S.O. 1990, c. M-56, ss.2, 6–15.

10 See also the provincial Ontario Student Record (OSR) guideline, which lays out the conditions of access to confidential student information in the OSR: http://www.edu.gov.on.ca/eng/document/curricul/osr/osr.html#fn3, s.4.
11 Of course, as discussed in chapter 5, there can be pitfalls – workers can be concerned that schools over-communicate when they know a case is pending with CAS.
12 In the spirit of Michael Lipsky (1980), "Teachers, social workers, public interest lawyers, and police officers in part seek out these occupations because of their potential as socially useful roles. Yet the very nature of the work prevents them from coming even close to the ideal conception of their jobs. Large classes or huge caseloads and inadequate resources combine with the uncertainties of method and the unpredictability of clients to defeat their aspirations as service workers"
13 (1999) 2 SCR 817.
14 See chapter 4.

4 Not "in the Game of Maximizing Potential": Corporate Parenthood, Policy Silence, and Limited Services for Children Who Stay at Home

1 In Ontario, under the Child and Family Services Act, a child is a Crown ward if there is a permanent shift of custody and a society ward if there is a temporary shift of custody. Where a child is in kinship care, they are not referred to as wards but there may still be a transfer of custody and the child is still considered to be "in care."
2 S.63, 63(2), s.105(2)
3 Of course, child custody disputes or agreements in the context of separation or divorce are likely the most litigated (and negotiated) areas of children's law, and in that context, it is common to differentiate legal and day-to-day responsibility by court order or agreement (see Mossman, 2004).
4 S.O. 2007, c.9, s.15: The functions of the Advocate are to (a) provide advocacy to children and youth who are seeking or receiving approved services under the Child and Family Services Act (c) promote the rights under Part V of the Child and Family Services Act of children in care (other provisions relate to children who are provincial schools for the deaf, schools for the blind, demonstration schools, children in holding cells, etc.).
5 There is a handful of smaller CASs in Ontario (Hamilton Catholic, Halton, Hastings, and Prince Edward County) where informants describe a practice that is more oriented towards children in the community being

served on a more equal basis. Hamilton Catholic and Halton have child welfare workers located in a number of schools and they have a strong prevention mandate, and Hastings and Prince Edward have a policy of providing services to all children.

6 See for example, s.1, purposes of the act, and s.34(1)(d) and s.35(3) dealing with residential placement advisory committees' duties to consider and recommend less restrictive alternatives to placement. So, for example, before making a finding that a child is in need of protection or making any order for supervision or custody, the court is required to consider a written plan of care (see s.56[1], s.105[1]). The plan of care sets out services to be provided and an explanation of why a child cannot be adequately protected in the care of their family, including an account of past efforts by the CAS. In fact, the court cannot order a child to be removed from parents unless the CAS can demonstrate that a child cannot be protected by services, in order to allow the child to stay at home.

5 Regulating Aspirations: Teachers' Responsibility and "The Whole Child"

1 With the notable exception of the duty to report suspected abuse or neglect, CFSA s.72, and see chapter 4.
2 Education Act, R.S.O. 1990, c.E.2, s.264 (hereinafter Education Act).
3 S.O. 1996, c.12.
4 Education Act, s.262.
5 O. Reg. 437/97.
6 Retrieved January 4, 2011 from http://www.oct.ca/standards/standards_of_practice.aspx?lang=en-CA
7 http://www.oct.ca/standards/ethical_standards.aspx?lang=en-CA
8 See for example, the Law Society of Upper Canada's Code of Professional Conduct, http://www.lsuc.on.ca/lawyer-conduct-rules/.
9 Available at http://www.oct.ca/members/complaints-and-discipline/decisions.
10 See for example, Collective Agreement between Toronto District School Board and Elementary Teachers Federation of Ontario for the 2008–09, 2009–10, 2010–11, and 2011–12 school years.
11 O. Reg 99/02. The new teacher induction program is governed by O. Reg 266/06.
12 Unlike educators, CAS workers tended to attribute a strong responsibility to both parents and the school around issues of attendance: school social workers tended to confirm that CAS expected schools to manage attendance issues. Comments by CAS workers attributed responsibility

to different members of the school administration rather than to teachers. The school social workers identified their own role in policing attendance as being one of the only points they dealt with families on anything other than a voluntary basis (e.g., Cory, a school social worker, reflected that "the school board can take students or families to court around attendance issues. CAS doesn't have that within their mandate – although one could argue that they have responsibility for the underlying issues. If a child isn't at school, where are they?"). A selection of comments by family service workers, below, underscore my finding that family service workers – while they view issues of attendance as important – don't hold teachers particularly responsible. For example, one family service worker, Kira, when asked about school's responsibility for educational success of the child, responded: "Attendance. And actually following up on attendance. They have means to enforce attendance. Oftentimes they don't want to use the whole truancy process, they want us to get involved." When Mallory was asked who she would work with at a school, she explained, "That depends on the issues, doesn't it? Sometimes you start with the social worker, or call perhaps for attendance with the VP ... Depending on the problems with the kids, if the problem is more about what's happening in the home, if the kid is acting up, I might talk to the social worker first, someone who sees them on a regular basis. If it is more issues with academics, or child non-attendance, I think it is the VP." Delilah, another family service worker, when asked if training on educational issues would be useful to her, shed light on her sense that attendance was a responsibility vested somewhere in the school, but not necessarily with the teacher: "It would be great to know everybody's role. The vice-principal, principal, guidance [counsellors], school officers – they are like guidance counsellors but roam around. Knowing what everybody's role is – who do you go to first? – if you have issues with attendance, say, or discipline."

13 A few examples reflect the tone of comments from mothers and educators. Melanie, who had actively (though with mixed results) advocated for her children through a range of special education and discipline issues, said: "I am in there a lot, they see me a lot, so if something is going wrong, I know right away ... If you need my help, need me to intervene, then call me." Ruby, a mother who comes to meetings at the school during the day 8 to 10 times a year, despite being enrolled in a full-time ESL program, explained, "when I go there they tell me, they know I try to help my son. Always they call me. I pay attention when they have meeting. I tried my best in coming so they are happy for that." This view was

mirrored by teachers: Dana, a veteran teacher, when asked what a parent's responsibility for children's educational success was, explained, "One of the key things is for them to relate to their child's teacher, connect with the child's teacher in some way, be willing to come in for parent interviews, look at agendas, notes sent home by teachers." Speaking about one of the mothers in my study, Vizheh, another veteran teacher, said "She was one of the best mothers ... she always wanted to know how she could help, wanted to know what we were doing, what she could do at home."

14 Operation of Schools – General, R.R.O. 1990, Reg. 298, ss.20(i), (k).
15 An Act to Amend the Education Act, "Keeping our Kids Safe at School Act," S.O. 2009, c.17, s.300.3.
16 Education Act, s.308(2)2, 309, 311(1)(b), 311.1(3), 311.1(9), 311.3(3).
17 Education Act, s.8(3), in Ontario Regulation 181/98 (as amended), which sets out special education procedures, parental notice, and participation as a part of almost every provision. Parents have to be notified about (or can initiate) the development of any special education services, have the right to be present at all committee meetings, have to consent to assessments, have to be notified of all decisions, and must consent to placements or changes of placements. For an authorized account of the process, with an emphasis on the parental role, see also, Individual Education Plan: A resource guide (Government of Ontario, 2004).

6 Between Labour and Love: Individualizing Teachers' Responsibility for the Work of Care

1 http://www.oct.ca/standards/ethical_standards.aspx?lang=en-CA.
2 The risk of "over-involvement" may be particularly potent if there is a perception of some shortcoming on the part of the children's own caregivers, usually mothers. Sara Lawrence Lightfoot (1978) observed a mirroring in the cultural notion of mother and teacher: "The notion is that there is a need for strong teachers when mothers are perceived as being less than adequate. So implicitly at least, a kind of competition exists between who is doing better at their respective social functions" (p. 63).

Conclusion – Revisiting the Dilemmas of Collective Responsibility: Implications for Research, Practice, and Policy

1 Senator Michael Kirby remarks from the Ontario Children Mental Health Summit, June 2, 2011.
2 Provincial Child and Youth Advocate Act, s.18.

Appendix Two

1 The Canadian Incidence Study 2008 (Public Health Agency of Canada, 2010) reported that 78 per cent of caregivers faced one or more significant stressors. The most common were being a victim of domestic violence (46 percent), lack of social support (39 per cent), and mental health issues (27 per cent).

References

Abrahams, N., Casey, K., & Daro, D. (1992). Teachers' knowledge, attitudes, and beliefs about child abuse and its prevention. *Child Abuse & Neglect, 16*(2), 229–38. http://dx.doi.org/10.1016/0145-2134(92)90030-U

Acker, S. (1999). *The realities of teachers' work: Never a dull moment.* London: Cassell.

Administration for Children, Youth and Families (U.S.). (2012). Information Memorandum ACYF – CB – IM – 12- 04, Apr. 17, 2012. Washington: Department of Health and Human Services.

Alexander, R. (Ed.). (2010). *Children, their world, their education: Final report and recommendations of the Cambridge Primary Review.* London: Routledge.

Alvarez, K.M., Kenny, M.C., Donohue, B., & Carpin, K.M. (2004). Why are professionals failing to initiate mandated reports of child maltreatment, and are there any empirically based training programs to assist professionals in the reporting process? *Aggression and Violent Behavior, 9*(5), 563–78. http://dx.doi.org/10.1016/j.avb.2003.07.001

American Association of University Professors. (2006). *Research on human subjects: Academic freedom and the Institutional Review Board.* Washington, DC: AAUP.

Andrews v. Law Society of British Columbia, 1 Supreme Court Review 143 (1989).

Apple, M.W. (2005). Education, markets and audit culture. *Critical Quarterly, 47*(1), 395–414.

Barber, M. (2004). The virtue of accountability: System redesign, inspection, and incentives in the era of informed professionalism. *Journal of Education, 185*(1), 7–38.

Belogolovsky, E., & Somech, A. (2010). Teachers' organizational citizenship behavior: Examining the boundary between in-role behavior and extra-role behavior from the perspective of teachers, principals and parents. *Teaching* and Teacher Education, 26(4), 914–23. http://dx.doi.org/10.1016/j.tate.2009.10.032

Ben-Arieh, A. & Goerge, R.M. (Eds.). (2006). *Indicators of children's well-being: Understanding their role, usage and policy influence.* Dordrecht: Springer. http://dx.doi.org/10.1007/1-4020-4242-6.

Berlin, M., Vinnerljung, B., & Hjern, A. (2011). School performance in primary school and psychosocial problems in young adulthood among care leavers from long-term foster care. *Children and Youth Services Review, 33*(12), 2489–97. http://dx.doi.org/10.1016/j.childyouth.2011.08.024

Berliner, B. (2010). *Grappling with the gaps: Towards a research agenda to meet the educational needs of children and youth in foster care.* Santa Cruz, CA: Center for the Future of Teaching and Learning.

Berridge, D. (2012). Educating young people in care: What have we learned? *Children and Youth Services Review, 34*(6), 1171–5. http://dx.doi.org/10.1016/j.childyouth.2012.01.032

Berridge, D., Henry, L., Jackson, S., & Turney, L. (2009). *Looked after and learning: An evaluation of the virtual school head pilot.* London: Department of Children, Schools and Families.

Biglan, A. (2014). *A comprehensive framework for nurturing the well-being of children and adolescents.* Washington, D.C.: Children's Bureau/Department of Health and Human Services.

Biklen, S.K. (1995). *School work: Gender and the cultural construction of teaching.* New York: Teachers College Press.

Black, J. (2002). Regulatory conversations. *Journal of Law and Society, 29*(1), 163–96. http://dx.doi.org/10.1111/1467-6478.00215

Black, J. (2008). Constructing and contesting legitimacy and accountability in polycentric regulatory regimes. *Regulation & Governance, 2*(2), 137–64. http://dx.doi.org/10.1111/j.1748-5991.2008.00034.x

Blackstock, C. (2011). The Canadian Human Rights Tribunal on First Nations Child Welfare: Why, if Canada wins, equality and justice lose. *Children and Youth Services Review, 33*(1), 187–94. http://dx.doi.org/10.1016/j.childyouth.2010.09.002

Blackstock, C., Cross, T., George, J., Brown, I., & Formosa, J. (2006). *Reconciliation in child welfare: Touchstones of hope for First Nations children, youth and families.* Ottawa: First Nations Child and Family Caring Society/National Indian Child Welfare Association.

Blome, W.W. (1997). What happens to foster kids? Educational experiences of a random sample of foster care youth and a matched group of non-foster care youth. *Child & Adolescent Social Work Journal, 14*(1), 41–53. http://dx.doi.org/10.1023/A:1024562813809

Bovens, M. (1998). *The quest for responsibility: Accountability and citizenship in complex organisations*. Cambridge: Cambridge University Press.

Brown, A.F., & Zuker, M.A. (2007). *Education law* (4th ed.). Toronto: Carswell.

Brown, D.J. (2006). Working the system: Re-thinking the institutionally organized role of mothers and the reduction of "risk" in child protection Work. *Social Problems, 53*(3), 352–70. http://dx.doi.org/10.1525/sp.2006.53.3.352

Brownell, M., Chartier, M., Au, W., MacWilliam, L., Schultz, J., Guenette, W., & Valdivia, J. (2015). *The educational outcomes of children in care in Manitoba*. Winnipeg, MB: Manitoba Centre for Health Policy.

Brownell, M.D., Roos, N.P., MacWilliam, L., Leclair, L., Ekuma, O., Fransoo, R. (2010). Academic and social outcomes for high-risk youths in Manitoba. *Canadian Journal of Education, 33*(4), 804–36.

Bullock, R., Courtney, M.E., Parker, R., Sinclair, I., & Thoburn, J. (2006). Can the corporate state parent? *Children and Youth Services Review, 28*(11), 1344–58. http://dx.doi.org/10.1016/j.childyouth.2006.02.004

Burley, M., & Halpern, N. (2001). *Educational attainment of foster youth: Achievement and graduation outcomes for children in state care*. Olympia, WA: Washington State Institute for Public Policy.

Cameron, G., Coady, N., & Adams, G.R. (2007). *Moving towards positive systems of child welfare: Current issues and future directions*. Waterloo, Ontario: Wilfrid Laurier University Press.

Casey, K., & Apple, M.W. (1989). Gender and the conditions of teachers work: The development of understanding in America. In S. Acker (Ed.), *Teachers, gender and careers* (pp. 171–86). London: Falmer.

Charmaz, K. (2000). Grounded theory: Objectivist and constructivist methods. In N.K. Denzin & Y.S. Lincoln (Eds.), *Handbook of Qualitative Research* (2nd ed., pp. 509–35). Thousand Oaks, CA: Sage.

Chief Inspector of Schools. (2005). *Every child matters: Framework for assessment of children's services*. London: OFSTED.

Children's Aid Society of Toronto. (2008). *Greater trouble in Greater Toronto: Child poverty in the GTA*. Toronto: Author.

Chunn, D.E. (1988). Rehabilitating the deviant family through family courts: The birth of socialized justice in Ontario, 1920–1940. *International Journal of the Sociology of Law, 16*, 137–58.

Cohen, D.K., Raudenbush, S.W., & Ball, D.L. (2003). Resources, instruction and research. *Educational Evaluation and Policy Analysis, 25*(2), 119–42. http://dx.doi.org/10.3102/01623737025002119

Coleman, J.S. (1966). *Equality of educational opportunity*. Washington, D.C.: U.S. Department of Health, Education and Welfare, Office of Education.

Commission to Promote Sustainable Child Welfare (Ontario). (2010). *Towards sustainable child welfare in Ontario*. Toronto: Government of Ontario.

Commission to Promote Sustainable Child Welfare. (2012a). *Realizing a sustainable child welfare system in Ontario: Final report*. Toronto: Government of Ontario.

Commission to Promote Sustainable Child Welfare. (2012b). *A new approach to accountability and system management*. Toronto: Government of Ontario.

Contenta, S., Monsebraaten, L., & Rankin, J. (2014, December 11). Why are so many black children in foster care? *Toronto Star*.

Corbett, T. (2006). The role of social indicators in an era of human service reform in the United States. In A. Ben-Arieh & R.M. Goerge (Eds.), *Indicators of children's well-being: Understanding their role, usage, and policy influence* (pp. 3–20). Dordrecht: Springer. http://dx.doi.org/10.1007/1-4020-4242-6_1

Corter, C., & Pelletier, J. (2005). Parent and community involvement in schools: Policy panacea or pandemic? In N. Bascia, A. Cumming, K. Leithwood, & D. Livingston (Eds.), *International Handbook of Educational Policy* (pp. 295–327). New York: Springer. http://dx.doi.org/10.1007/1-4020-3201-3_15

Cossman, B. (2002). Family feud: Neo-liberal and neo-conservative visions of the reprivatization project. In B. Cossman & J. Fudge (Eds.), *Privatization, law and the challenge to feminism* (pp. 169–217). Toronto: University of Toronto Press.

Cossman, B., & Fudge, J. (2002). Privatization, law and the challenge to feminism. In B. Cossman & J. Fudge (Eds.), *Privatization, law and the challenge to feminism* (pp. 3–38). Toronto: University of Toronto Press.

Courtney, M.E., Barth, R.P., Berrick, J.D., Brooks, D., Needell, B., & Park, L. (1996). Race and child welfare services: Past research and future directions. *Child Welfare*, 5(2), 99–137.

Daly, M., & Lewis, J. (2000). The concept of social care and the analysis of contemporary welfare states. *British Journal of Sociology*, 51(2), 281–98. http://dx.doi.org/10.1111/j.1468-4446.2000.00281.x

Daly, M., & Rake, K. (2004). Gender and the welfare state: Care, work and welfare in Europe and the USA. *British Journal of Sociology*, 55(4), 531–43.

den Dunnen, W. Drouillard, D., Lescheid, A. (2014). Supporting the 90% of children served through Ontario's child welfare resources: An empirically derived appreciation of what it takes to support child safety through community support and differential response initiatives. Unpublished manuscript.

Department of Children, Families and Schools [England]. (2008). *HM Government information sharing guidance: Further guidance on legal issues*. London: Government of England.

Department of Health and Human Services/Administration for Children and Families (U.S.). (2010). *Results of the 2007 and 2008 Child and Family Services Reviews.*

DeVault, M.L. (1991). *Feeding the family: The social organization of caring as gendered work.* Chicago: University of Chicago Press.

DeVault, M.L. (2006). Institutional ethnography: Using interviews to investigate ruling relations. In D.E. Smith (Ed.), *Institutional ethnography as practice* (pp. 13–44). Lanham: Rowman & Littlefield.

Downs, L.L. (2010). *Writing gender history* (2nd ed.). London: Bloomsbury.

Dreikurs, R., & Soltz, V. (1964). *Children: The challenge.* New York: Hawthorn Books.

Dryfoos, J. & Quinn, J. (Eds.). (2005). *Community schools: A strategy for integrating youth development and school reform.* San Francisco: Jossey Bass/Wiley.

Dryfoos, J.G., & Nissani, H. (2006). Interventions in schools in the U.S. In C. MacAuley, P. Pecora, & W. Rose (Eds.), *Enhancing the well-being of children and families through effective interventions: International evidence for practice* (pp. 289–99). Philadephia: Jessica Kingsley Publishers.

Eckenrode, J., Laird, M., & Doris, J. (1993). School performance and disciplinary problems among abused and neglected children. *Developmental Psychology, 29*(1), 53–62. http://dx.doi.org/10.1037/0012-1649.29.1.53

Eichler, M. (1997a). *Family shifts: Families, policies and gender equality.* Toronto: Oxford University Press.

Eichler, M., & Albanese, P. (2007). What is household work? A critique of assumptions underlying empirical studies of housework and an alternative approach. *Canadian Journal of Sociology, 32*(2), 227–58. http://dx.doi.org/10.2307/20460633

Elmore, R.F., Abelmann, C.H., & Fuhrman, S.H. (1996). The new accountability in state education reform: From process to performance. In H.F. Ladd (Ed.), *Holding schools accountable: Performance-based reform in education* (pp. 65–98). Washington, D.C.: Brookings Institution.

Elmore, R.F., & McLaughlin, M.W. (1988). *Steady work: Policy, practice, and the reform of American education.* Santa Monica: RAND.

Engel, D.M., & Munger, F.W. (2003). *Rights of inclusion: Law and identity in the life stories of Americans with disabilities.* Chicago: University of Chicago Press. http://dx.doi.org/10.7208/chicago/9780226208343.001.0001

Epstein, J. (1998). *School and family partnerships: Preparing educators and improving schools.* Boulder, CO: Westview.

Etzioni, A. (Ed.). (1969). *The semi-professions and their organization.* New York: Free Press.

Falconer, J., Edwards, P., & MacKinnon, L. (2008). *The road to health: A final report on school safety.* Toronto: School Community Safety Panel, Toronto District School Board.

Ferguson, H.B. (2014). *Physical and mental health: The keys to success.* Toronto: People for Education.

Ferguson, H.B., & Wolkow, K. (2012). Educating children and youth in care: A review of barriers to school progress and strategies for change. *Children and Youth Services Review, 34*(6), 1143–9. http://dx.doi.org/10.1016/j.childyouth.2012.01.034

Fineman, M.A. (2005). Cracking the foundational myths: Independence, autonomy, and self-sufficiency. In M.A. Fineman & T. Dougherty (Eds.), *Feminism confronts Homo Economicus* (pp. 179–92). Ithaca: Cornell University Press.

First Nations Child and Family Caring Society of Canada v. Attorney General of Canada. (2016). Canadian Human Rights Tribunal. 2016 CHRT 2.

Fluke, J., Merkel-Holguin, L., Yuan, Y.Y., & Fuller, T. (2014). Differential response. Paper presented at the 16th Annual Child Welfare Waiver Demonstration Projects Meeting.

Flynn, R.J. & Byrne, B.A. (2005). Overview and findings to date of research in the Ontario Looking After Children project. *Ontario Association of Children's Aid Societies Journal, 49*(1), 12–21.

Flynn, R.J., Ghazal, H., & Legault, L. (2006). *Looking after children: Good parenting, good outcomes. Assessment and action records (Second Canadian adaptation, AAR-C2).* Ottawa, ON and London, UK: Centre for Research on Community Services.

Flynn, R.J., Marquis, R.A., Paquet, M.P., Peeke, L.M., & Aubry, T.D. (2012). Effects of individual direct-instruction tutoring on foster-children's academic skills: A randomized trial. *Children and Youth Services Review, 34*(6), 1183–9. http://dx.doi.org/10.1016/j.childyouth.2012.01.036

Folbre, N. (2001). *The invisible heart: Economics and family values.* New York: New Press.

Forsman, H., & Vinnerljung, B. (2012). Interventions aiming to improve school achievements of children in out of home care: A scoping review. *Children and Youth Services Review, 34*(6), 1084–91. http://dx.doi.org/10.1016/j.childyouth.2012.01.037

Fost, N., & Levine, R.J. (2007). The dysregulation of human subjects research. *Journal of the American Medical Association, 298*(18), 2196–8. http://dx.doi.org/10.1001/jama.298.18.2196

Foucault, M. (1977). *Discipline and punish: The birth of the prison.* New York, Vintage Books.

Freedberg, S. (1993). The feminine ethic of care and the professionalization of social work. *Social Work, 38*(5), 535–40.

Frempong, G., & Willms, J.D. (2002). Can school quality compensate for socio-economic disadvantage? In J.D. Willms (Ed.), *Vulnerable Children* (pp. 277–303). Edmonton: University of Alberta Press.

Fullan, M. (2008). *The new meaning of educational change* (4th ed.). New York: Teachers College Press.

Gannerud, E. (2001). A gender perspective on the work and lives of women primary school teachers. *Scandinavian Journal of Educational Research, 45*(1), 55–70. http://dx.doi.org/10.1080/00313830020023393

Gavigan, S.A.M. (1996). Familial ideology and the limits of difference. In J. Brody (Ed.), *Women and public policy in Canada* (pp. 255–78). Toronto: Harcourt Brace.

Gavigan, S.A.M., & Chunn, D. (2007). From mothers' allowance to mothers need not apply: Canadian welfare law as liberal and neo-liberal reforms. *Osgoode Hall Law Journal, 45*(4), 733–72.

Geenen, S., & Powers, L. (2006). Are we ignoring youths with disabilities in foster care? An examination of their school performance. *Social Work, 51*(3), 233–41. http://dx.doi.org/10.1093/sw/51.3.233

Gelles, R. (1997). *The book of David: How family preservation can cost children's lives*. New York: Basic Books.

Gilligan, C. (1982). *In a different voice: Psychological theory and women's development*. Cambridge, MA: Harvard University Press.

Goerge, R.M., Voorhis, J.V., Grant, S., Casey, K., & Robinson, M. (1992). Special education experiences of children in foster care: An empirical study. *Child Welfare, 71*(5), 419–37.

Government of England. (2004). *Every Child Matters: Change for children*. London: HMSO.

Government of England. (2005). *Every Child Matters: Change for children in schools*. London: HMSO.

Government of Ontario. (2004). *Individual Education Plan: A resource guide*. Toronto: Government of Ontario.

Griffith, A.I., & Smith, D.E. (2005). *Mothering for schooling*. London: RoutledgeFalmer.

Grubb, N., & Lazerson, M. (1982). *Broken promises: How Americans fail their children*. Chicago: University of Chicago Press.

Guiton, G., & Oakes, J. (1995). Opportunity to learn and conceptions of educational equality. *Educational Evaluation and Policy Analysis, 17*(3), 323–36. http://dx.doi.org/10.3102/01623737017003323

Haggerty, K.D. (2004). Ethics creep: Governing social science research in the name of ethics. *Qualitative Sociology, 27*(4), 391–414. http://dx.doi.org/10.1023/B:QUAS.0000049239.15922.a3

Halse, C., & Honey, A. (2005). Unravelling ethics: Illuminating the moral dilemmas of research ethics. *Signs (Chicago, Ill.), 30*(4), 2141–62. http://dx.doi.org/10.1086/428419

Hamilton, L.S., Stetcher, B.M., & Yuan, K. (2005). *Standards-based reform in the United States: History, research and future directions.* Washington, DC: RAND Corporation.

Hargreaves, A. (2000). Mixed emotions: Teachers' perceptions of their interactions with students. *Teaching and Teacher Education, 16*(8), 811–26. http://dx.doi.org/10.1016/S0742-051X(00)00028-7

Harper, J., & Schmidt, F. (2012). Preliminary effects of a group-based tutoring program for children in long-term foster care. *Children and Youth Services Review, 34*(6), 1176–82. http://dx.doi.org/10.1016/j.childyouth.2012.01.040

Health and Human Services. (2011). *Federal Child and Family Services Reviews: Aggregate Report Round 2: 2007–10.* Washington: Children's Bureau.

Heath, A., Colton, M., & Aldgate, J. (1994). Failure to escape: a longitudinal study of foster children's educational attainment. *British Journal of Social Work, 24*(3), 241–60.

Hill, F. (2009). *Partnership study between York Children's Aid Society and York Catholic School Board.* Unpublished manuscript, York Region.

Hochschild, A.R. (1983). *The managed heart: The commercialization of human feeling.* Berkeley: University of California Press.

Hong, S. (2011). *A cord of three strands: A new approach to parent engagement in schools.* Cambridge, MA: Harvard Education Press.

Howard, S., Dryden, J., & Johnson, B. (1999). Childhood resilience: Review and critique of literature. *Oxford Review of Education, 25*(3), 307–23. http://dx.doi.org/10.1080/030549899104008

Hunt, D., & Levin, B. (2012). *18th OISE survey: Public attitudes towards education in Ontario.* Toronto: Ontario Institute for Studies in Education.

Ingersoll, R.M. (2003). *Who controls teachers' work? Accountability, power and the structure of educational organizations.* Cambridge, MA: Harvard University Press.

Interagency Secretariat on Research Ethics. (2005). Tri-council policy statement ethical conduct for research involving humans. Ottawa: Supply and Services.

Jackson, S., Ajayi, S., & Quigley, M. (2005). *Going to university from care.* London: Institute of Education.

Jackson, S., & Cameron, C. (2012). Leaving care: Looking ahead and aiming higher. *Children and Youth Services Review, 34*(6), 1107–14. http://dx.doi.org/10.1016/j.childyouth.2012.01.041

Jackson, S., & Simon, A. (2006). The costs and benefits of educating children in care. In E. Chase, S. Jackson, & A. Simon (Eds.), *In care and after: A positive perspective* (pp. 44–62). London: Routledge.

Jenson, J. (2004). Changing the paradigm: Family responsibility or investing in children. *Canadian Journal of Sociology, 29*(2), 169–92. http://dx.doi.org/10.2307/3654692

Jeynes, W.H. (2005). A meta-analysis of the relation of parental involvement to urban elementary student academic achievement. *Urban Education, 40*(3), 237–69. http://dx.doi.org/10.1177/0042085905274540

Jimmieson, N.L., Hannam, R.L., & Yeo, G.B. (2010). Teacher organizational citizenship behaviours and job efficacy: Implications for student quality of school life. *British Journal of Psychology, 101*(3), 453–79. http://dx.doi.org/10.1348/000712609X470572

Kemp, S., Marcenko, M., Hoagwood, K., & Vesneski, W. (2009). Engaging parents in child welfare services: Bridging family needs and child welfare mandates. *Child Welfare, 88*(1), 101–26.

Kennedy, M.K. (2010). The uncertain relationship between teacher assessment and teacher quality. In M.K. Kennedy (Ed.), *Teacher assessment and the quest for teacher quality* (pp. 1–6). San Francisco, CA: Jossey Bass.

Kenny, M.C. (2004). Teachers' attitudes toward and knowledge of child maltreatment. *Child Abuse & Neglect, 28*(12), 1311–19. http://dx.doi.org/10.1016/j.chiabu.2004.06.010

Kortenkamp, K., & Ehrle, J. (2002). *The well-being of children involved with the child welfare system: A national overview* (Vol. B-43). Washington, DC: Urban Institute.

Kufeldt, K. (2006). The Looking After Children in Canada project: Educational outcomes. In K. Kufeldt & B. McKenzie (Eds.), *Child welfare: Connecting research, policy, and practice* (pp. 177–90). Waterloo: Wilfrid Laurier University Press.

Langlois, L., & Lapointe, C. (2010). Can ethics be learned? Results from a three-year action research project. *Journal of Educational Administration, 48*(2), 147–63. http://dx.doi.org/10.1108/09578231011027824

Lareau, A., & Shumar, W. (1996). The problem of individualism in family-school relations. *Sociology of Education, 69*, 24–39. http://dx.doi.org/10.2307/3108454

Lavergne, C., Dufour, S., Trocmé, N., & Larrivée, M.C. (2008). Visible minority, Aboriginal and Caucasian children being investigated by Canadian Protective Services. *Child Welfare, 87*(2), 59–76.

Lee, V.E., & Smith, J.B. (1999). Social support and achievement for young adolescents in Chicago: The role of school academic press. *American Educational Research Journal, 36*(4), 907–45. http://dx.doi.org/10.3102/00028312036004907

Leiter, J. (2007). School performance trajectories after the advent of reported maltreatment. *Children and Youth Services Review, 29*(3), 363–82. http://dx.doi.org/10.1016/j.childyouth.2006.09.002

Leiter, J., & Johnsen, M.C. (1994). Child maltreatment and school performance. *American Journal of Educational Research, 102*(154–89), 154.

Leithwood, K., & Beatty, B. (2008). *Leading with teacher emotions in mind.* Thousand Oaks, CA: Corwin.

Lerner, R.M., Rothman, F., Boulos, S., & Castellino, D.R. (2002). Developmental systems perspective on parenting. In M.H. Bornstein (Ed.), Handbook of Parenting (Vol. 2). *Biology and ecology of parenting* (pp. 407–37). Englewood, N.J.: Erlbaum.

Lescheid, A., & den Dunnen, W. (2015). *Do we have the right outcome measures for the 90% of the children we serve.* Toronto: OACAS.

Liabo, K., Gray, K., & Mulcahy, D. (2013). A systematic review of interventions to support looked-after children in school. *Child & Family Social Work, 18*(3), 341–53. http://dx.doi.org/10.1111/j.1365-2206.2012.00850.x

Lightfoot, S.L. (1978). *Worlds apart: Relationships between families and school.* New York: Basic Books Inc.

Lincoln, Y.S., & Tierney, W.G. (2004). Qualitative research and institutional review boards. *Qualitative Inquiry, 10*(2), 219–34. http://dx.doi.org/10.1177/1077800403262361

Lipsky, M. (1980). *Street-level bureaucracy: Dilemmas of the individual in public services.* New York: Russell Sage Foundation.

Lortie, D.C. (2002). *Schoolteacher* (2nd ed.). Chicago: University of Chicago Press. (Original work published 1975).

MacKinnon, I. (2006). *BC's children in care: Improving data and outcomes reporting.* Victoria: Government of British Columbia – BC Children and Youth Review.

Maiter, S., Alaggia, R., & Trocmé, N. (2004). Perceptions of child maltreatment by parents from the Indian subcontinent: Challenging myths about culturally based abusive parenting practices. *Child Maltreatment, 9*(3), 309–24. http://dx.doi.org/10.1177/1077559504266800

Mapp, K.L. (2011). *Title I and parent involvement: lessons from the past, recommendations for the future.* Washington, D.C.: American Enterprise Institute.

Maynard-Moody, S., & Portillo, S. (2010). Street-level bureaucracy theory. In R. Durant (Ed.), *Oxford Handbook of American Bureaucracy.* Oxford: Oxford University Press (pp. 252–77). http://dx.doi.org/10.1093/oxfordhb/9780199238958.003.0011

McLaughlin, M.W. (1987). Learning from experience: Lessons from policy implementation. *Educational Evaluation and Policy Analysis, 9*(2), 171–8. http://dx.doi.org/10.3102/01623737009002171

McLaughlin, M.W. (1993). What matters most in teachers' workplace context? In M.W. McLaughlin & J.W. Little (Eds.), *Teachers' work: Individuals, colleagues and contexts* (pp.77–103). New York: Teachers College Press.

McLaughlin, M.W., & Marsh, D.A. (1978). Staff development and school change. *Teachers College Record, 80*(1), 69–94.

McMurtry, R., & Curling, A. (2008). The review of the roots of youth violence (Vol. 1). *Findings, analysis and conclusions*. Toronto: Queen's Printer of Ontario.

Mill, J.S. (1956). *On liberty; Representative government; on the subjection of women: Three essays*. Oxford: Oxford University Press.

Ministry of Children and Youth Services. (2005). *Child welfare transformation 2005: A strategic plan*. Toronto: Government of Ontario.

Ministry of Children and Youth Services. (2007, February). *Child protection standards in Ontario*. Toronto: Government of Ontario.

Ministry of Children and Youth Services. (2015). *Report on the 2015 review of the Child and Family Services Act*. Toronto: Government of Ontario.

Ministry of Children and Youth Services and Ministry of Education. (2015). *Joint protocol on student achievement*. Toronto: Government of Ontario.

Ministry of Education. (2014a). *Achieving excellence: A renewed vision for education in Ontario*. Toronto: Government of Ontario.

Ministry of Education. (2014b). *Improving the educational outcomes of children and youth in care. Capacity building series #37*. Toronto: Government of Ontario.

Minow, M. (1990). *Making all the difference: Inclusion, exclusion and American law*. Ithaca, NY: Cornell University Press.

Mnookin, R.H., & Kornhauser, L. (1979). Bargaining in the shadow of the law: The case of divorce. *Yale Law Journal, 88*(5), 950–97. http://dx.doi.org/10.2307/795824

Mossman, M.J. (2004). *Families and the law in Canada: Cases and commentary*. Toronto: Emond Montgomery.

Myers, J.B. (2005). *Myers on evidence in child, domestic and elder abuse cases* (3rd ed.). New York: Aspen Publishers (Kluwer).

National Committee for the Prevention of Child Abuse. (1997). *Current trends in child abuse reporting and fatalities: The results of the 1996 annual fifty state survey*. Chicago: University of Chicago Press.

National Research Council (U.S.). (2002). *Achieving high educational standards for all*. Washington: National Academies Press.

National Research Council Institute of Medicine (U.S.). (2004). *Engaging schools: Fostering high school students' motivation to learn*. Washington: National Academies Press.

Nespor, J., & Hicks, D. (2010). Wizards and witches: Parent advocates and contention in special education in the USA. *Journal of Education Policy, 25*(3), 309–34. http://dx.doi.org/10.1080/02680931003671954

Noddings, N. (1983). *Caring: A feminine approach to ethics and moral education*. Berkeley: University of California Press.

O'Brien, M. (2012). Knowledge transfer from the Improving Educational Outcomes for Children in Care conference: How it is helping a child welfare organization build a long term educational strategy. *Children and Youth Services Review*, *34*(6), 1150–3. http://dx.doi.org/10.1016/j.childyouth.2012.01.043

O'Higgins, A., Sebba, J., & Luke, N. (2015). *What is the relationship between being in care and children's educational outcomes: An international systemic review*. Oxford: Rees Centre for Fostering & Education, Oxford University.

Ong-Dean, C. (2009). *Distinguishing disability: Parents, privilege and special education*. Chicago: University of Chicago Press. http://dx.doi.org/10.7208/chicago/9780226630021.001.0001

Ontario Association of Children's Aid Societies. (2007). *Crown ward education championship teams*. Toronto: OACAS.

Ontario Association of Children's Aid Societies. (2008). *Gateway to success survey of the educational status of Crown Wards and former Crown Wards*. Toronto: OACAS.

Ontario Association of Children's Aid Societies. (2014). *Ontario Association of Children's Aid Societies submission to standing committee on government agencies, Bill 42, Ombudsman Amendment Act (Children's Aid Societies), 2013*. Toronto: OACAS.

Ontario Association of Children's Aid Societies. (2015). *Performance indicators for child welfare*. Toronto: OACAS.

Ontario Child Welfare Outcomes Expert Reference Group. (2010). *Defining key outcomes for children and youth in Ontario's child welfare system*. Toronto: Government of Ontario.

Organisation for Economic Co-operation and Development (OECD). (2005). *Teachers matter: Attracting, developing and retaining effective teachers*. Paris: OECD.

Organisation for Economic Co-operation and Development (OECD). (2014). *PISA 2012 results: Excellence through equity - Giving every child a chance to succeed*. Paris: OECD.

Panel on Research Ethics (2014). *Tri-council policy statement: Ethical conduct for research involving humans*. Ottawa: Government of Canada.

Parker, R. (ed.) (1980). *Caring for separated children*. London: MacMillan. http://dx.doi.org/10.1007/978-1-349-16294-9

Pateman, C. (1997). Beyond the sexual contract. In G. Dench (Ed.), *Rewriting the sexual contract: Collected views on changing relationships and sexual division of labour* (pp. 165–90). London: Institute of Community Studies.

Pecora, P.J. (2012). Maximizing educational achievement of youth in foster care and alumni: Factors associated with success. *Children and Youth Services Review, 34*(6), 1121–9. http://dx.doi.org/10.1016/j.childyouth.2012.01.044

Pecora, P.J., Kessler, R.C., O'Brien, K., White, C.R., Williams, J., Hiripi, E., . . ., & Herrick, M.A. (2006). Educational and employment outcomes of adults formerly placed in foster care: Results from the Northwest Foster Care Alumni Study. *Children and Youth Services Review, 28*(12), 1459–81. http://dx.doi.org/10.1016/j.childyouth.2006.04.003

Pelton, L. (2008). Informing child welfare: The promise and limits of empirical research. In D. Lindsey & A. Shlonsky (Eds.), *Child welfare research: Advances for policy and practice* (Ch. 2). Oxford, New York: Oxford University Press. http://dx.doi.org/10.1093/acprof:oso/9780195304961.003.0002

People for Education. (2011). *The measure of success: What really counts. Annual report on Ontario's publicly funded schools.* Toronto: People for Education.

People for Education. (2013). *Broader measures of success: Measuring what matters in education.* Toronto: People for Education.

Phillips, E. (2008). When parents aren't enough: External advocacy in special education. *Yale Law Journal, 117*(8), 1802–53. http://dx.doi.org/10.2307/20454695

Pianta, R.C., & Walsh, D.J. (1996). *High-risk children in schools: Constructing sustaining relationships.* London: Routledge.

Pressman, J.L., & Wildavsky, A. (2005). Implementation: How great expectations in Washington are dashed in Oakland: Or, why it's amazing that federal programs work at all, this being the saga of the economic development administration as told by two sympathetic observers who seek to build morals on a foundation of ruined hopes. *Canadian Public Administration, 48*(2), 268–73.

Public Health Agency of Canada. (2010). *Canadian incidence study of abuse and neglect 2008.* Ottawa: Government of Canada.

Public Health Officer of Canada. (2009). *The chief public health officer's report on the state of public health in Canada 2009: Growing up well - priorities for a healthy future.* Ottawa: Government of Canada.

Public Sector and MPP Accountability and Transparency Act, (2014). S.O. 2014, C.13

Pushor, D. (2007). *Parent engagement: Creating a shared world.* Toronto: Government of Ontario.

Quinton, D. (2004). *Supporting parents: Messages from the research.* London: Jessica Kingsley.

R. v. M. (M.R.), 3 S.C.R. 393, (1998).

Raudenbusch, S.W., & Willms, J.D. (1991). *Schools, classrooms, and pupils: International studies of schooling from a multi-level perspective.* San Diego: Academic Press.

Reed, R.P., Joens, K.P., Walker, J.M., & Hoover-Dempsey, K.V. (2000). *Parents' motivations for involvement in children's education: Testing a theoretical model.* Paper presented at the American Educational Research Association, New Orleans.

Rivière, D. (2011). Looking from the outside/in: Re-thinking research ethics review. *Journal of Academic Ethics,* 1–12. http://dx.doi.org/10.1007/s10805-011-9139-y.

Roberts, D. (2008). The racial geography of child welfare: Towards a new research paradigm. *Child Welfare, 87*(1), 125–50.

Rosenberg, R. (1983). *Beyond separate spheres: Intellectual roots of modern feminism.* New Haven: Yale University Press.

Rothstein, R. (2008). Whose problem is poverty? *Educational Leadership, 65*(7), 8–13.

Rutman, D., Barlow, A., Alusik, D., Hubberstey, C., & Brown, E. (2003). Supporting youth people's transitions from government care. In K. Kufeldt & B. Mackenzie (Eds.), *Child welfare: Connecting research, policy and practice* (pp. 227–38). Waterloo: Wilfrid Laurier University Press.

Rutter, M. (1987). Psychosocial resilience and protective mechanisms. *American Journal of Orthopsychiatry, 57*(3), 316–31. http://dx.doi.org/10.1111/j.1939-0025.1987.tb03541.x

Sander, J.B., Sharkey, J.D., Olivarri, R., Tanigawa, D.A., & Mauseth, T. (2010). A qualitative study of juvenile offenders, student engagement and interpersonal relationships: Implications for research directions and preventionist approaches. *Journal of Educational & Psychological Consultation, 20*(4), 288–315. http://dx.doi.org/10.1080/10474412.2010.522878

Scarth, S., & Sullivan, R. (2008). Child welfare in the 1980s: A time of turbulence and change. In L.T. Foster & B. Wharf (Eds.), *People, politics and child welfare in British Columbia* (pp. 83–96). Vancouver: UBC Press.

Scholte, E.M., Colton, M., Casas, F., Drakeford, M., Roberts, S., & Williams, M. (1999). Perceptions of stigma and user involvement in child welfare services. *British Journal of Social Work, 29*(3), 373–91. http://dx.doi.org/10.1093/oxfordjournals.bjsw.a011463

Scherr, T.G. (2007). Educational experiences of children in foster care: Meta-analyses of special education, retention and discipline rates. *School Psychology International, 28*(4), 419–36.

Scott, J.W. (1986). Gender: A useful category of historical analysis. *American Historical Review, 91*(5), 1053–75. http://dx.doi.org/10.2307/1864376

Scott, J.W. (2008). Unanswered questions: AHR forum on gender: A useful category in historical analysis. *American Historical Review, 113*(5), 1422–30. http://dx.doi.org/10.1086/ahr.113.5.1422

Scott, W.R., & Meyer, J.W. (1997). Institutional environments and organizations: Structural complexity and individualism. *Organization, 4*(2), 289–92.

Sears, A. (2014). *Measuring what matters: Citizenship domain.* Toronto: People for Education.

Sears, M., & Sears, W. (1995). *The discipline book: Everything you need to know to have a better-behaved child from birth to age 10.* Boston: Little Brown.

Shanker, S. (2014). *Social-emotional skills: The new basics.* Toronto: People for Education.

Shea, C. (2000). Don't talk to the humans: The crackdown on social science research. *Lingua Franca, 10*(6), 27–34.

Shlonsky, A., & Wagner, D. (2005). The next step: Integrating actuarial risk assessment and clinical judgment into an evidence-based practice framework in CPS case management. *Children and Youth Services Review, 27*(4), 409–27. http://dx.doi.org/10.1016/j.childyouth.2004.11.007

Skrtic, T.M. (2010). Distinguishing disability: Parents, privilege, and special education. *Contemporary Sociology, 39*(2), 188–90. http://dx.doi.org/10.1177/0094306110361589jj

Smith, D.E. (2006a). Incorporating texts into ethnographic practice. In D.E. Smith (Ed.), *Institutional ethnography as practice.* (pp. 65–88). Lanham: Rowman and Littlefield.

Smith, D.E. (Ed.). (2006b). *Institutional ethnography as practice.* London: Rowman & Littlefield, Inc.

Smithgall, C., Gladden, R.M., Howard, E., Goerge, R.M., & Courtney, M.E. (2004). *Educational experiences of children in out of home care.* Chicago: Chapin Hall Center for Children.

Staden, H. (1998). Alertness to the needs of others: A study of the emotional labour of caring. *Journal of Advanced Nursing, 27*(1), 147–56. http://dx.doi.org/10.1046/j.1365-2648.1998.00498.x

Stone, D. (2011). *Policy paradox: The art of political decision-making* (3rd ed.). New York: Norton & Co.

Stone, S. (2007). Child maltreatment, out-of-home placement and academic vulnerability: A fifteen-year review of evidence and future directions. *Children and Youth Services Review, 29*(2), 139–61. http://dx.doi.org/10.1016/j.childyouth.2006.05.001

Sullivan, R. (2007). *Statutory interpretation* (2nd ed.). Toronto: Irwin Law.

Swift, K. (1995). *Manufacturing bad mothers.* Toronto: University of Toronto Press.

Swift, K.J. (2011). Canadian child welfare: Child protection and the status quo. In N. Gilbert, N. Parton, & M. Skivenes (Eds.), *Child protection systems: International trends and orientations* (pp. 36–59). New York, Oxford: Oxford University Press. http://dx.doi.org/10.1093/acprof:oso/9780199793358.003.0003

Swift, K.J., & Callahan, M. (2009). *At risk: Social justice in child welfare and other human services*. Toronto: University of Toronto Press.

Sykes, J. (2011). Negotiating stigma: Understanding mothers' responses to accusations of child neglect. *Children and Youth Services Review, 33*(3), 448–56. http://dx.doi.org/10.1016/j.childyouth.2010.06.015

Tamanaha, B.Z. (1995). An analytical map of social scientific approaches to the concept of law. *Oxford Journal of Legal Studies, 15*(4), 501–35. http://dx.doi.org/10.1093/ojls/15.4.501

Thompson, D.F. (1980). Moral responsibility of public officials: The problem of many hands. *American Political Science Review, 74*(4), 905–16. http://dx.doi.org/10.2307/1954312

Tideman, E., Vinnerljung, B., Hintze, K., & Isaksson, A.A. (2011). Improving foster children's school achievements: Promising results from a Swedish intensive study. *Adoption & Fostering, 35*(1), 44–56. http://dx.doi.org/10.1177/030857591103500106

Tilbury, C., Creed, P., Buys, N., Osmond, J., & Crawford, M. (2014). Making a connection: School engagement of young people in care. *Child & Family Social Work, 19*(4), 455–66. http://dx.doi.org/10.1111/cfs.12045

Trocmé, N., MacLaurin, B., Fallon, B., Shlonsky, A., Mulcahy, M., Esposito, T. (2009a) National Child Welfare Outcomes Matrix. Montreal: McGill Centre for Research on Children and Families. Retrieved from https://www.mcgill.ca/crcf/files/crcf/NOM_09Final.pdf

Trocmé, N., & Caunce, C. (1995). The educational needs of abused and neglected children: A review of the literature. *Early Child Development and Care, 106*(1), 101–35. http://dx.doi.org/10.1080/0300443951060110

Trocmé, N., Knoke, D., & Blackstock, C. (2004). Pathways to overrepresentation of Aboriginal children in Canada's child welfare system. *Social Service Review, 78*(4), 577–600. http://dx.doi.org/10.1086/424545

Trocmé, N., Knoke, D., Fallon, B., & MacLaurin, B. (2009). Differentiating between substantiated, suspected and unsubstantiated maltreatment in Canada. *Child Maltreatment, 14*(1), 4–16. http://dx.doi.org/10.1177/1077559508318393

Trocmé, N., MacLaurin, B., Barbara, F., Knoke, D., Pitman, L., & McCormack, M. (2005). *Understanding the overrepresentation of First Nations children in Canada's child welfare system: An analysis of the Canadian incidence study of reported child abuse and neglect (CIS-2003)*. Toronto: Centre for Excellence for Child Welfare.

Truth and Reconciliation Commission (2015). *Honouring the truth, reconciling for the future: Summary of the final report of the Truth and Reconciliation Commission*. Ottawa: The Commission. Retrieved from: http://www.trc.ca/websites/trcinstitution/File/2015/Findings/Exec_Summary_2015_05_31_web_o.pdf

Ungar, M. (2009). *Enhancing the development of resilience in early adolescents: Literature review*. Toronto: The Learning Partnership.

Upitis, R. (2014). *Creativity: The state of the domain*. Toronto: People for Education.

Upshur, R. (2009). Overcoming the problem of calibration: Towards a scholarly agenda for research ethics. In F. Lolas (Ed.), *Dimensiones ethicas de las regulaciones en salud* (pp. 61–9). Santiago: Universidad de Chile.

Vincent, C., Moffat, S., Paquet, M.P., & Flynn, R. J. (2010). Asset-building and the Ontario Looking After Children project: Fostering resilient outcomes in children and youth in out of home care. *Outcome Network: An International Database and eJournal for Outcome-Evaluation and Research* (72).

Waldegrave, S., & Coy, F. (2005). A differential response model for child protection in New Zealand. *Social Policy Journal of New Zealand, 25*, 32–49.

Waldfogel, J. (1998). *The future of child protection: How to break the cycle of abuse and neglect*. Cambridge, MA: Harvard University Press.

Waldfogel, J. (2009). Differential response. In K.A. Dodge & D.L. Coleman (Eds.), *Preventing child maltreatment: Community approaches* (pp. 139–55). New York: Guilford Press.

Williams v. Eady (1893) 10 T.L.R.41 (C.A.)

Withler v. Canada (Attorney General), [2011] 1 Supreme Court Review 396.

Wulczyn, F., Smithgall, C., & Chen, L. (2009). Child well-being: The intersection of schools and child welfare. *Review of Research in Education, 33*(1), 35–62. http://dx.doi.org/10.3102/0091732X08327208

Index

academic press, 123, 134, 139
Acker, Sandra, 122, 125
advocacy, 41, 61–62, 69, 77–8, 82–91, 97, 137, 142, 144–5, 150, 152–3
autonomy, 101, 103, 160, 169–71, 174, 176, 178

Bovens, Mark, 9–10, 143
bureaucracy, 15, 19, 62, 87, 149, 152, 156, 174; bureaucratic control, 102, 103. *See also* street-level bureaucracy

Canadian Incidence Study of Reported Child Abuse and Neglect (CIS), 4–6, 162, 181n1, 182n12, 188n1
Canadian Mental Health Commission, 136
caring work, 4, 22–3, 122–4, 135–9
case study method, 160
child advocate. *See* Provincial Advocate for Children and Youth
Child and Family Services Act (CFSA), 6, 10, 14–15, 25, 27, 57, 72, 79, 81, 91, 181n3, 181n6, 184n1
Child and Family Services Review Board, 92

Child and Family Services Reviews (U.S.), 19, 153
Child Welfare Education Championship Teams, 17
Child Welfare Outcomes Expert Reference Group, 17, 81, 94
Child Welfare Transformation (Ontario), 9
CFSA. *See* Child and Family Services Act (CFSA)
collaterals, 3, 25, 27–8, 145, 152, 165
collective agreement, 99, 104, 106, 180, 185n10
collective responsibility for dependency, 10–14, 22, 23–4, 141, 147
Commission to Promote Sustainable Child Welfare, 15, 90, 94, 96, 143
confidentiality, 55–61, 133, 170–1, 173–4
consent: corporate consent, 175, 182n10; to participate in research, 20–1, 160–3, 165, 166, 167, 169–71, 175–6, 178; to sharing information, 17, 28, 55–8, 69, 82, 87, 91, 148, 150–1, 153, 183n4
constant comparison, 165
corporate consent. *See under* consent
corporate parenthood, 3, 72–4, 146

Crown wards, 7, 72, 83, 184n1; compared to children in the community, 17, 183n8; Crown Ward Education Championship Teams, 17, 149
"culture of fear," 174

differential response, 49, 72, 92, 94–6
"dilemma of difference," 130
discipline: student, 1, 16, 55, 63, 82, 85, 104, 127, 149, 185n12, 186n13; teacher, 106–7, 180; of subjects (Foucault), 65–6, 68; parental discipline of children, 67–8, 70
do no harm, 100
"dual captivity," 128
duty to report, 2, 5, 24, 25–7, 56, 60, 111, 183n4, 185n1

Education Act, 10, 56, 98–9, 104–7, 133, 180, 181n2, 185n2, 185n4, 187n17
education advocate, 16, 22, 47, 54, 57, 61, 69, 83, 84–5, 89, 92, 112, 129, 131, 136, 160, 162, 164, 177. See also Provincial Advocate for Children and Youth
educational interventions, 9, 82–5, 148–9
Educational Success Plan, 16–17, 154
educational supports, 81–6
emotional labour. See caring work
equal moral status, 169, 174, 179
ethical review, 167–71
ethical standards, 106, 124, 180, 185n7
Every Child Matters (U.K.), 17–18, 153
Fineman, Martha, 10–12, 22, 141

foster care, 2, 5–9, 16, 18–19, 83–4, 93, 137–8, 150, 154, 182n8
Freedom of Information and Protection of Privacy Act (FIPPA), 50, 56, 59, 153, 183n4

grounded theory, 165

high expectations, 82–3, 123
holistic student success/development, 46, 100, 104, 108, 121, 125, 131, 146
human dignity, 167, 169, 175

Identification, Placement and Review Committee (IPRC), 52, 83, 87, 113
in loco parentis, 125–6, 144
incidence of abuse and neglect, 4; across cultural/racial groups, 65
Individual Complaints Review Panel, 92
Ingersoll, Richard, 101–3, 123, 128
institutional ethnography, 20, 159–60, 165
instructional triangle, 124
integrated indicators of well-being/outcome measures, 18–19, 155
IPRC. See Identification, Placement and Review Committee

Joint Protocol for Student Achievement, 16, 19, 82, 142, 149, 151, 154

Lightfoot, Sara Lawrence, 11, 187n2
linked interviews, 20–1, 160, 164, 167, 170
Looking After Children project (Canada), 94, 148

Index 209

Looking After Children project (Ontario), 81, 90, 94
Lortie, Dan C., 101–3, 120, 123
lower-risk cases of child welfare, 9, 92, 95–6

mandatory reporting. *See* duty to report
Manufacturing Bad Mothers (Swift), 12–13, 181n4
micro-macro connections, 159
Ministry of Education, 14–15, 104, 137, 151, 155–6, 160. *See also* Education Act
Ministry of Children and Youth Services, 15, 17, 78, 81–2, 88, 153–4, 160, 181n6. *See also* Child and Family Services Act (CFSA)
Municipal Freedom of Information and Protection of Privacy Act, 183n4

"no excuses," 130

OACAS. *See* Ontario Association of Children's Aid Societies
OECD. *See* Organisation for Economic Cooperation and Development
Office of the Provincial Advocate for Children and Youth. *See* Provincial Advocate for Children and Youth
OnLAC. *See* Looking After Children (Ontario)
Ontario Association of Children's Aid Societies (OACAS), 7, 16–17, 76, 82, 92, 94
Ontario College of Teachers, 99, 105, 124, 165
Ontario Student Record (OSR) 55, 57–8, 133, 184n10

Organisation for Economic Cooperation and Development (OECD), 102, 110, 123–4
organizational citizenship behaviour, 104, 120, 136
OSR. *See* Ontario Student Record
overrepresentation of racialized/ Aboriginal children in child welfare, 3, 65, 69, 145

parent communication, 113–19
People for Education, 84, 156
performance indicators, 17, 19, 81, 94, 154–5
policy manuals, CAS, 28
privatization, 13
problem of many hands, 9–10, 143–4, 147, 154
professional conduct, standards of, 99
professional responsibility, 4, 98, 104, 119, 124, 132, 141, 165, 180
Provincial Advocate for Children and Youth, 15, 62, 71, 78, 93, 154, 160, 162, 164, 182n7, 184n4

racism, 68–9, 118. *See also* overrepresentation of racialized/ Aboriginal children in child welfare
REACH (Realizing Educational Achievement for Children and Youth) Teams, 16–17
Rees Centre for Fostering and Education, Oxford University, 18
relationships: importance of, 123–4, 127–38; regulating, 136–9
reporting, mandatory. *See* duty to report
research review by agencies, 167, 172–3
resilience, 9, 61–2, 99, 138, 151

responsibility: for instruction, 110–12; for safety, 117–19

separate spheres, 2–3, 25–7, 31
Smith, Dorothy, 12, 20, 159, 165
society ward, 183n8, 184n1
special education 1, 7, 16, 17, 51, 55, 60–1, 63, 69, 83–7, 108, 113, 155, 186n13, 187n17
Standards of Practice (teachers), 27, 106, 180, 185n6
Standards of Practice (CAS), 27
stereotypes: about mothers in child welfare system, 148; about abuse and neglect in cultural groups, 67, 70, 146, 150, 152

stigma of CAS involvement, 12, 25, 33–4, 36, 43, 54–61, 117, 144, 153, 177–8
street-level bureaucracy, 20, 99
student achievement, 10, 41, 104. *See also* holistic student success
substantive equality, 22
surveillance, 3, 26, 28–9, 42–3, 59, 61–2, 64–6, 165
Swift, Karen, 12–13, 181n4

teacher evaluation, 107, 180
Tri-Council Policy Statement on Ethical Research Involving Humans, 21, 175, 182n10